The Plays
from Alienation and Freedom

I0591931

Also Available from Bloomsbury

Chronicles of Nonsensual Times, Jacques Rancière

Mallarme: The Politics of the Siren, Jacques Rancière

Thousand Plateaus, Gilles Deleuze

Francis Bacon, Gilles Deleuze

The Three Ecologies, Felix Guattari

What Is Art?, Leo Tolstoy

Dissemination, Jacques Derrida

Marx, Michel Henry

The Pornographic Age, Alain Badiou

Happiness, Alain Badiou

Logics of Worlds, Alain Badiou

Clandestine Theology, François Laruelle

Anti-Badiou, François Laruelle

Jean-François Lyotard: The Interviews and Debates,
Jean-François Lyotard

Libidinal Economy, Jean-François Lyotard

The Selected Writings of Pierre Hadot, Pierre Hadot

Branches, Michel Serres

Hominescence, Michel Serres

The Incandescent, Michel Serres

The Five Senses, Michel Serres

Maine de Biran's 'Of Immediate Apperception', Maine De Biran

After Finitude, Quentin Meillassoux

Key Writings, Henri Lefebvre

Beyond the Chains of Illusion, Erich Fromm

Entre Nous, Emmanuel Levinas

Evolution and Conversion, René Girard

Aesthetic Theory, Theodor W. Adorno

The Beginning of Knowledge, Hans-Georg Gadamer

Mindfulness, Martin Heidegger

THE PLAYS
FROM ALIENATION AND FREEDOM

FRANTZ FANON

Edited by Jean Khalfa and Robert J.C. Young
Translated by Steven Corcoran

BLOOMSBURY ACADEMIC

LONDON • NEW YORK • OXFORD • NEW DELHI • SYDNEY

BLOOMSBURY ACADEMIC
Bloomsbury Publishing Plc
50 Bedford Square, London, WC1B 3DP, UK
1385 Broadway, New York, NY 10018, USA

BLOOMSBURY, BLOOMSBURY ACADEMIC and the Diana
logo are trademarks of Bloomsbury Publishing Plc

First published in *Ecrits sur L'Alienation et La Liberte* in France © Editions
LA DÉCOUVERTE, Paris, France, 2015
Reprinted 2019

First published in English in *Alienation and Freedom*, Great Britain, 2018

Paperback edition first published in Great Britain, 2021

Copyright to the collection and editorial material © Jean Khalfa and
Robert J. C. Young, 2018, 2021
Copyright to the English translation © Steven Corcoran, 2018, 2021

For legal purposes the Acknowledgements on pp. xiii–xiv constitute
an extension of this copyright page.

Cover design by Charlotte Daniels

All rights reserved. No part of this publication may be reproduced or transmitted
in any form or by any means, electronic or mechanical, including photocopying,
recording, or any information storage or retrieval system, without
prior permission in writing from the publishers.

Bloomsbury Publishing Plc does not have any control over, or responsibility for,
any third-party websites referred to or in this book. All internet addresses given
in this book were correct at the time of going to press. The author and publisher
regret any inconvenience caused if addresses have changed or sites have
ceased to exist, but can accept no responsibility for any such changes.

A catalogue record for this book is available from the British Library.

A catalog record for this book is available from the Library of Congress.

ISBN: PB: 978-1-3501-2657-2
      ePDF: 978-1-3501-2658-9
      eBook: 978-1-3501-2659-6

Typeset by Integra Software Services Pvt. Ltd.

To find out more about our authors and books visit www.bloomsbury.com
and sign up for our newsletters.

Contents

Frantz Fanon: Works Cited

Peau noire, masques blancs, Seuil, 1952. English translation, *Black Skin, White Masks*, trans. Richard Philcox, New York: Grove Press, 2008.

L'An V de la révolution algérienne, Maspero, 1959. English translation, *A Dying Colonialism*, trans. Haakon Chevalier, New York: Grove Press, 1965.

Les Damnés de la terre, Maspero, 1961. English translation, *The Wretched of the Earth*, trans. Richard Philcox, New York: Grove Press, 2004.

Pour la révolution africaine, Écrits politiques, Maspero, 1964. English translation, *Toward the African Revolution*, trans. Haakon Chevalier, New York: Grove Press, 1967.

Œuvres, Paris: La Découverte, 2011.

Editors' Preface

Jean Khalfa and Robert J.C. Young

In 2015 we published an edition of Frantz Fanon's uncollected and unpublished writings *Écrits sur l'alienation et la liberté* (Paris: La Découverte), translated into English in 2018 as *Alienation and Freedom* (London: Bloomsbury). For this paperback English edition, the publisher suggested that given the size of the original it would make sense to break it up into three books. *Alienation and Freedom* was in fact already divided into three main sections, plays, psychiatry and politics, and these form the basis of the division of the material for the paperbacks: *The Plays from Alienation and Freedom, The Psychiatric Writings from Alienation and Freedom and The Political Writings from Alienation* and *Freedom.*

During his lifetime, Fanon published three books: *Black Skin, White Masks* (1952), *A Dying Colonialism* (1958), and *The Wretched of the Earth* (1961). After his death in 1961, his publisher François Maspero collected up some of Fanon's political writings in the volume translated as *Toward the African Revolution* (1964). As he announced in the Preface to that volume, Maspero intended to follow it with a further collection that would bring together Fanon's psychiatric writings. For a variety of reasons, this was never published. Maspero and Fanon's friend Giovanni Pirelli had intended if possible to publish all Fanon's unpublished or uncollected work that was available to them: in putting together *Alienation and Freedom,* we have been able to complete their task, some fifty years later. With the passage of time, some of the original material has disappeared, while new material has been found.

Fanon has always been celebrated for his passionate language, but his early writing for theatre was long thought to be lost. In *The Plays from Alienation and Freedom* we print two remarkable plays that he wrote during his medical studies in Lyon. Never before published, they throw a striking philosophical light on the texts published during his lifetime. These first texts are steeped in the poetry of Césaire and the theatre of Claudel and of Sartre. In them, however, we can also glimpse passages which foreground the unbearable, raw light that one must risk preferring to the reassuring choice of an obscurity in which conflict is avoided; the relation of words to action; the desire to accept the event as such rather than the comfort of the known, a comfort akin to death – a Nietzschean conception of the tragic that informed Fanon's political thinking on disalienation and independence. In Sartre, the thinker he probably admired most, he had already discerned the thought of the present that would be developed in *Critique de la raison dialectique*, about which he later gave seminars to officers of the Algerian National Liberation Army.

The Psychiatric Writings from Alienation and Freedom completes the plan for the collection of Fanon's psychiatric work first announced by Maspero in 1964:

> Since becoming a psychiatrist at Blida Hospital [in Algeria], and even more so after the outbreak of the [November 1954] insurrection, Fanon also came to be a militant in the Algerian revolutionary organization. At the same time, he carried on a remarkable medical activity, innovating at many levels, deeply, viscerally close to his patients, whom he regarded as primarily victims of the system he was fighting. He collected clinical notes and developed analyses of phenomena of colonialist alienation as seen through mental illnesses. He explored local traditions and their relations to colonization. This essential material remains untouched, but it is too scattered, and we hope to be able to assemble it and present it in a separate volume.[1]

In the current collection of psychiatric texts, the reader will find not only Fanon's dissertation in psychiatry (defended viva voce in November 1951) and the scientific articles, both single-authored and collaborative, that he published throughout the 1950s, but also manuscripts and fragments that we have discovered. We have reprinted editorial texts that were originally published in the ward newspaper of Saint-Alban Hospital, where, in 1951 and 1952, Fanon was an intern of the revolutionary psychiatrist François Tosquelles, and further editorials from the newspaper that he set up at Blida-Joinville Hospital (today the Frantz-Fanon Hospital, Blida, Algeria), which formed an essential element of the 'socialtherapy' he helped to pioneer. Many of these texts that he wrote between 1954 and 1956 were long forgotten, ignored, or, for some manuscripts, unknown.

The wealth and impact of his political oeuvre are such that, given his short life (of only thirty-six years),[2] it was no doubt difficult to think that Fanon could have produced psychiatric research of any importance alongside it. On occasion, this psychiatric work was perhaps somewhat obscured or played down when seemingly out of sync with later fashions. But it would have been surprising had someone of Fanon's rigour been satisfied with a slapdash philosophy. As the reader shall see, the political work is in fact grounded on an astonishingly lucid epistemology and innovative scientific work and clinical practice. The dissertation in psychiatry aimed to establish

---

[1] Frantz Fanon, *Toward the African Revolution*, 1967, p. viii (translation modified – SC).
[2] Some key dates are to be found in the Chronology at the end of each volume.

a scientific distinction between the psychiatric and the neurological, by underlining the importance of the body and movement, of social and spatial relations, in structuring consciousness, or else in the alienation of consciousness when the aforementioned are hindered. The scientific articles explore and unfold the consequences of this intuition, in particular as part of a critique of the biologism of colonial ethnopsychiatry, and enable him to revisit culture in its relation both to the body and to history. Such work clearly underlies the famous talk on 'National Culture' that he delivered at the Second Congress of Black Artists and Writers, held in Rome in 1959. This psychiatric work also leads toward the overall mental health programme that he implemented while in Tunis, where he founded the Neuropsychiatric Day Centre of Charles-Nicolle Hospital, which he headed from 1957 to 1959 and which was one of the first open psychiatric clinics in the Francophone world. Moreover, some psychiatrists whose practice, it seems, he shook up, could not stop themselves, albeit much later, from claiming his heritage.[3]

Tunisian sociologist Lilia Ben Salem has entrusted us with the notes she took of Fanon's lectures on society and psychiatry at the Institut des Hautes Études in Tunis: the lectures synthesize and broaden the meaning of his works, and tell us about the books and films that excited him at the time. But leafing through the editorials of Saint-Alban and Blida, which Fanon compared to the pages of a logbook, we already see some of the structuring themes of his thinking: vigilance as the essence of being human, a theme he presents when remarking upon the difference between wakefulness and insomnia; his constant reminders to the orderlies that he was training to inquire into the meaning of all their actions; and the distrust of institutionalization that, in his last writings, informs the critique of the neocolonial elites that emerged in many countries after winning independence.

The Political Writings from Alienation and Freedom focuses on Fanon's political writings, where we reprint articles originally published in *El Moudjahid* from 1958 on. These texts were not collected in *Toward the African Revolution*, but, on the basis of precise contemporary testimonies and crosschecking done by his editors immediately after his death, it seems to us that Fanon's thinking at least strongly influences them, even if they were perhaps only partly authored by Fanon himself.[4] Along with a

---

[3]On this point, see the Introduction to the *Psychiatric Writings, from Alienation and Freedom*. p. 36, footnote 70.

[4]Anonymity was the rule at *El Moudjahid*. The articles retained in 1964 were done so 'under the control of Mme F. Fanon'. The editor stipulated that he had conserved only 'those of which we had irrefutable certainty that Frantz Fanon had written them. His contribution, naturally, was not limited to these precise texts. But, as in every team, and particularly in this revolution in full ferment, there was constant osmosis, interaction, mutual stimulation' (x; translation modified – SC). We provide the reasons for our selections in the introduction to the articles we have selected.

previously untranslated speech offering a justification for the FLN use of violence, the reader will also find here two previously unpublished texts dealing with important issues: a propaganda pamphlet published in Accra, Ghana, where Fanon was the ambassador of the Provisional Government of the Algerian Republic – the pamphlet develops an acerbic critique of some new African elites, whom he calls 'stooges of imperialism', and of neocolonialism more generally; and, in a letter to Iranian philosopher Ali Shariati, kindly provided to us by Dr Sara Shariati, we find his reflections and doubts on the role of religion in a revolutionary process. However, much of Fanon's political correspondence remains undiscovered.

We have also consulted the family library[5] and provide in each paperback a list of the works from the collection that most probably belonged to Fanon himself, reproducing his marks and annotations whenever significant.

Finding and assembling these texts was not a simple process. In this task, Fanon's Italian editors, Giovanni Pirelli and Giulio Einaudi, of course preceded us, as did François Maspero, who drew up the first inventory of Fanon's writings. The essential part of the correspondence containing this inventory is presented in the third volume in the section titled 'Publishing Fanon'. Retracing the work of these pioneers, who radicalized publishing with a view to creating a new society, we saw that the works that we now take as fixed, Fanon rather viewed as elements of shifting arrangements. Their plans to publish Fanon's complete works, which they arranged in a somewhat different fashion from what we consider today as the Fanon corpus, nevertheless did not come about. For over a decade now, we have sought to tackle this corpus anew.

There is no substantive archive of Fanon's work that contains all his original typescripts, drafts or letters in the manner of those preserved for many eminent European writers. Fanon does not seem to have been too concerned with conserving his writings or his preparatory works (even if he was proud of the plays he wrote in his youth). Moreover, he did not exactly write, but, for the most part, dictated, without notes, as is still the practice for many doctors. The texts gathered in these volumes were therefore assembled over a considerable period of time by putting together disparate material drawn from a multiplicity of sources from four continents. We were first required to engage in painstaking work to identify everything

---

[5]In 2013 the family library was given to the Centre National de Recherches Préhistoriques, Anthropologiques et Historiques (CNRPAH) in Algiers (see http://www.cnrpah.org/index. php/fondset- catalogues).

that he had written – in Algeria, in France and in Martinique – whether published or not. Through our works and persistence, we eventually won the trust of Fanon's descendants and of others who were in possession of documents, which were sometimes discovered following our encounters. In some cases, we had to restore texts that were too damaged to be immediately legible.[6] We warmly thank all those who placed their trust in us and helped us in our editorial work.

Alienation and Freedom is based on the surmise that an author of this magnitude cannot genuinely be understood without knowing all his work, in its continuities as much as in its transformations. In approaching it, the two of us took a different point of departure: one of us, Jean Khalfa, set out from the history of psychiatry and a longstanding interest in Francophone writings from the Antilles and the Maghreb, the other, Robert J.C. Young, from the history of colonialism and decolonization, in particular in the Anglophone and Francophone regions. We were both similarly dissatisfied with reductive interpretations of Fanon, interpretations that eliminate either the historical/political dimension or the philosophical/psychological dimension, depending on the social imperatives of the moment. By turning him into a political icon, his well-argued and very lucid critiques of the possible despotic future of postcolonial societies get buried. By seeing him as the thinker of contemporary identity issues, his essential aim is forgotten: namely, to think and construct freedom as disalienation within a necessarily historical and political process. Even Fanon's most technical psychiatric writings seem to us to add depth to an understanding of his other texts, which are already known the world over. Through editorial notes, we have endeavoured to indicate how this is so. Everything in this thinker's work has its intelligibility. Fanon had a very precise idea of what mattered to him and made use of anything that could enrich his perspective (he devoured in equal measure literature, philosophy, psychiatry, history, politics, sociology and ethnology). We also talked at length with many people who knew Fanon well and who kindly provided information on the detail of his work methods and on his own understanding of his work's significance. In retrospect, this collection has far exceeded our original hopes, something for which we are very glad. The persistence and talents of our French publisher, François Gèze, in mediating between all the interested parties, was extraordinary. He belongs to the tradition of those aforementioned great publishers. But we also view this edition as only one stage along the road and as an appeal to the future. Other texts by Fanon,

---

[6]For these documents, restored on the basis of poor quality manuscripts or typescripts (as in the case of the two plays), we have indicated in brackets the words that remained unclear.

in particular from his correspondence as well as his Blida and Tunis case notes, and his seminars for officers of the Algerian National Liberation Army remain unavailable. The interest of what we present in this edition will, we hope, give rise to further enrichments.

Note to the paperback edition

We have taken the opportunity of the reprinting of the English edition in three paperback volumes to correct errors present in the original hardback. This edition should be considered the definitive English text.

Acknowledgements

In our work to prepare this edition of the Plays, Psychiatric work and Political writings of Fanon, we have received help from numerous parties. We are especially indebted to the British Academy, the Leverhulme Trust, New York University, Trinity College, Cambridge and Wadham College, Oxford, all of which helped make this research possible. The role of Mireille Fanon-Mendès France (president of the Fondation Frantz-Fanon, which was established in Paris and in Montréal in 2007 and boasts an international network) was decisive. In 2001, she took the initiative, along with her brother Olivier, to deliver to the Institut Mémoires de l'édition contemporaine (IMEC, Paris and Caen), a Fanon Collection that includes a large part of the documents on which we worked and to which she gave us access, something for which we are deeply thankful. We owe a special debt of gratitude to the IMEC archivists, who always willingly facilitated our work there. Olivier Fanon (president of the National Association Frantz-Fanon, created in Algiers in 2012) authorized us to consult the documents that he had also deposited at IMEC, and permitted us, along with Professor Slimane Hachi, to consult and arrange the Frantz Fanon Collection that he set up at the *Centre national de recherches préhistoriques, anthropologiques et historiques in Algiers* (CNRPAH).

Jacques Azoulay's family kindly passed onto us the complete text of his PhD dissertation and Numa Murard gave us access to the transcription of the interviews he conducted with Jacques Azoulay. Charles Geronimi replied at length to our questions and gave us access to his beautiful text on Fanon at Blida. Marie-Jeanne Manuellan – who was Fanon's assistant in Tunis – was generous in providing us with many indications and clarifications about Fanon's method of writing, his clinical practice and his life and encounters. We are especially grateful to Neelam Srivastava, who located the Fanon-Pirelli correspondence and has introduced it here, as well as to Sara Shariati, who did the same for Fanon's correspondence with her father. Mireille Gauzy and association SACPI (Saint-Alban arts culture psychothérapie institutionnelle) provided us with copies of the Saint-Alban hospital ward newspaper containing editorials by Fanon. Amina Bekkat provided us with a considerable number of copies of the Blida hospital ward newspaper and Paul Marquis kindly gave us a number of the issues we were still missing, issues he discovered during his research. For their help with our research, we thank Norman Ajari, A. James Arnold, Margaret Atack, Levanah Benke, Elina Caire, J. Michael Dash, Olysia Dmitracova, Louise Dorignon, Jessica Galliver, Lucy Graham, Azzedine

Haddour, Joshua Heath, Ellen Iredale, Andrew Lanham, Nicholas Mirzoeff, Mélina Reynaud, Weimin Tang, Daniel Wunderlich and Heather Zuber. James Kirwan from the Wren Library restored the illegible parts of the plays typescripts. Mélanie Heydari offered considerable editorial support throughout the preparation of this volume, in particular with translation issues. We are very grateful to Gabriel Quigley for assistance in copy-editing the volumes for this paperback edition.

Introduction: Fanon, Revolutionary Playwright

ROBERT J.C. YOUNG

The following two plays, *The Drowning Eye* (*L'Oeil se noie*), and *Parallel Hands* (*Les Mains parallèles*), written in 1949, represent the earliest texts by Frantz Fanon that survive.[1] Fanon is also reported to have completed a third play, *The Conspiracy* (*La Conspiration*), but the manuscript has been lost.[2]

---

[1]Dating of the plays is given by Joby Fanon (*Frantz Fanon, De la Martinique à l'Algérie et à l'Afrique*, Paris: L'Harmattan, 2004, p. 129. Since the English translation, *Frantz Fanon, My Brother: Doctor, Playwright, Revolutionary*, trans. Daniel Nethery, Lanham, MD: Lexington Books, 2014, omits some chapters and interpolates additional material, I here reference and translate from the original French edition), and corroborated by Josie Fanon in her interview with Abdelmadjid Kaouah, *Révolution Africaine*, no. 1241, 11 December 1987, p. 33.

[2]Geismar lists the third play, *La Conspiration*, last (Peter Geismar, *Frantz Fanon*, New York, NY: The Dial Press, 1969, p. 49); Fanon may have gone on to write this after completing *Parallel Hands* in the summer of 1949. For many years, it was presumed that the manuscripts of all the plays were lost, as Fanon's wife Josie had suggested. She does not mention the third play, and neither does Joby Fanon in his 2004 biography *Frantz Fanon*. Jean Khalfa, however, records that Joby Fanon told him in 2001 that there were three plays, and confirmed this in a letter of 21 January 2004 in these terms: 'In particular three plays, which Frantz asked me to destroy in August 1961, because they did not correspond to his intellectual evolution and were far removed from his political choices at that time' (my translation).The two typescripts transcribed here were passed by Joby in the 1980s to Fanon's daughter, Mireille Mendès-Fanon, who deposited them with IMEC in 2001. *La Conspiration* may have owed something to Paul Nizan's celebrated novel *La Conspiration* which was reviewed by Sartre on its publication in 1938 (*The Conspiracy*, trans. Quentin Hoare, London: Verso, 1988). The novel recounts the story of an idealistic philosophy student at the École normale supérieure in Paris. Seeking to prove his commitment to the cause of revolution by moving from words to deeds, he involves his small group of disciples in a conspiracy that ends in betrayal and death. One should also note the publication in *Esprit* (the journal in which Fanon published his two earliest essays) in 1951 of an unpublished fragment on suicide by Charles Baudelaire, entitled 'La Conspiration' (*Esprit* 176, 1951, pp. 161–2).

Fanon's early passion for theatre

Philosophical influences

Fanon's interest in theatre developed during the years that he was studying medicine between 1946 and 1951. Whilst in Lyon, he frequented Les Célestins, Théâtre de Lyon, whose programme, during the years that he lived in the city, offered an extraordinary sequence of 252 'spectacles'. These included contemporary plays by Sartre,[3] Camus,[4] as well as Jean-Louis Barrault's celebrated production of Paul Claudel's *Partage de midi*, given in February 1949.[5] Although Peter Geismar claims that at that time Fanon began to think of pursuing a career in the theatre, his only recorded attempt to get his plays performed was to send *Parallel Hands* to Barrault.[6] No response from Barrault survives. By 1950/1951, Fanon's interests seem to have moved on: his focus shifted to completing his medical doctoral thesis and writing *Peau noire, masques blancs*; in January 1953 he announced that he was working on a study of the novels of Richard Wright, whilst by June of the same year he had qualified as a psychiatrist and was able to take up a temporary

---

[3]The following performances of plays by Sartre were staged while Fanon was in Lyon: *Morts sans sépulture* (*Men Without Shadows/The Victors*), February 1947; *Les Mains sales* (*Dirty Hands*), May 1949; *Huis Clos* (*No Exit*), October 1949, April 1950, May 1951, *La Putain respectueuse* (*The Respectful Prostitute*), February 1947, October 1949, April 1951 ('Mémoire des Célestins: Histoire d'un théâtre' http://www.memoire.celestins-lyon.org/index.php/Saisons/(offset)/60). The last play is cited by Fanon in *Black Skin, White Masks*, p. 118. The Sartrean theme of authenticity at the opening of *The Drowning Eye* recalls *No Exit*, though authenticity in love is not at issue in Sartre's play. In October 1949 at Les Célestins, Fanon would also have had the opportunity to see Katherine Dunham's 'Caribbean Rhapsody', an ethnographic 'black tumult', sponsored by Richard Wright and Aimé Césaire, intended to bring together Caribbean and African culture. See Geneviève Fabre, 'Katherine Dunham on the French Stage (No Repeat of La Revue Nègre)' *The Scholar and Feminist Online* vol. 6, nos.1–2, 2007/2008, http://sfonline.barnard.edu/baker/print_fabre.htm.
[4]*Caligula* was performed in February 1950. Camus' *Les Justes* (*The Just*) was in Fanon's library.
[5]A copy of Claudel's *Théâtre*, volume 1, containing *Partage de Midi* (*Break of Noon*), was in Fanon's library (though this is not the Barrault version that he could have seen at the theatre).
[6]Geismar, *Frantz Fanon*, p. 43. Alice Cherki reports that, according to Josie Fanon, Fanon sent *Parallel Hands* to Barrault, but received no response (*Frantz Fanon, A Portrait*, trans. Nadia Benabid, Ithaca, NY: Cornell University Press, 2006, p. 16).

position in Pontorson.[7] By November he had gone to Algeria and was at work at the hospital in Blida. Three years later he was expelled from Algeria and went to Tunis to work for the Front de libération nationale (FLN).

The philosophical context in which Fanon became immersed in France was that of post-war French existentialism and phenomenology rather than Marxism. Although biographers have assumed that Jean-Paul Sartre was the dominant influence on the plays – David Macey suggests that 'they were variants on the themes of Sartre's plays of the 1940s'[8] – this turns out to be somewhat less the case than expected. Along with his medical studies, Fanon was reading widely in contemporary philosophical literature, certainly Sartre and Camus, but also the foundational nineteenth-century 'existentialist' philosophers Friedrich Nietzsche and Søren Kierkegaard, as well as Gaston Bachelard, Henri Bergson, Karl Jaspers, Emmanuel Levinas, Maurice Merleau-Ponty and Jean Wahl, among others.[9] As 'The Black Man and Hegel' discussion in *Peau noire* suggests, he also read Georg Wilhelm Friedrich Hegel's *Phenomenology* (1807) and Alexandre Kojève's *Introduction à la lecture de Hegel* (*Introduction to the Reading of Hegel*), first published in 1947.[10] Indeed his readings in contemporary philosophy, as evidenced by the volumes marked up in his library, were so extensive that it is remarkable that he was able to follow his courses in medicine at the same time.

Together with the pervading authority of the Greek idiom of French classical drama, which Fanon knew well having been through the French education system in Martinique, all these theatrical and philosophical influences can be discerned in his

---

[7]Fanon's statement that he had thought of submitting *Black Skin* as his thesis (*Black Skin*, pp. 30–1) suggests that some of it at least was drafted before the submission of the thesis in November 1951; *Black Skin* was published April 1952. For the Richard Wright project, see the 1953 letter to Wright in *The Political Writings from Alienation and Freedom*, p. 101, footnote 1.

[8]David Macey, *Frantz Fanon: A Life*, London: Granta, 2000, p. 128.

[9]Geismar, *Frantz Fanon*, p. 43; Macey, *Frantz Fanon*, p. 126. All these philosophers are represented in Fanon's library.

[10]Copies of both texts have been read and marked in Fanon's library. On Hegel's master-slave, see also Jean-Paul Sartre, *L'Être et le néant. Essai d'ontologie phénoménologique. Édition corrigée par Arlette Alkaïm-Sartre*, Paris: Gallimard, 1976, pp. 274–83 (*Being and Nothingness*, trans. Hazel E. Barnes, London: Methuen, 1957, pp. 236–44).

plays.[11] Whilst generating the intense emotions prescribed for drama by Jean Racine,[12] the plays could be best described as philosophical dramatizations: they are primarily plays of ideas and expression not of character. However, as the emphasis on the body in the titles of both plays already suggests, they are not merely cerebral: as a result of the distinctive poetic-surrealist idiom of Fanon's language, they come across as '*lived* things', intensely physical, visceral, full of affect, with the sensations of the trembling, dispersed body emphasized as much as that of the psyche and indeed often indistinguishable from it.[13] It is remarkable that this poetry and prose of great linguistic inventiveness and complexity was composed not on the page but spoken out loud and recorded directly on to the page through the medium of dictation. Nietzsche's claim with regard to his own work – 'I have always composed my writings with all my body and all my life' – would seem to be far more the case for Fanon than for the German philosopher.[14] Fanon's compelling language, bursting with an energy that brings to life a somatic psychology, sets his drama apart from any of the influences cited above.

What makes the plays distinctive from any contemporary theatre written by Camus or Sartre is the pervading imaginative and linguistic presence of Aimé Césaire. There is a violence present in the language throughout that also communicates an intense physicality; as in Césaire, the image of violation is often articulated or implied

---

[11]Tosquelles reports that, in conversation, Fanon demonstrated a deep familiarity with the texts of classical French tragedy. François Tosquelles, 'F. Fanon at St Alban', *L'Information psychiatrique*, vol. 51, no. 10, 1975, pp. 9–14. Cf. Fanon's later remarks on how the colonized intellectual 'will endeavour to make European culture his own' (*The Wretched of the Earth*, p. 156).

[12]Joby Fanon recalls that Fanon knew the 'Preface' to *Bérénice* and *Britannicus* by heart, *Frantz Fanon*, p. 50.

[13]'I speak only of *lived* things and do not simply present cerebral processes', quotation, ascribed to Nietzsche, *Thus Spoke Zarathustra*, cited in the dedication to his brother Joby in Fanon's medical doctoral thesis. The language of Fanon's plays seems to instantiate a condition that Nietzsche describes in *The Genealogy of Morals*: 'sensuality is not suspended as soon as we enter the aesthetic condition, as Schopenhauer believed, but is only transfigured and no longer enters the consciousness as a sexual stimulus', Friedrich Nietzsche, '*On the Genealogy of Morality' and Other Writings*, trans. Keith Ansell-Pearson, 3rd edition, Cambridge: Cambridge University Press, 2017, p. 82. In his copy, Fanon has marked this passage and added the comment 'good'.

[14]Cited in Karl Jaspers, *Nietzsche: Introduction à sa philosophie*, Paris: Gallimard, 1950, p. 387. This quotation comes two lines above the quotation which Fanon used as a dedication for his brother Joby in his thesis cited in the previous note.

through metaphoric language. Given his personal acquaintance with Césaire, and the circulation of Césaire's work amongst Martiniquan intellectuals, it is hard to know exactly how much of Césaire's writing Fanon may have known in its many different versions.[15] He certainly knew the *Cahier d'un retour au pays natal* (*Notebook of a Return to The Native Land*), passages of which he could recite by heart;[16] in both *Peau noire* and *Les Damnés de la terre* he cites the play *Et les chiens se taisaient* (*And the Dogs Were Silent*) from *Les Armes miraculeuses* (*The Miraculous Weapons*) (1946).[17] Fanon may have also known Césaire's third, most extreme, volume of the 1940s, *Soleil cou coupé* (*Solar Throat Slashed*) (1948), at the very least in the selection included in Léopold Sédar Senghor's *Anthologie de la nouvelle poésie nègre et malgache de langue française* (1948). The *Discours sur le colonialisme* (*Discourse on Colonialism*), cited at the very beginning of *Peau noire* was not published until 7 June 1950, and therefore post-dates the plays.[18]

Fanon's surrealist existentialism

For readers familiar with Fanon's later writings on race and politics, the plays come as something of a surprise: they give little explicit evidence of the concerns and themes of the mature work, offering

---

[15]There is no evidence that Fanon read any issues of Césaire's journal *Tropiques*, published from 1941 to 1945, though it is very likely that he was aware of the journal. With an overall anticolonial agenda set out in Césaire's *Introduction* to the first issue, *Tropiques* featured articles on surrealism and its poetic tradition going back to Lautréamont and Mallarmé, the paintings of Wifredo Lam, as well as contemporary poets such as Reverdy and Césaire himself.

[16]In *Black Skin*, pp. 172–3. Fanon cites the *Cahier* from the 1947 Paris Bordas edition, the more explicitly anti-colonial, but not yet Marxist version, which has never been translated into English; this is the version used here.

[17]*Black Skin*, pp. 174–5; *Wretched*, pp. 44–6. Macey points out (*Frantz Fanon*, pp. 425–6) that the quotation in *Wretched* was a very late addition to the 'On Violence' essay and repeats some of the same lines that are cited in *Black Skin*. Symptomatically, the repeated lines are those in which the slave murders the white master in his bed. *Les Armes miraculeuses* (1946) is the only volume by Césaire to be found in Fanon's library.

[18]Often incorrectly cited as first published in 1955, that date rather refers to the revised French version credited on the copyright page of the English translation (*Discourse on Colonialism*, trans. Joan Pinkham, New York, NY: Monthly Review Press, 1972). The earliest version of the *Discours* was published in 1948 as 'L'impossible contact' in *Chemins du Monde* 5–6 (1948), 105–111.

rather existentialist and phenomenological preoccupations about consciousness and identity evoked, staged and conveyed in a dense, surrealistic language. The strangeness of the language of the plays is the greater as a result of the fact that their primary influence, the poetry and plays of Césaire, is not widely known in the forms in which Fanon read them.

As Césaire realized so brilliantly, the idiom of surrealism was exactly right for the irrational disjunctive world of coloniality in which he had grown up. Moving into a more dense and violent surrealistic mode after his meeting with André Breton in Martinique in 1941, Césaire subsequently rewrote the *Cahier* in the 1950s to inflect it with a more recognizable left-wing anticolonial politics, and either rewrote his early poetry and plays or suppressed them. The result is that much of the Césaire that influenced Fanon has, until very recently, lain almost as unread as Fanon's plays in manuscript. As is perhaps indicated by the unexpected presence of only one of Césaire's volumes in Fanon's library, Fanon's relationship to Césaire was always ambivalent, particularly regarding the latter's political and cultural programme of *négritude*. Whilst Césaire's influence is very prominent with respect to Fanon's surrealistic linguistic style, the plays are marked by the notable absence of explicit reference to any of Césaire's political concerns of the 1940s; they therefore constitute, by force of omission, an emphatic rejection of *négritude*.[19] Nor, on the other hand, are they simply Sartrean in their preoccupations, even if the influence of Sartre is at times discernible. Whilst emphasis is placed on various levels of consciousness, action, and the necessity of choice as a defining act of the will and the production of the event, there is no explicit interest in the political concepts of freedom or commitment in Sartrean terms. Embedded rather in Césaire's disruptive linguistic politics, conceptually the plays develop what amounts to a distinctive form of surrealist existentialism that more closely affiliates to the Nietzscheanism of the earlier Césaire or the Camus of *Caligula*, projecting a view of the world as an irresolvable paradoxical dualism that is either absurd or tragic.

Fanon's medical studies also took him to analyses of surrealism in contemporary psychology such as in Henri Ey's *La Psychiatrie*

---

[19]In *The Wretched of the Earth* Fanon implicitly criticizes Césaire for 'those bitter, desperate recriminations, those loud, violent outbursts that, after all, reassure the occupier' (*Wretched*, p. 173).

devant le surréalisme (*Psychiatry in the Face of Surrealism*) (1948).[20] Ey's account of surrealism as a revolutionary, subversive anti-realist aesthetic, in which the 'thought dictation' of the unconscious spontaneously produces surrealism's extravagantly magical, absurd qualities, its words resonating with performative immediacy rather than expressing hidden meaning,[21] also supported the direction that Fanon's own writing—itself dictated spontaneously—was taking. Whilst he drew on broader practices and analyses of surrealist poetry, it was Césaire who provided the dominant linguistic influence on his own work. This is evident from an imperative style of declarative exclamations and the use of a characteristic range of vocabulary common to both writers evoking the presence of violent overwhelming natural forces, for example words such as convulsion, scattered, lightning/dazzling/searing, burnt-out, throbbing, snigger, tidal wave, vertiginous, volcanic. Like Césaire, Fanon utilizes a wide variety of erudite medical and biological vocabulary to create a further sense of a strange, unrecognizable universe.[22] Sometimes the two are conflated, as in the use of 'orbits' to mean at once eye sockets and stars. Moving between prose and verse, Fanon's language is also marked by the use of Césaire's distinctive mode of *métaphore filée* (extended metaphor) which develops the surrealistic technique best described by Max Ernst in his 1936 essay on collage: 'The coupling of two realities, reconcilable in appearance, upon a plane which apparently does not suit them', a technique ideal for work that focuses on the irresolvable paradox of the dualism of the human condition.[23] The convulsive, 'volcanic' tension of the unexpected juxtaposition, famously characterized by André Breton in 1937 as 'explosante-fixe' ('exploding-fixed'),[24] is typically reinforced and repeated by running the association through a number of lines (or

---

[20]Henri Ey, *La Psychiatrie devant le surréalisme*, Paris: Centre d'éditions psychiatriques, 1948. Fanon discusses Ey's pamphlet in his thesis which, to judge by the different coloured marginal markings, he seems to have read at least three times. The mysterious voice in *The Drowning Eye* mimics the reality-disturbing forms of the surrealist proverbs cited by Ey, p. 14.

[21]Ey, *La Psychiatrie devant le surréalisme*, pp. 11–14, 47.

[22]See René Hénane, *Aimé Césaire, le chant blessé: biologie et poétique*, Paris: Jean-Michel Place, 1999.

[23]Max Ernst, 'Au delà de la peinture', *Cahiers d'art*, vol. 11, no. 6, 1936, p. 166. A more detailed study of Fanon's language would also include comparison to the poetry of other contemporaries, notably René Char,* as well as Louis Aragon, André Breton, Edouard Glissant*, Paul Claudel*, Léon Damas, Paul Éluard, Pierre Reverdy, Léopold Senghor*, and the hermetic Saint-John Perse* (*represented in Fanon's library).

[24]André Breton, *L'Amour fou* (*Mad Love*), Paris: Gallimard, 1937, p. 26.

indeed the whole work), emphasized by devices such as anaphora, rhythmical repetition, caesura, capitalization and 'vers en scalier' ('stepped verse') falling across the page.[25]

In Césaire's case, as in Fanon's, these startling combinations are not arbitrarily produced by the processes of automatic writing. The technique typically involves an abstract concept brought to life so that it becomes an embodied presence through being deliberately articulated with an incongruous physical or material image, sometimes reversing its familiar associations, as in the following lines from the opening of the *Cahier*:

> At the end of the small hours, the extreme, deceptive desolate eschar on the wound of the waters; the martyrs who do not bear witness; the flowers of blood that fade and scatter in the empty wind like the cries of babbling parrots; an aged life mendaciously smiling, its lips opened by vacated agonies; an aged poverty rotting under the sun, silently; an aged silence bursting with tepid pustules.[26]

Here the sea is evoked with the violent physical imagery of a wound, a metaphor more appropriate to the human body which is then carried over to describe the withering flowers of blood and the tepid pustules of the silence. The smile of old life is then physicalized by the description of its lips, just as in *The Drowning Eye* Ginette describes the lips of the waves in the mouth of the conch (the Martiniquan 'lambi' also makes an appearance in the *Cahier*) which she will transform into the lips of the world:

> The waves invited to the seabed return late,
> Quickly abandon their foam outfits and retire bare-footed,
> their cold lips in the throat of the conch. (Scene 3, p. 91)

---

[25]On Césaire's particular use of language, see Carrie Noland, *Voices of Negritude in Modernist Print*, New York, NY: Columbia University Press, 2015, pp. 29–60.

[26]Césaire, *Cahier d'un retour au pays natal*, 1947, *Œuvres complètes*, p. 74, *The Complete Poetry of Aimé Césaire*, trans. A. James Arnold and Clayton Eshleman, Middletown, CT: Wesleyan University Press, 2017, p. 13. Since there is no translation of the 1947 Bordas edition from which Fanon cites, English translations have been taken from other published versions, and modified as appropriate. These lines were present in the 1939 edition, suggesting that Césaire's meeting with André Breton only increased his interest in surrealism, which was already a feature of the Martiniquan journal *Légitime Défense* of 1932 (of which Fanon seems to have been unaware).

In *Parallel Hands* the same linguistic technique of startling, inappropriate conjunctions is developed in a similar, though often more abstract, way:

> Stop, choruses of criminal children, drops of clotted blood in the trough of orbits, set out to storm the firmament. Stop, the rediscovered man, inhabiting his consciousness of icy imminence, inhale the false fogs.
>
> Man, stupefying illusion, absurd gratuity, seizes, limited by serene darkness, the incontestable secret. (Act I. 1, p. 109)

Whilst both plays at times invoke the absurdity of life, they follow Césaire in situating this existential crisis within the context of a wider cosmos of natural and superhuman forces, reinforced in the French by the frequent use of pronominal verb forms that depersonalise the self while personalising abstractions and cosmic events, so that they operate indistinguishably as events in the same register. The abrupt flow of lines of *métaphore filée* means that the meaning of the speeches are often as much found in their performative impact, through an accumulative emotional affect produced by the density of intense physical metaphors, as in any sense of conventional 'content' or developing syntactic exposition, just as François in the play 'wouldn't speak, he would express' (p. 84). It was this disjunctive characteristic of the language that allowed Joby Fanon, in his chapter on 'Frantz Fanon playwright', to string together across two pages of his text odd lines or extracts taken from the entire length of either or both plays as if they formed a single poetic statement by Fanon *in propria persona*.[27] His claim that for Fanon language 'was the prelude to the act' articulates an important sentiment voiced in *Parallel Hands*, but in its practice Fanon's verbal style comes closer to another of Joby's descriptions: 'The word must be a movement of penetration and emergence. It must be a movement supported by movement.'[28] This idea of

---

[27]Joby Fanon, *Frantz Fanon*, pp. 130–4. In 'Frantz and the Idea of Death', introduced with the words 'He wrote to me in 1950', thus attributing the sentiments to Fanon directly, Joby cites a collection of jumbled lines taken from the manuscripts of *The Drowning Eye* and *Parallel Hands* (p. 139. Note that the date given here is a year later than his original dating of the plays on p. 129). While Joby sometimes omits words within a line or occasionally changes them from singular to plural, his citations of individual lines are generally taken accurately from the manuscript. This suggests that the lines cited from other manuscripts, now lost, are probably also accurate.
[28]Joby Fanon, *Frantz Fanon*, pp. 130, 141.

language as a moving, active agent supporting itself, functioning almost as an autonomous actor in the drama, is illuminated by a vivid quotation provided by Joby from a lost manuscript, possibly from the plays, in which Fanon invokes the violent language of the *clochard*:

> Take the words of the tramp and restore their teeth. Words have fangs and must hurt. Soft and supple words must disappear from this hell. Man speaks too much. He must be taught to reflect. To do that he must be made afraid. Very afraid. For that I have the bow-words, bullet-words, saw-words, words that are ionic charge carriers. Words that are words. And before uttering a word, I want to see a mask of suffering, a mask of the searcher, of the disillusioned. For words must be agile, cunning. They have to appear, avoid giving the eye, vanish.[29]

Fanon's words here, with their 'must' and their infinitives themselves sound a little like a manifesto, proposing the idea of the transformative power of words as violent weapons, saws, conductors carrying charged electrical particles. We can compare this, as Joby himself does, with Lucien's play on the close relations between *mot* (word) and *mort* (death) in *The Drowning Eye* (a semantic connection also articulated in *Parallel Hands*).

Lucien   He must live, for nothing, because he is there;
He must seize life with both hands, head-on like a gladiator.
He must be a constant insult to destiny.

Ginette   Mere words, Lucien. He's right.

Lucien   Then death is right against life.
Hearts must stop beating.
The spring must cease its wedding march.
Then, the smile must desert and give way to the hideous tenseness
of anxiety and death. (Scene 3, p. 88)

---

[29]Joby Fanon, *Frantz Fanon*, p. 141 (my translation). The comment 'he must be taught to reflect' correlates with *Black Skin* where Fanon aligns himself with Sartre's 'authoritative' essay 'What is Literature?' by declaring literature's 'only real task … is to get society to reflect and mediate', Fanon, *Black Skin*, p. 161. See also Sartre's comments on words as things not signs, as antennae for the body, underlined by Fanon, p. 210 below.

Joby Fanon completes his earlier *clochard* citation with the following lines which he puts into the mouth of Fanon himself instead of Lucien. The first line, about his needing words that have the power of boots that stride seven leagues per step,[30] is not in the play – there 'mere words' follows on from 'the hideous tenseness of anxiety and death' cited above:

> I need words that have seven-league boots.
> Mere words, you say?
> But words the colour of pulsating flesh
> Words the colour of mountains on heat.
> Of cities on fire.
> Of the resurrected dead.
> Words, yes, but battle flag words.
> Words like swords
> The love that makes you live to the power of two.
> A word,
> but a word strangled by life,
> bristling with life.
> A thirsty,
> hungry,
> screaming word that,
>   cries,
>   calls out,
>   is engrossed
>   and gets
>   lost.[31]

---

[30] A reference to a European folklore motif popularized by Charles Perrault about magical boots that cover with each step the three miles that a person normally takes an hour to walk. Fanon's immediate source, however, is more likely to have been *Either/Or* (a copy of which is in his library), where Kierkegaard tells the story of how the dwarf guarding the abducted princess in his castle put on his seven-league boots to catch her when she escaped (Søren Kierkegaard, *Either/Or*, Part I, trans. Howard V. Hong and Edna H. Hong, Princeton, NJ: Princeton University Press, 1987, p. 29).

[31] Joby Fanon, *Frantz Fanon*, p. 141; *The Drowning Eye*, Scene 3, p. 88. With these ideas of words strangled by life compare Césaire in the *Cahier*: 'Words while we handle quarters of earth, while we wed delirious continents, while we force streaming gates, words ah yes, words? but words of fresh blood, words that are tidal waves and erysipelas and malarias and lava and bush fires, and blazes of flesh, and blazes of cities ...' (Césaire, *Cahier*, 1947, *Œuvres complètes*, pp. 162–3, *The Collected Poetry*, trans. Clayton Eshleman and Annette Smith, Berkeley, CA: University of California Press, 1983, translation of 1956 edition modified to correlate to Bordas edition).

Whilst Lucien urges an activist use of words, his brother François is concerned rather to challenge any idea of *la clarté* by aligning himself with the obscurity and silence of the stars. The phrase 'Man speaks too much' is reminiscent of François' complaint that men do nothing but talk ('They come. They speak. They must speak') and his refusal to say a single word to his devoted friend Bussières or to Lucien his brother. Whilst for François words are largely superfluous, for Lucien or Bussières they are not real or material enough: 'When words scratch each other's eyes out, the only remaining resource is action', the latter remarks, adding mysteriously 'But when acts slip through one's fingers, all one can do is to lie down.'[32] The play questions whether words seduce one away from reality or lead us to a primordial reality beyond or behind the superficial compromises of everyday appearance. Words can move through their representation of reality to penetrate to a more profound insight into the world beyond the surface. Words operate in a combative, fluid relation, sliding a deceitful or truthful, white or black, mask over reality: in order to achieve their power, they must at once trick the eye, create a mask, avoid 'giving the eye', and vanish. Before words, the external eye of reality drowns. The role of language becomes a fundamental issue in determining the question of the value of living: can words be transformed into acts, or is it rather that they can be used to transform the scope and dimensions of life itself?

Fanon and Césaire's preoccupation with the value of words, their relation to physical reality, immediacy and action, can be situated in the wider context of a political preoccupation with the ideological role of language that followed on from the Second World War. The direct experience of language's deceptions, the ways in which it can produce meaning that is at odds with reality and truth, detaching signifier from signified, meant that many writers after the war (among them Edouard Glissant, Yves Bonnefoy, Roger Giroux, Sartre) shared a sense of the emptiness (*vacuité*) of language and became preoccupied with re-attaching it to the material world and reworking its power in more forceful ways. In *Peau noire* Fanon was to become more interested in the ways in which language was utilized to define racial attitudes and identity, but here the concern is focused on ideas about active, physical language, about words

---

[32]Scene 3, p. 82. Cf. Fanon's annotation to André Cresson, *Les Courants de la pensée philosophique française* (1946), 'No, knowledge is not opposed to action. The best knowledge is achieved *through* action.'

that are directly involved in life – bristling with it, or strangled by it – words that have physical effects on the listener and prompt him or her to transformative action, words that must be like burning cities and the resurrected dead, banners and swords. In this focus on language, we can see how far the composition of the plays enabled an apprenticeship in writing that enabled Fanon to develop his own distinctive, visceral linguistic style closely related to his belief in the necessity of political action in his later work.

Along with his language, Fanon's use of the Voice and the Chorus is of particular interest in these plays. Utilization of the chorus varies in French classical and contemporary theatre – Racine, for example, hardly ever uses a chorus, and neither does Sartre employ one in *Les Mouches* (*The Flies*) (1943), though it is written in the idiom of a Greek tragedy. Where it is found, the chorus tends to offer long, considered monologues, or interacts as another character as in *Oedipus Rex*. In both Fanon plays, neither the Voice or Chorus offers a position of detachment from the characters, neither adopt a position that is mid-way between stage and audience in the mode of Schlegel's 'ideal spectator', as described by Nietzsche in *The Birth of Tragedy*.[33] A closer model to Fanon's comes in Césaire's *Et les chiens se taisaient*, where we have a chorus, along with a semichorus, echo, narrators and various voices. These all function as 'characters' in the play who interact with the Rebel, the Lover and others, even as they articulate the Rebel's own dilemmas and self-questionings. In Fanon's plays the Voice/Chorus positions itself – as in Aeschylus – on the one side or other of the dialectic of positions staged in the play. In *The Drowning Eye*, the Voice aligns itself to the larger, darker, cosmic world beyond the human to which François wishes to assimilate himself. At strategic but often apparently random moments it delivers gnomic, ominous surrealist proverbs of Delphic obscurity, in an idiom that often evokes the elliptical poetry of René Char, offered from an apparently cosmic, godlike perspective, rebuking Lucien in particular and siding with François. The Chorus presents a visionary deterministic world of

---

[33]'The chorus is the "ideal spectator" inasmuch as it is the only *seer* – seer of the visionary world of the stage', Friedrich Nietzsche, *The Birth of Tragedy*, trans. Francis Golffing, New York: Doubleday, 1956, p. 54 (a marked-up copy of *The Birth of Tragedy* is in Fanon's library). Translations from *The Birth of Tragedy* have been modified to correspond more closely to Fanon's French translation, *L'Origine de la tragédie, ou hellénisme et pessimisme*, trans. Jean Marnold and Jacques Morland, Paris: Mercure de France, 1947.

necessity beyond the human. Its oracular statements are amongst the most evocative, but difficult to interpret, lines of the plays. They come across as the voice of the demiurgical cosmic order beyond the human that recalls that evoked by Césaire, who in turn draws on the primitive cosmogony of Frobenius.[34]

In *Parallel Hands*, the Chorus also appears as the representative of the world of the gods, but here the role of the gods has changed. The Chorus functions as the minder of King Polyxos their lackey, directly warning him in a repeated incantation about the dangers that await him. The play opens with the Chorus speaking a long prologue which sets up some of the main themes of the play from an apparently conservative perspective, and announces the necessity of stopping the spectacle that is to follow, that is its central event, the murder of Polyxos. In terms of the action, therefore, it wishes to stop the play itself. The role of the Chorus changes from that of the Voice in *The Drowning Eye* as a result of the different perspective of the second play. In *The Drowning Eye* the thrust of the Voice is to endorse the cosmic and inhuman over the everyday human social order, whereas in *Parallel Hands* the Chorus defends the current status quo of an alliance between 'the divine things' and its current rulers – the very thing that the hero Épithalos seeks to overturn and destroy.

The Drowning Eye

Fanon had completed *The Drowning Eye*, the first of the two plays, by July 1949.[35] Written in a single act with five scenes, the manuscript lacks Scene 4. The play has three characters, Lucien, his younger brother François, who will speak to no one but Ginette, a young woman who is emotionally committed to François but whom Lucien seeks to entice away from him; in addition to these three, there is an off-stage Voice, and a servant and cat who are both described as blind.[36] A painting in the corner, specified as being by the modernist

---

[34]Cf. Césaire, 'And it can be said that all true poetry, without ever abandoning its humanity, at the moment of greatest mystery ceases to be strictly human so as to begin to be truly cosmic', 'Poetry and Knowledge', trans. A. James Arnold, in Aimé Césaire, *Lyric and Dramatic Poetry, 1946–82*, Charlottesville, VA, and London: University Press of Virginia, 1990, p. xlix.

[35]Joby Fanon, *Frantz Fanon*, p. 129.

[36]The blind servant does not appear in any of the scenes of the play that have survived; at the end of Scene 2 Lucien describes him as being the one person to whom François will talk.

Cuban artist Wifredo Lam, immediately conjures up the presence of Aimé Césaire, who had been praising and invoking Lam since the second issue of *Tropiques* (July 1941).[37] The presence of the painting signals the intervention of the non-European artist within a domestic French environment.

The confrontation of the ordinary and the absolute

The first scene consists of a dialogue between François and Ginette, which recalls the erotic exchange between the Lover and the Rebel at the opening of *Et les chiens se taisaient*; the second involves a conversation between Lucien and Ginette in front of François who says nothing; the third comprises a long scene between Lucien and Ginette, who now begins to speak far more freely and indeed intelligently, defending her lover, than she did when with François; and the fifth concludes with a monologue by Ginette in front of François, who then finally speaks the last four lines with which the play ends. The opening scene initiates the metaphoric contrast of the play between night and day that symbolizes its basic existentialist choice between death and life, except that for François the day is associated with murder ('the moon has brought down the murderous hordes of the day'):[38] oppositions will always be challenged and categories transposed or dissolved in this drama. The morbid, taciturn François has withdrawn from life, which he sees as absurd. His indifference, incommunicativeness, *ennui*, lack of emotion and conviction of the absurdity of life recalls something of Meurseult in Albert Camus' *L'Étranger* (*The Outsider*) (1942). Structurally, of course, Fanon's alienation was the reverse of Meurseult's: the play expresses and attempts to transcend the oppression and alienation of the colonized. Whilst Meurseult famously ends his story by opening himself to the humanising 'tender indifference of the world', François seeks a form of transcendence through a structure of immanence by assimilating himself into the non-human material universe: obsessed with death, he wants to move from the human to the inhuman and become part of the larger celestial processes of the

---

[37]The 1947 Bordas version of *Cahier* from which Fanon cites included a frontispiece by Wifredo Lam.
[38]Scene 1, p. 72.

universe which seem anything but tender.[39] His resistance also takes the form of refusal: after the first scene, he says nothing until the very last lines of the play, when he takes Ginette's hand and leads her away. In contrast to the resistant passivity of François, Lucien, who enters in Scene 2, projects himself as life-affirming, but he cannot offer the intensity, depth and scope of François' dark cosmic vision. As the play begins, François challenges Ginette to tell him how much she loves him, and however much she protests that she does, he tells her that it is not enough, or too much in the idiom of the kind of bourgeois love that she has been brought up to desire and expect. Rejecting conventional modes of behaviour and morality as a beguiling imposture, he seeks authenticity. Her love for him, by contrast, seems above all intensely physical, an experience of being overpowered by him and helpless before him. By contrast with Ginette's sexual, masochistic passion for François, his questioning is cerebral and detached, and seeks to produce some form of a pure, absolute love which she is unable to articulate in the manner that he desires. The scene involves an obvious rewriting of Hegel's master-slave dialectic: François sits passively at her feet whilst he demands her recognition.[40] She offers him everything, complete submission, but it is not enough. He declares that he rather wants to violate her against her will ('I would have wanted to enter into you in spite of yourself') and force her to absorb him.[41] He does not want her recognition of him according to a structure in which she constructs him in any way as other to herself. Her conventional love must be negated – the dialectic will only be fulfilled in the final scene when she has left him and then returned to him repentant.

In the second scene, Lucien enters and François stops speaking – indeed he does not utter another word until the very end of the play.

---

[39]This transcendentalist metaphysics is not rational, like Spinoza's, but aleatory, for Fanon particularly emphasizes the prevalence of random chance, of colliding stars, an issue also to be understood in the context of contemporary questions about contingency and determinacy, freedom and necessity, in the work of Merleau-Ponty, Sartre and others.

[40]Fanon's reading of Hegel in *Black Skin* (pp. 191–7), in which he revises Hegel by bringing in the question of race to the master-slave relation, is clearly anticipated here without being developed in explicit racial terms (though see the discussion below). On Hegel and slavery, see Susan Buck-Morss, *Hegel, Haiti and Universal History*, Pittsburgh, PA: Pittsburgh University Press, 2009.

[41]Scene 1, p. 76.

Lucien, who later reveals that François has not spoken to him for a very long time, proceeds to cajole him and taunt him, telling him to stop being so morose, to get up and seize life in a positive fashion. Ginette repeatedly steps in to defend him and protests that Lucien is making him suffer. Lucien responds that François only makes others suffer. The third, longest scene, between Lucien and Ginette, takes the form of a dialogue in which the former seeks to destroy François whilst the latter defends him. At one level, this is a seduction scene: Lucien seeks to win Ginette over to himself by discrediting his brother, urging her to go beyond *ressentiment* and negation to an affirmation of an active life in all its possibilities. Having been overpowered by François' charisma, Ginette is gradually persuaded by Lucien's positive arguments. Though she fiercely defends François, she also suggests that at times she has wanted to kill him, to get rid of him too. As the scene proceeds, Lucien and Ginette seem to enact through their verbal exchanges a ritual of a purgative sacrifice, moving towards a union in which all opposites, sun and moon, night and day, death and life, are resolved. The result is that she finally, somewhat reluctantly, yields to Lucien. The lost Scene 4 may have involved a presentation of an increasingly fractious interaction between the two new lovers. In Scene 5, Ginette returns to François to tell him that she found being absent from him unbearable; it opened up an abyss within her that must be filled. In her last words, she begs him: 'Fashion me frighteningly!' He accepts that negativity as proof of her love's authenticity at last: her love and recognition of him are no longer dependent on her construction of him as other to herself. With his masculinist control and incorporation of her complete, he stands up and gets ready to leave, announcing that he wishes to lead her 'to the ABSOLUTE gates / where life is seized'.[42]

The play's structural and dramatic focus is centred on the long seduction scene in which Ginette vacillates between the two brothers. This recalls the explicit sexual drama of Claudel's *Partage de Midi*, where in successive acts of the play the coquettish heroine Ysé oscillates in her passion between her husband de Ciz, the lonely and misanthropic Mesa, and Amalric, her former lover. Scene 4 of *The Drowning Eye* may have been similar to the disastrous new relationship portrayed in the second act of *Partage de Midi*. However, in Fanon's play, despite the intense sexuality of Ginette's passion,

---

[42]Scene 5, p. 106.

and the sexualized language (though less explicit than in Césaire), sexuality as such does not come across as the play's primary focus. The consistent centre of attention is François, his own identity and his conflictual relationship with his brother Lucien. Through its progressive dialectical structure, the play presents an intense debate about an existential choice between two possible forms of life: between a life that embraces the everyday and one that disdains the ordinary and seeks an absolute beyond it. In François' case this involves the rejection of conventional reason in favour of a strange and mystical 'secret' that is the product of communion with the celestial, material world of the stars, imaged through intense, violent sexual desire of the body that shatters individuality and effects deliverance from the self in the face of a primordial oneness. All these values are opposed to Lucien's hedonistic alternative of seizing life as it is lived on earth as an aesthetic form of positive pleasure and assertion of the self.

From boyhood, François has always disdained the everyday, refusing the socialized reality of ordinary society and remaining alienated from it: Lucien recounts a mysterious incident when a star, 'green with fire', came down to earth in front of him: he watched whilst François appeared to have some sort of communion with it. Although Lucien claims that he saw the star, the fact that it is specifically described as green suggests that it must, in some sense, have been imaginary, since for physiological optical reasons no green stars are observable to human sight. Since that incident, he tells Ginette, François has always been removed, and lived for himself, in what Lucien characterises as an egotistical preoccupation with the visionary (François disdains human company, never speaks to Lucien, but on the other hand spends a whole night talking to a blind man). François combines a Nietzschean conjunction of the inhuman with superhuman aspirations to achieve a 'direct intuition of the cosmic idea'.[43] The celestial, supernatural element is reinforced in the play by the inclusion of a chorus in the form of a Voice who utters enigmatic sentiments at strategic, unpredictable intervals, beginning with the opening line delivered by the anonymous Voice off-stage: 'The rain that chaps the overly essential clarity of the night, yesterday, in full grip, surprised the confession-less rivers.'[44] These words immediately

---

[43]Nietzsche, *The Birth of Tragedy*, p. 128.
[44]Scene 1, p. 72.

set up surrealistic images of disruption and disturbance, of the existence of some other level of reality, with the oxymoron 'clarity of the night' invoking, echoing and subsuming Corneille's line from *Le Cid*: 'Cette obscure clarté qui tombe des étoiles' ('This darkling light that from the stars descends').[45] Thus fraternal difference is transformed into a cosmic drama between the indifferent world of the stars, things, and primal Being, and the small world of humans, who have created their own meaning out of their conformist lives invested in normative bourgeois assumptions.

A work of personal exorcism

Peter Geismar and Joby Fanon both depict *The Drowning Eye* as an autobiographical self-interrogation and analysis. By renaming himself François, Fanon draws our attention to the fundamental problem of his own unusual Germanic first name, Frantz, which not only means 'Frenchman', but, as pronounced in French, forms a homophone with the word 'France' itself. It would hardly be too much to say, à la Michèle Montrelay, that the fundamental issue for Fanon's whole psychic and intellectual landscape was determined from the first by his having to live with the excruciating situation of being named after the imperial country under whose power he lived as a colonized subject in Martinique. His writings involve a series of attempts to work through and beyond this: in life he would later assume his second name Omar. In a letter from François Maspero to Giovanni Pirelli of 6 September 1963, Maspero mentions the existence of a play by Fanon which he describes as follows: 'It is a sort of work of personal exorcism, one that often attains an extraordinary formal beauty, but is not devoid of hermeticism.'[46] Whether he was discussing *The Drowning Eye* or *Parallel Hands*, Maspero's characterization of Fanon's theatre as a 'work of personal exorcism' was as acute as his description of its aesthetic. It is noticeable that the constant, indeed almost only, topic of conversation and debate

---

[45]Pierre Corneille, *Le Cid*, Act IV.iii.66 (*The Cid, the Cinna, the Theatrical Illusion*, trans. John Cairncross, London: Penguin, 1975, p. 88). Compare Roland Barthes' later critique of *La clarté* on the grounds that such language conceals a hidden ideological or at the very least class agenda in *Critique et vérité*, Paris: Éditions du Seuil, 1966, pp. 27–35 (*Criticism and Truth*, trans. Katrine Pilcher Keuneman, London: The Athlone Press, 1987, pp. 9–13).
[46]*The Political Writings from Alienation and Freedom*, p. 182.

in the first play concerns the character of François and 'the hideous tenseness of anxiety and death' from which he suffers.[47] As Lucien tries to seduce Ginette away from him, they debate his ideas and personality at great length, the result being that for the most part, François does not represent himself, but is represented by others – negatively by Lucien, and positively by Ginette. Whilst at one level Lucien and François clearly stage a dialectical division with Fanon himself, it is also not difficult to see in the rivalry between these two brothers projected images of Joby and Frantz. Such an interpretation is encouraged by Joby himself in the chapter that immediately follows 'Frantz Fanon Playwright', 'Frantz and the Idea of Death', where he describes Frantz as a version of François in this period, a visionary obsessed with death.[48] The lines he quotes from Fanon's letter to his 'marraine de guerre' sound remarkably close to some of the sentiments voiced by François:

> You tell me that you are surprised by my silence. But you are not unaware that the things that haunt me and obsess me cannot be translated…. I do not want that larval life, gathered up, old-fashioned, which awaits me once my studies are completed. I do not want '*marriage*', children, home, the family table. I wonder if I have the right to impose on Paule[49] my life, my convictions, my tendencies. In fact, my greatest sin was to exile myself to Lyons. There I became accustomed to detach myself, to detest everything, to hate everything.[50]

Fanon's dark account of himself here correlates closely with the sentiments expressed by François. For his part, taking the idiom of Lucien, Joby speaks of 'My incessant criticism of the fact that he has his head in the clouds ("qu'il est dans la lune") and that he ought to put his feet back on the ground.' He notes that the quotation from

---

[47]Scene 3, p. 88.

[48]Joby Fanon, *Frantz Fanon*, p. 135. Fanon himself remarks in a footnote in *Black Skin* that 'When we began this work we wanted to devote a section to a study of the black man's attitude towards death' (p. 193).

[49]'A young girl with whom he had established intimate relations during his convalescence in Paris in 1945 after being wounded in the Bouches de Doubs' (note by Joby Fanon).

[50]Joby Fanon, *Frantz Fanon*, p. 111 (my translation). 'Marraine de guerre' was a term used to describe French women who wrote to, and sent gifts to, soldiers at the front in order to keep up their morale.

Nietzsche addressed to him in Fanon's dedication in his medical doctorate thesis, 'I speak only of *lived* things and do not simply present cerebral processes', formed Fanon's combative response.[51]

The lived experience of the black man: Issues of race

What were these '*lived* things' to which Fanon here refers? The phrase recalls the title of Fanon's essay 'The Lived Experience of the Black Man' published earlier the same year.[52] But Fanon's play, despite its literary closeness to the work of his fellow-Martiniquan Césaire, hardly seems to give us the lived things or experience of the black man. Despite the clear influence of Césaire's surrealistic language, we might well ask what has happened to Césaire's anticolonial politics, to his politics of race if not of *négritude*? Their apparent disappearance might seem less strange, were it not that Fanon's own book on race, *Peau noire, masques blancs*, was published less than three years after *The Drowning Eye* was completed. Moreover, in the Introduction to *Peau noire* where he discusses the situation of the black man, Fanon remarks: 'This book should have been written three years ago … But then the truths burned us.'[53] Three years before would have been 1949, the very year in which he wrote *The Drowning Eye*.

Despite their not appearing as the overt subject of the play, with a little probing we can, however, detect deep concerns about language, identity, race and the ways in which these issues are played out in and through consciousness and the dynamics of inter-racial relationships, all of which can be directly linked to the ideas explored in *Peau noire, masques blancs*. The language of *The Drowning Eye* correlates directly to the visceral language of affect and its effect on the body that is so remarkable and insistent a characteristic of *Peau noire*. Recall the famous analyses in chapter 5 of being pointed out in the street, or the incident in the railway carriage when a child points at Fanon and he feels his blackness precipitated into the cold whiteness of winter and transformed into white ash. Whiteness and blackness exist in a shifting, symbiotic relationship.

---

[51]See *The Psychiatric Writings from Alienation and Freedom*, p. 40. The thesis was defended on 29 November 1951.

[52]First published in *Esprit* in May 1951, and subsequently included as chapter 5 of *Black Skin*.

[53]Fanon, *Black Skin*, p. xiii (translation modified).

As with Fanon in *Peau noire*, so François in *The Drowning Eye* seems caught in an irresolvable dialectical bind between black and white, past and future, body and world, desire and insentience, consciousness and transcendent immanence. Nothing, in other words, if not ambivalent, a condition of alienation that François wants to escape. The stage directions specify that the characters of the play continually move on the stage between light and obscurity, enforcing the way in which the play is all about whiteness and darkness, transparency and opacity, vision and blindness: red and white suns, white moons, black night and white night, white death. Like Césaire, Fanon belonged to a generation of Antillean intellectuals for whom the experience of living in France forced them to realize for the first time that they were not French because they were black.[54] The problem for Fanon was that as an *evolué* from Martinique he did not think of himself easily as 'black' either. As he himself suggests, to the extent that he identified himself with being French, he identified with being white. Geismar suggests that Fanon wrote the plays in order to relieve the tensions of being in what Karl Jaspers calls a psychic 'border situation' in Lyon where he found himself alienated from both black and white communities: 'Not yet white, no longer completely black, I was damned.'[55] Being in a border situation certainly describes *The Drowning Eye* with remarkable astuteness.

Characteristically, these antitheses and oppositions break down, dissolve, invert and circulate: we shall see that François can be both black and white. As in *Peau noire*, whiteness and blackness are not absolute oppositions but relative, positional, on a scale of gradations. You become white or black, according to clothing, education, language, money, the look of others. The phenomenology of blackness is a matter of perception. The stage directions already suggest some difference between the characters by describing each one as a person of colour produced as an effect of the lighting. They are not, however, created in conventional racial colours. Lucien's face is the 'colour of pewter', which is an interesting metal since when it is polished it can look both black and silver, in other words indistinguishably black and white. François on the other hand is 'the colour of new blotting paper': since new, therefore unstained with

---

[54]A. James Arnold, 'Introduction', *in Aimé Césaire, Lyric and Dramatic Poetry, 1946–82*, Charlottesville, VA: University Press of Virginia, 1990, p. xxvii.
[55]Geismar, *Frantz Fanon*, p. 50; *Black Skin*, p. 117.

dark ink. Ginette, meanwhile, is 'the colour of a rain drop', that is, transparent, with no colour of her own, rather reflecting the colours around her. The characters, in other words, mirror or absorb the light of the colours around them. The play thus positions itself in relation to its audience, who watch the play according to their own racial perspectives. Fanon puts everyone in the position of the in-between, of being neither and both at once, which is in fact precisely what he complained of feeling whilst he was in Lyon.

Unlike *Peau noire*, in *The Drowning Eye* Fanon develops these issues without foregrounding the question of race or skin colour explicitly. In doing so, he was putting into practice the argument that difference should be a matter of indifference: the oppressive sense of being racialized as a minority and therefore objectified by a white society is exactly what Fanon wished to get away from. He wanted to erase that person and reconstruct himself otherwise. He did not want to be marked out and regarded as different, nor to turn that projected difference into the grounds of his own social and cultural identity. He wished to be allowed the dignity of being ordinary, unremarkable, indifferently the same. 'I wanted quite simply to be a man among men.... I wanted to be a man, and nothing but a man.'[56] Having been brought up as French and rejecting *négritude*, however, the painful paradox for Fanon was that his idea of man was white, even as he sought to undo the dehumanisation of the racial epidermal schema.[57]

The Drowning Eye explores psychological effects of racialization without foregrounding the social milieu that has produced them, or indeed overtly discussing the question of race as such – the characters, as it were, wear white masks. It is easy, therefore, to miss the idea that the play is at one level about race – or perhaps more accurately, about the radical alienation of being between race or the shifting constructions of race. There are, however, a succession of further

---

[56]*Black Skin*, p. 92. Cf. the famous Ernest C. Withers civil rights photograph, '*I Am A Man, Sanitation Workers Strike, Memphis, Tennessee*, March 28, 1968'. In the context of the customary language of address of whites to blacks in the US South, the strikers' placards asserting 'I am a Man' have the added implication that as African-Americans they are not a 'boy'.

[57]'As painful as it is for us to have to say this: there is but one destiny for the black man. And it is white', *Black Skin*, p. xiv, a statement that is repeated at the end of the book, p. 202. It should always be remembered that *Black Skin* is written as a phenomenological sequence of dramatic 'voiced' dialogic assertions, each of which extends and revises the last.

indicators beyond the descriptions of the colours of the characters. Readers of Césaire will hear in the phrase 'white death' in Lucien's declaration to Ginette – 'White death, slain, wrested from its shroud rises up dripping and disappears'[58] – an allusion to the lines in the *Cahier* describing Toussaint l'Ouverture's imprisonment in Europe in which a deathly whiteness is set against an accumulation of positive images of blackness:

> a lone man defying the white screams of white death
> (TOUSSAINT, TOUSSAINT LOUVERTURE)
> a man who mesmerizes the white sparrow hawk of white death[59]

Already in Scene 1, there are indications of a racialized consciousness in the strange master-slave scene which opens the play.[60] One of François' confessions offers perhaps the most personal articulation in the plays, certainly in a more upfront way, of emotional insecurity, alienation, and of a feeling that people's responses to the speaker are either hurtful and hostile, or if positive and loving, inauthentic, here based on the explicit grounds of racial prejudice. François' alienation dream is sketched out in vivid terms that are drawn from the world of the American South:

> You, you really do not know what it's like not to understand. Not to understand what's happening to you! You're in your big white bed, as light as if flying in a dream, you get a knock at the door, men enter. You see them dimly, very dimly. They speak, you hear them faintly, very faintly, and then they start hitting and lynching you, and you get hurt, badly hurt. They leave and you've understood nothing, and you are beaten down by blows.

---

[58]Scene 3, p. 86.

[59]*Cahier*, Césaire, *Œuvres complètes*, p. 158, *The Complete Poetry*, pp. 29, 31. The phrase 'white death' is also to be found in Richard Wright's *Black Boy* (1945): the following passage, describing Wright's reaction when Bob, a black boy, is shot because he has had sex with a white prostitute, is marked in Fanon's French translation, published in 1947: 'Inside of me my world crashed and my body felt heavy. I stood looking down the quiet, sun-filled street. Bob had been caught by the white death, the threat of which hung over every black male in the South' (Richard Wright, *Black Boy*, London: Vintage Books, 2000, pp. 172–3). *Black Boy* was first serialized in *Les Temps modernes* during 1946–1947; Fanon also marked up Sartre's comments on the novel in *Situations II*.

[60]See note 40.

> Later they return, you get up, you want to talk to them and you
> think you will understand. Then you are told that you are also a
> tough guy and they leave you alone with a medal and you are
> beaten down by blows.[61]

This nightmare seems to come straight out of the world of Richard Wright and Sartre's *La Putain respectueuse* (*The Respectable Prostitute*), possibly seen by Fanon in Lyon and discussed by him in *Peau noire*.[62] Describing to Ginette his nightmarish world that does not allow him to participate in everyday existence, François recounts a dream of being lynched – a nightmare that would haunt Fanon to the end of his life.[63] Unexpectedly in the dream, the men return, acknowledge that he is 'a tough guy' and give him a medal.[64] He is left at once with a medal and a body heavy with blows: beaten up because he is a black man, and then acknowledged and rewarded as human. Ginette responds problematically to François' nightmare of the dualism of being identified racially or as a human being, by also seeing him as black and affirming his desirable blackness:

> I love you and if you love me, I will tell you why those men beat you down with blows and medals. I love you and I want to repeat to you what the manchineel tree confided in me one evening when, naked, I scattered grains of love on the riverbank. *(She stands up and moves close to him.)*
>
> I love you, oh my God, and I want to tell you why your body has the audacity of the coconut tree and the muted brutality of a negro tom-tom.[65]

Speaking of him as if he were black, she immediately invokes the stereotypical images of black people amongst Europeans, the coconut and the 'negro tom-tom'.[66]

---

[61]Scene 1, pp. 74–5.
[62]Fanon, *Black Skin*, p. 118.
[63]Cf. *Black Skin* where Fanon quotes the following lines from Césaire's *Et les chiens se taisaient* as a headnote to chapter 4: 'There is not in the world one single poor lynched bastard, one poor tortured man, in whom I am not also murdered and humiliated' (*Black Skin*, p. 64; Césaire, *Œuvres*, p. 298).
[64]After experiencing racial prejudice in the army, Fanon was himself awarded war medals. Macey, *Frantz Fanon*, p. 102.
[65]Scene 1, p. 75.
[66]On black stereotypes, compare Césaire, 'Tam Tam de nuit', 'Tam-Tam I', 'Tam-Tam II', *Œuvres*, pp. 254, 263–4, *The Complete Poetry*, pp. 115, 135, 137.

The dynamics of this exchange correlate with the ambivalent antitheses developed in the play between whiteness and blackness, lightness and heaviness, day and night. And right away, the polarities reverse, as it begins to appear that in the absoluteness of her desire she herself loves François in the slavish mode of the black woman for the white man as described by Fanon in *Peau noire*. At one level, indeed, *The Drowning Eye* offers a dramatization and exploration of some of the psychological traits, different positionalities produced by the inter-racial relationships that would be analysed in the second and third chapters of that book, all fuelled by the black Martiniquan dream of becoming white.[67] So chapter 2 of *Peau noire*, 'The Woman of Colour and the White Man', begins with a discussion of how love ordinarily involves an affirmation of the self by the other, 'my beloved will support me energetically in assuming my virility',[68] a phenomenon of 'failed love' that Fanon pointed out was an example of 'bad faith' and inauthenticity in Sartre's *L'Être et le néant*.[69] Fanon argues that authentic love is impossible in the presence of sentiments of inferiority and exaltation in the power structure of a relationship between a woman of colour and a European. In *The Drowning Eye* he explores similar dynamics of power without specifying that those feelings emerge as a result of racial difference.

In *Peau noire*, Fanon analyses the recent book by Mayotte Capécia, *Je suis Martiniquaise* (*I am a Martinican Woman*) (1948) in which Mayotte's relationship operates on the same structure of absolute devotion as Ginette's: 'Mayotte loves a white man unconditionally. He is her lord. She asks for nothing, demands nothing, except for a little whiteness in her life.'[70] As part of this mental landscape of the desire for lactification, Mayotte projects stereotypical images of whiteness and blackness that for her, as Fanon puts it, 'represent the two poles of this world, poles in perpetual conflict: a genuinely Manichaean notion of the world. There, we've said it – Black or

---

[67]See Jock McCullock, *Black Soul, White Artifact: Fanon's Clinical Psychology and Social Theory*, Cambridge: Cambridge University Press, 1983, pp. 65ff.

[68]Fanon, *Black Skin*, p. 24.

[69]Fanon, *Black Skin*, p. 24; Sartre, *L'Être et le Néant*, pp. 404ff, *Being and Nothingness*, pp. 364ff.

[70]Fanon, *Black Skin*, p. 25. Fanon marked a related observation by Capécia in his copy of *Je suis Martiniquaise*: 'With her mentality of the slave, she was devoted body and soul to Isaure', Mayotte Capécia, *Je suis Martiniquaise*, Paris: Editions Corrêa, 1948, p. 36 (my translation).

White, that is the question'.[71] With this last phrase, Fanon has turned Hamlet's existential moment of uncertain choice between life and death into one of choosing to be white or black:

> I am white; in other words, I embody beauty and virtue, which have never been black. I am the color of day.
> I am black: I am in total fusion with the world, in sympathetic affinity with the earth, losing my ego in the heart of the cosmos.... I am black, not because of a curse, but because my skin has been able to capture all the cosmic effluvia. I am truly *a drop of sun* (goutte de soleil) under the earth.[72]

The antithesis that Fanon describes Mayotte developing here is comparable to the difference between Lucien and Ginette/François in *The Drowning Eye*, where the one is identified with beauty, the day, the other identified with night and a fusion with the cosmos:

Lucien   I love you Ginette, almond forgotten by the night.

Ginette   I love you Lucien, *Sun drop* (goutte de Soleil).[73]

In *Peau noire*, Fanon goes on to critique overtly these positions associated with stereotyped ideas of whiteness and blackness, including those of *négritude*, but here the Manichaean antithesis resonates in the opposition between the two brothers, one predominantly white and associated with the daylight, the other linked on two occasions to blackness and associated with a Frobenian desire for 'a complete fusion with the world', whilst Ginette the lover alternates from one to the other. The play shows the author working though the psychic dimensions of being 'haunted by a series of corrosive stereotypes', stereotypes that as a black man he had internalized and needed to work through in order to overcome the alienation that they had produced.[74]

The play thus presents a drama that was being played out around and inside Fanon himself. It amounts to a staged self-analysis, with Fanon dramatizing through different masks the ambivalence of his own consciousness and forms of subjectivity, of being split

---

[71]Fanon, *Black Skin*, p. 27.
[72]Fanon, *Black Skin*, p. 27, my emphasis (translation modified).
[73]Scene 3, p. 101, my emphasis.
[74]Fanon, *Black Skin*, p. 108.

between being both black and white at the same time, 'un écorché vif' as Edouard Glissant put it, a phrase which means a tormented soul, literally someone flayed alive.[75] As a Martiniquan, Fanon, Macey points out, was an honorary *toubab* – white man – not a native (*indigène*).[76] He did not support Césaire's reinscription of black identity in the concept of *négritude*. Césaire's *négritude* was a provocative and deliberate statement of his identification with Africanness, very different from Fanon's own identification of himself as 'quasi-metropolitan'.[77] Fanon left for Lyons because there were, he said, 'too many Negroes (nègres) in Paris, I want something more milky' – by 'nègres' he did not mean fellow Martiniquans such as Césaire, but Africans.[78] Fanon used the term 'nègres' exclusively to describe Africans, not Antilleans whom he describes at once as 'noir' and 'European'.[79] He hated being treated in any way that gestured towards his colour, for example being complemented on his good French, a sensitive subject for Fanon that forms the topic of the first chapter of *Peau noire*.[80] He recounts scathingly there that having given a lecture in Lyon, a French comrade warmly congratulated him, 'Basically, you're a white man.'[81] Sensing an identification of himself with Frenchness and therefore culturally with whiteness, one of his fellow medical students provocatively nicknamed Fanon 'Blanchette' ('Whitey').[82] Without advertising its racial component, *The Drowning Eye* analyses the split consciousness of a man who sees himself as both black and white, caught between the two: *noir* but not *nègre*, his mentality European and therefore culturally white.

In *Peau noire*, Fanon would return to Shakespeare's *Hamlet* to articulate the consciousness of the black man who identifies with being white:

---

[75]Macey, *Frantz Fanon*, p. 119.

[76]Macey, *Frantz Fanon*, p. 143.

[77]'In every West Indian, before the war of 1939, there was not only the certainty of a superiority over the African, but the certainty of a fundamental difference. The African was a Negro and the West Indian a European', Fanon, *Toward the African Revolution*, p. 20.

[78]Cherki, *Frantz Fanon*, p. 15; Macey, *Frantz Fanon*, p. 118.

[79]Fanon, *Toward the African Revolution*, pp. 20–1.

[80]'The Antillean who wants to be white will succeed, since he will have adopted the cultural tool of language', Fanon, *Black Skin*, p. 21.

[81]Fanon, *Black Skin*, p. 21.

[82]Joby Fanon, *Frantz Fanon*, p. 89.

> Out of the blackest part of my soul, through the cross-hatched zone, surges up this desire to be suddenly *white*.
> I want to be recognized not as *Black*, but as *White*.
> But – and this is the form of recognition that Hegel never described – who better than the white woman to bring this about? By loving me, she proves to me that I am worthy of a white love.
> I am loved like a white man.
> I am a white man.[83]

In order to analyse such ambivalent, contradictory feelings, Fanon invokes the principle character, Jean Veneuse, of René Maran's recent novel, *Un homme pareil aux autres* (*A Man the Same as the Others*) (1947):

> Jean Veneuse is not a 'Negro', and does not want to be a 'Negro'. Yet unbeknownst to him, a hiatus has occurred. There is something indefinable, irreversible, indeed the *that within* of Harold Rosenberg.[84]

The reference here is to an article by Rosenberg on *Hamlet*, recently translated in *Les Temps Modernes* 1948, and heavily marked up in Fanon's own copy. The hiatus, the gap, missing part or lacuna, 'split' (*clivage*),[85] that operates within Jean Veneuse, the nègre who is not a nègre, is indefinable and irreversible: his 'that within' is the 'existential deviation' that 'white civilization and European culture have imposed … on the black man'.[86] Just as Jean Veneuse needs the love of the white woman in order to affirm himself as white, so in *The Drowning Eye* François needs Ginette's love to affirm his own identity and sense of inner self, except that initially François can never be satisfied by Ginette's protestations of love as such. It is only when she declares that he has opened a wound within her that only he can heal ('this open wound that

---

[83]Fanon, *Black Skin*, p. 45.
[84]Fanon, *Black Skin*, p. 52. For further analysis of Fanon's use of Maran, see David Marriott, 'En moi: Frantz Fanon and René Maran', in Max Silverman (ed.), *Frantz Fanon's Black Skin, White Masks: New Interdisciplinary Essays*, Manchester: Manchester University Press, 2005, pp. 146–79.
[85]Fanon, *Black Skin*, p. 63.
[86]Fanon, *Black Skin*, p. xviii.

your hands made in me had to be stitched')[87] that her choice and recognition of him becomes enough.

In the article by Rosenberg that Fanon cites, the phrase that describes the inner wound of consciousness, the 'that within' which Fanon quotes in English, appears as part of André Gide's translation of Hamlet's speech to his mother in Act 1, Scene II of the play.[88] Hamlet, like François, is a gloomy man of the night and the shadows, pursuing authenticity beyond or behind the appearances of the everyday, nursing inside him the grieving wound of his father's death. It festers within, beneath any surface or epidermal appearance, but dominates his relations with others. The 'nighted' Hamlet's insistence on reality rather than seeming and show, on the painful 'that within' of the wound of his father's death, and his interrogation of the ways in which language can both articulate and evade this condition, anticipates François' preoccupation with authenticity, with the role of language, and with his choice of the 'interior life' over the outer world. So the sullen and gloomy François becomes the morbid prince of darkness who inhabits the shadows and the night: 'It is night and François' reign has come.'[89]

---

[87]Scene 5, p. 104. In Scene 3, Lucien speaks of the 'Sun who dresses the cold wounds of humans' (Scene 3, p. 97) and tells Ginette that 'It is with my needle and your thread to stitch the world's wound' (Scene 3, p. 101), Cf. Nietzsche in *The Birth of Tragedy*: 'heal the eternal wound of life' (p. 108, English translation modified to correspond to the French translation), marked by Fanon in his copy. The image of the wound is repeatedly invoked in Césaire's *Cahier*, *Les Armes miraculeuses*, and elsewhere in his poetry.

[88]The *Hamlet* discussion is relevant to the concerns of *The Drowning Eye*: Hamlet picks up his mother's use of the words 'seems' to deny that what she can see is just show. Gide, whose translation Rosenberg's translator uses, translates Hamlet's '"Seems, madam". Nay, it is; I know not "seems"' into a more philosophical antithesis of reality and appearance: 'Appearance! Eh! No Madam. Reality. What have I to do with appearance?' Hamlet's response, 'But I have that within which passeth show; / These but the trappings and the suits of woe' (1.2.85–6) becomes 'But I have something there (that within) [phrase in English] that passes show. The rest is nothing but pomp and adornment of grief' (my back translations from the French). Rosenberg's comment has been underlined by Fanon: 'But in the man there is that within which cannot be played by an actor; it exceeds the stage; it is a remainder of the common part. It is a particular which is [really].' 'Du jeu au je: esquisse d'un géographie de l'action', *Les Temps Modernes*, April 1948, p. 1733; 'The Stages: Geography of Action', *Possibilities*, vol. 1, 1947–1948, p. 50.

[89]Scene 3, p. 92.

Existentialist questions

In *The Drowning Eye*, we thus see the characters moving between psychological characteristics of the different racialized positionalities described in *Black Skin* – the very neuroses that Fanon sought to cure in writing that book. Whilst at times Ginette enslaves herself to François as if he were white and she was black, so she also adores him sexually as if he were black; so too François demands repeated and unsatisfiable recognition from her as if he was black and she was white. In contrast to this vacillating world of fluid transpositions of black and white, reinforced through the alternating imagery of the sun and moon, day and night, stars and death, *The Drowning Eye* presents a set of mutually exclusive alternatives – 'a man will always have to choose between life and death'[90] as Lucien puts it, variously following Hamlet or Jaspers[91] – that becomes the focus of debate throughout the long third scene which dramatizes an existential discussion about the meaning of life in the face of the view that it is absurd.[92] This proposition is introduced not as a radical thought but as a conventional class assignment that François was given in school, '"What possible reasons does a human have to exist?"'[93]

With this question we find ourselves firmly in the post-war world of existential writers from Nietzsche ('man is aware everywhere of the ghastly absurdity of existence'[94]) to Kierkegaard, in the secularized form of a religious substitute developed by Jaspers and Wahl, to Sartre and Camus. Whilst the class assignment seems to come almost directly from Camus, the antiphonal dialogical form of *The Drowning Eye* recalls the Kierkegaard of *Either/Or* which Fanon had been reading.[95] Though the two brothers in the play do

---

[90]Scene 3, p. 87.

[91]'One must live now, in the present moment, or renounce living absolutely' (my translation). Heavily marked in pen in Fanon's copy of Joseph de Tonquédec, *Une philosophie existentielle: L'Existence d'après Karl Jaspers*, Paris: Beauchesne, 1945, p. 31.

[92]Scene 3, p. 86.

[93]Scene 3, p. 85.

[94]Nietzsche, *The Birth of Tragedy*, p. 51.

[95]Sœren Kierkegaard, *Ou bien ... ou bien*, translated from Danish by F. and O. Prior and M. H. Guignot; introduction of F. Brandt, Paris: Gallimard, 1943. Five texts by Kierkegaard are represented in Fanon's library: *Either/Or*, *Fear and Trembling*, *Philosophical Crumbs*, *Stages on Life's Way* and *Works of Love*. He also possessed and marked up a copy of Jean Wahl's seminal essay on 'Heidegger et Kierkegaard',

not correlate simply to the antitheses represented by A, the aesthete, and Judge Vilhelm in Kierkegaard's text, the issues debated in the play oscillate between those of the *Either/Or*, namely the aesthetic, dedicated to 'immediacy', the ethical turned towards the universal, and the religious, with faith conceived as the expression of a limit to what can be thought. These found the opposition between Lucien's hedonistic aesthetic life of pleasure and the aboulic or apathetic religiosity of François who can't be bothered with life whilst he is preoccupied with death, asserting the most profound singularity of his individuality against the universal by railing against the life of the crowd, represented by 'they'.[96] François' weariness with existence, his indolence whilst in pursuit of a personal transcendence, draws on a common existentialist motif, as described in the opening of Emmanuel Levinas' *Existence and Existents* (1947).[97]

The philosophical debates can also be interpreted in Sartrean terms, dramatized into the antithetical choices that Ginette has to make between the two brothers, whose personalities evoke the Sartrean division between being-in-itself and being-for-itself. François seeks the condition of the first, the mode of existence that Sartre says is that of animals or inanimate objects, but which manifests itself in humans as the longing for control and an absolute god-like state – for Sartre, a Hegelian and Heideggerian desire that constitutes bad faith. In his pursuit of being-in-itself François rejects what he considers the inauthenticity that follows from making 'compromises' to the social pressure to conform. Lucien, on the other hand, follows the second way, being-for-itself, and affirms his decision to enjoy living into the future. He has willed his own form of freedom and achieved consciousness even if he cannot transcend his own subjectivity. Lucien presents this as a deliberate choice, but Ginette denies it and claims that only François' refusal

---

in *Recherches philosophiques. 1932–1933*, vol. 2, Paris: Boivin & Cie, 1932. According to Ian Alexander Moore, this essay both 'legitimated Soren Kierkegaard in French academic and inaugurated French existentialism' and 'laid the groundwork for the anthropologist humanist reading of Martin Heidegger' in France (Jean Wahl, *Transcendence and the Concrete: Selected Writings*, eds. Alan D. Schrift and Ian Alexander Moore, New York, NY: Fordham University Press, 2017, pp. 107–31).
[96]Cf. Wahl on the 'Domain of the "They"', 'Heidegger and Kierkegaard', pp. 112–3.
[97]Emmanuel Levinas, *De l'existence à l'existant* (1947) (*Existence and Existents*, trans. Alphonso Lingis, Pittsburgh, PA: Duquesne University Press, 1978, pp. 11–12). Fanon's marked-up copy is in his library.

merits the title of a real choice.[98] These two possibilities which the play pits against each other are irresolvable in their own terms. Whereas Sartre pushes against the first in favour of the second, *The Drowning Eye* shows itself fascinated with Sartre's rejected Hegelian other. This correlates with Fanon's observation on Sartre in *Peau noire*: 'For once, this born-Hegelian had forgotten that consciousness needs to get lost in the night of the absolute, the only condition for attaining self-consciousness.'[99] Fanon rejects any construction of the self that involves its relation to the other, for othering is precisely what opens up the demeaning condition of black consciousness: 'What is certain is that at the very moment when I endeavored to grasp my being, Sartre, who remains "the Other", by naming me stripped away every illusion.'[100] Far from being simply 'Sartrean', therefore, *The Drowning Eye* stages a critical engagement with Sartre, corroborated by François' demand for Ginette to recognize him as part of herself, not as an other, and by his identification with the material though hardly inert world of things which causes Roquentin such nausea in *La Nausée* (*Nausea*) (1938).[101]

Hint of a further source of philosophical influence on the play comes in its emphatic, half-rhyming but elusive title, *The Drowning Eye*. At first, it is hard to see its relevance.[102] In the manuscript the play has no title at all, but both Joby and Josie Fanon refer to it independently as 'The Drowning Eye'. In the syntax of the French, 'L'Œil se noie', the phrase hovers between activity and passivity, between volition, the eye actively drowns, perhaps even drowns itself,

---

[98]Ginette – *(Breathless.)* He's right, because he chose.

Lucien – I've also chosen.

Ginette – No! You know that you did not choose; that we did not choose.

We want to live, but we want to know why *he* wants to die.

(Scene 3, p. 90)

[99]Fanon, *Black Skin*, p. 112 (translation modified).

[100]Fanon, *Black Skin*, p. 116 (translation modified).

[101]Jean-Paul Sartre, *La Nausée*, Paris: Gallimard, 1938 (*Nausea*, trans. Robert Baldick, London: Penguin, 2000). Unless, that is, one would wish to identify François with the Absolute permitted by Sartre, that of the artist. See the essay on Giacometti, 'La recherche de l'absolu', *Situations*, vol. III, 1949, pp. 289–306.

[102]Though Fanon's play would seem to have no direct relation to Georges Bataille's *Story of the Eye* (1928), Nietzsche's *Augenblick* (moment), his concern with vision and seeing, permeates both texts.

and the passivity of being overwhelmed, the eye is drowning. As this suggests, 'se noie' could be translated in the present simple, a single act, or present continuous, which would emphasize the temporality of the process of drowning, as in the title of Stevie Smith's poem, 'Not Waving but Drowning'. The drowning eye could simply refer to the act of crying, as in J.-A.-A. Maltrait's late nineteenth century Creole poem, 'Le chapeau de prêcheur'.[103] However, a line in Victor Hugo's poem 'Passing Through Louis XV Square on a Public Holiday', published in *Rays and Shadows* (1840), comes much closer to the spirit of the play and its central question of the relation of the eye to external reality:

> –Oh! I thought, strange and superhuman power
> Of the one who keeps us throbbing in his hand!
> Oh will of heaven! Abyss where the eye drowns![104]

Hugo's romantic exclamation articulates ideas that would be reconceptualised by Fanon over a hundred years later. Towards the end of Scene 3, Ginette exclaims: 'In a suit the mountain whistler welcomes the jealous oyster and the violated red anemones cry in their corner again. / It's over Lucien, humans have lost. / The mocking sun drowned itself after the cry of blood just now' (p. 96). Ginette here announces that Lucien's human world of the day has thrown itself into the abyss of the night. In its oscillations between light and darkness, *The Drowning Eye* plays on identifications between the sun, the eye and the 'I' or the self. The word 'eye' itself only appears once in the singular, a few lines after Lucien describes the moment when François saw a green star: he then looked at Lucien with wet eyes and cried for a long time. Lucien continues:

Lucien   Yes I loved him! As never before a brother has loved. I loved his eyes.
Some morsel of our being is both source and mouth, he would say.
One day he confided to me that he would like to be blind.

Ginette   Why?

---

[103]'He adds, drying a poor drowning eye', in Norman R. Shapiro (ed.), *Creole Echoes: The Francophone Poetry of Nineteenth-Century Louisiana*, Urbana, IL: University of Illinois Press, 2003, p. 124.
[104]Victor Hugo, 'En passant dans la place Louis XV un jour de fête publique' (*Œuvres poétiques*, ed. Pierre Albouy, I, Paris: NRF, 'Bibliothèque de la Pléiade', p. 1082, ll. 29–31 (my translation).

Lucien   The eye, he answered, must be worthy of the spectacle, but the spectator himself must have a certain dignity.[105]

François' desire to be blind sets up the theme developed throughout the play of his disdain for the everyday appearances of the ordinary world and of his desire to see through the spectacle by means of the inner eye into a visionary cosmic world: 'And my eyes a back door that one has not closed.'[106] One source of this concept of the spectacle, of the 'abyss where the eye drowns', can be found in Nietzsche's *The Birth of Tragedy*.

For Nietzsche, the 'spectacle' for which the eye must be worthy is the Apollonian spectacle which the Dionysian artist can see beyond. Nietzsche writes:

He will have seen more, and more deeply, than ever and yet wished to be blinded.... In that myth the world of appearance is pushed to its limits, where it denies itself and seeks to escape back into the world of the true and unique reality.[107]

In wishing to be blind, to be worthy of the spectacle in order to see the elemental reality behind it, François follows the logic of Nietzsche's Apollonian and Dionysian dialectic according to which the Dionysian artist pushes the human world of appearance (*Schein*) to its limits in order to perceive the essence of what lies behind or beyond. The drowning eye of the play's title evokes Nietzsche's clairvoyant eye that is able to go beyond the superficial layer of semblance and perceive the 'primordial spectacle'.[108] This ultimate reality, according

---

[105]Scene 3, p. 84.

[106]Scene 3, p. 91.

[107]Nietzsche, *The Birth of Tragedy*, p. 132, English translation modified to correspond to the French. Cf. the discussion on p. 141. There are marked-up copies of both *The Birth of Tragedy* and *The Genealogy of Morals*, as well as Andler's *Le Pessimisme esthétique de Nietzsche*, 1921, Bachelard's *L'Air et les Songes*, 1943, *Le Nouvel Esprit scientifique*, 1949, Bernard Groethuysen, *Introduction à la pensée philosophique allemande depuis Nietzsche*, 1926, Jaspers, *Nietzsche et le christianisme*, 1949, among other secondary works on or influenced by Nietzsche, in Fanon's library. Fanon refers to *The Will to Power* in *Black Skin* (p. 197) and, as already mentioned, cites some lines from Nietzsche in the dedication of his thesis (see *The Psychiatric Writings from Alienation and Freedom*, p. 40). His substitution of Nietzsche for Descartes in *Black Skin, White Masks* is indicative (see below, footnote 155).

[108]*Parallel Hands*, Act IV. 1, p. 155. Cf. *Black Skin*, 'I had subtly established the real world. The essence of my world was my property.... I had rediscovered the primordial One' (p. 107).

to Nietzsche, embodies a continual 'artistic' process of indifferent creation and destruction, a remote realm evoked in the play by the interventions of the Voice in lines such as the following which also link directly to the title of the play: '*Silence! Two captive stars commit suicide at the bottom of orbits / eye-sockets.*'[109] The faltering eye represents the movement of the play from the show of observable reality to the primal world that François perceives, whilst its identification with the 'I' also signals the disappearance of François' individuation as he moves towards the realm of the absolute. The complete negation of the self through accession to the realm of the non-human absolute would mean death itself.[110] François is in love with easeful death, but he does not seek it altogether: as the repeated emphasis on doors throughout the play suggests, he reaches the portal of primal experience without entirely losing himself in it – the classic, ecstatic experience of the sublime since Longinus. He stands on the edge, but does not plunge irrevocably into the void. Compare Nietzsche's description of *Oedipus Rex* in *The Birth of Tragedy*: 'we see that the poet's entire conception was nothing more nor less than the luminous image which is offered to us by helpful nature after our glances into the abyss'.[111] And here with the afterimage of the look into the abyss, we find a second source of inspiration for the title of the play – the transcendent, self-sacrificial moment which ends Césaire's *Cahier* as he watches the rising dove imaged in the cornea of his eye ascend to the great black hole in the sky in which he had wanted to drown himself:

> then, strangling me with your lasso of stars
> rise, Dove
> rise
> rise

---

[109]Scene 3, p. 87.

[110]Cf. Sartre, *L'Être et le néant* 'Death has always been … considered as the final boundary of human life. As such it was natural that a philosophy which was primarily concerned to make precise the human position in relation to the non-human which surrounded it, would first consider death as a door opening upon the nothingness of human-reality, and that this nothingness would be the absolute cessation of being or else existence in a non-human form. Thus we may say that there has been … a realistic conception of death such that death appeared as an immediate contact with the non-human.' Thus death escaped man at the same time that it rounded him off with the non-human absolute' (*Being and Nothingness*, p. 532).

[111]Nietzsche, *The Birth of Tragedy*, p. 61, English translation modified to correspond to the French translation.

rise
I follow you who are imprinted on my ancestral white cornea
rise sky licker
and the great black hole where a moon ago I wanted to drown
it is there I will now fish the malevolent tongue of the night in its
immobile veerition![112]

Césaire's sublime ending is complicated by its dialectical structure: the poet had wanted to be like the dove and drown in the great black hole of the sky, but that was a moon ago. Now he will fish the malevolent tongue /language of the night: self-extinction has been replaced by triumphant poetic production.

In *The Drowning Eye* we can thus detect the influence of Fanon's reading of *The Birth of Tragedy* mediated by the Césaire of the *Cahier*.[113] Césaire had discovered in Nietzsche's critique of European culture and its Christian values (not to be underestimated given the importance of the Catholic church in colonial Martinique), together with his stress on the necessity of the self-creation of new values as a form of self-affirmation, a fulcrum that could be utilized for the colonized person of colour who had been relegated to the negativity of the position of an inferior and uncivilized race. Whilst Fanon was generally familiar with the post-war French Left reading of Nietzsche, he took from Césaire a recognition of the transformative

---

[112]Césaire, *Cahier* 1947, *Œuvres complètes*, pp. 177–8, *The Complete Poetry*, p. 61 (translation modified to correspond to 1947 Bordas edition). Fanon explicitly echoes Césaire's final image at the end of the Introduction to *Black Skin*: 'And with feverish lips and frenzied heart he plunges into the great black hole' (p. xviii); cf. also Fanon citing the Rebel from *Et les chiens se taisaient* in *Black Skin*: 'When the black man plunges, in other words, goes down, something extraordinary happens. Listen to Césaire again: "And here I find myself again in the rush of metamorphosis / Drowned blinded / Afraid of myself…. / Gods … you are not gods. I am free"' (p. 174).
[113]In his discussion of *Et les chiens se taisaient*, Césaire frequently invoked Paul Claudel's Nietzschean *Tête d'or* as among the works most important to him in his student years (A. James Arnold, *Modernism and Négritude: The Poetry and Poetics of Aimé Césaire*, Harvard: Harvard University Press, 1990, p. 53). On Césaire and Nietzsche, see also Arnold, *Modernism and Negritude*, pp. 114–18; Eshleman and Smith, *Collected Poetry*, p. 3; Donna V. Jones, *The Racial Discourses of Life Philosophy : Négritude, Vitalism, and Modernity*, Columbia University Press, 2010; on Nietzsche, Césaire and Fanon, Françoise Lionnet, *Autobiographical Voices: Race, Gender, Self-Portraiture*, Ithaca, NY: Cornell University Press, 1989: 'Césaire and Fanon have a larger debt to Nietzschean views of culture than to any other Western conceptual apparatus, unsurprisingly so in light of the radical critique of Western ideology and dogmatism that Nietzsche's works incorporate …', p. 73.

possibilities that Nietzsche's philosophy held out for the colonized person. The attraction of Nietzsche for Fanon can be understood through a passage in Karl Jaspers' *Nietzsche et le Christianisme* that Fanon marked in his copy, in which Jaspers argues that it is Nietzsche who holds out the possibility that the *ressentiment* of disempowerment can be reconstructed by the dispossessed into a form of creative empowerment. Jaspers writes: 'It is Nietzsche who discovered, in the domain of psychology, that the *ressentiment* aroused by powerlessness, under the action of the will to power even in impotence, can become creative, engender values, ideals, interpretations.'[114] This reversal, or as Fanon would later put it, transmutation, in many ways correlated with the thinking of Fanon's later therapeutic practice and provided the structure of individual and social transformation that he would articulate in both *Peau noire* and *Les Damnés de la terre*. The political relevance of Nietzsche for both Césaire and Fanon should be understood within this conceptual framework of the impotence of the colonized transformed into the will to power. In both *The Drowning Eye* and *Parallel Hands*, Fanon follows such a model of self-affirmation, as he will at the end of *Peau noire*: 'In the world I am heading for, I am endlessly creating myself.... I am my own foundation.'[115]

Layered onto the dynamics of the racial binary discussed above, the dialogue between the two brothers in *The Drowning Eye* also offers a philosophical debate between Apollonian light and Dionysian darkness, between a commitment to the values and aesthetic pleasures of bourgeois life and a disposition to believe that everyday reality is an illusion that hides a more profound cosmic reality. Whilst the pragmatic Lucien complains that François 'always refused to see things as they are',[116] François sees himself as a dissident who has broken 'the yoke of individuation' and seen through the veil of appearance to the lunar cosmic world in his desire to accede to the realm of 'the absolute One' ('l'Un-absolu').[117] The

---

[114]Karl Jaspers, *Nietzsche et le christianisme*, Paris: Minuit, 1949, p. 38 (my translation). Fanon makes this argument, citing Nietzsche, whereby negation, *ressentiment*, and reaction can be transformed into affirmation and the actional in the conclusion to chapter 7 of *Black Skin*, p. 197.

[115]Fanon, *Black Skin*, pp. 204–5.

[116]Scene 3, p. 85.

[117]Nietzsche, *The Birth of Tragedy*, pp. 97, 27 (translation modified to correspond to Fanon's French edition).

play's fierce, antagonistic Apollonian-Dionysian opposition plays out in the imagery of life, sun and transparency attached to Lucien, whose very name means light, and that of death, darkness and obscurity associated with François.[118] *The Drowning Eye* precipitates us into the existential situation of being caught between being light and darkness, white and black, mediated through a preoccupation with nothingness, with mortality and death, with 'white death', 'the hideous tenseness of anxiety and death', leading to an assumption into the freedom of an absolute otherness of inhuman cosmic materiality presented in the Nietzschean terms of the return, nakedness and the seizing of Life: 'Man is a YES resonating from cosmic harmonies.'[119] It might be expected that the Dionysian unites with the Apollonian at the end of the play, but the reconciliation with Ginette hardly provides a substitute for Lucien. Far from reconciling or synthesizing the two poles, she eliminates all form of otherness by allowing herself to be totally absorbed into her controlling lover, according to a characteristic surrealist trope whereby Eros or woman allows the alienated self to ascend to a desired fullness of being, here conforming to François' demand that her love for him should not involve any structure of alterity.[120]

In the final moment of the last scene, the Apollonian human world is left behind, as François incorporates Ginette within him and leads her forwards towards full self-realization at the doors of the Absolute where life is grasped:

François   (Takes her hand and gets ready to go.)
O Return, exuberance not yet torn
My foaming nudity takes you, broken with horror and I want to lead you to the ABSOLUTE gates
where life is seized.[121]

---

[118]With the theme of light in both plays, compare Levinas, *Existence and Existents*, pp. 38–44, 85–6. The antimony of light and darkness is also to be found in Camus and is central to Césaire's *Cahier*.
[119]*Black Skin*, p. xii (translation modified).
[120]Compare the metaphors of absorbing blotting paper, of being opened and then finished like a book: 'Then he goes leaving my body open like a novel that one will finish later' (Scene 3, p. 94), 'I implore you, restart me. / I implore you, complete me' (Scene 5, p. 104).
[121]Scene 5, p. 106.

This closing act of self-realization initially sounds as much Hegelian as Nietzschean, as Fanon's own language, echoing and evoking the *Phenomenology*'s 'night of the absolute' suggests. We find a comparable mix of Hegel with Nietzsche at the end of Césaire's *Cahier* which stages its own Hegelian sublation in the final leap of the speaker to a new poetic consciousness. Just as the *Cahier* has a Hegelian three-part dialectical structure, so we can see *The Drowning Eye* also working in the same sequence, with the extended critique of François in the second and third scenes, ending in his rejection by Ginette, functioning as the long labour of the negative before its *Aufhebung* in the dramatic moment of the final scene where François finally acts – by standing up and beginning to walk away. But the anticipated sublation into the absolute is not the absolute itself. He leads Ginette towards the doors from which they can look out on to the prospect of a Nietzschean form of primordial unity (*das Ur-Eine*), the non-individuated reality of what Fanon in *Peau noire* calls 'the primordial One' that exists beyond all forms of appearance.[122] If they went through the doors they would be choosing death or the absolute, but instead they will stand naked before the beyond, before the 'abyss where the eye drowns', the antechamber of death where it is possible to grasp the most intense experience of life. We are left with the affirmation of an aspirational Nietzschean moment of becoming, an assertion of the human will to the absolute but not its final Hegelian achieved resolution.

Unlike Césaire's *Cahier*, *The Drowning Eye* therefore does not conclude with a turn towards language as the proffered form of the sublime: it ends with a more explicit desire for a freedom through transcendence, an absolute otherness, which looks towards a self-achieved erasure of alienated consciousness and its social milieu. The meaning of such transcendence remains inevitably elusive given that transcendence here seems to follow from what Georg Lukács described as 'the negation of any meaning in the world or the life of man'.[123] The final moment of the play which moves towards transcendence offers a vision beyond the exigencies of the oppressive every day which are left behind: unsupportable alienated self-consciousness, the sense of being caught in a perpetual volleying between nothingness and the infinite – all this is apparently

---

[122]*Black Skin,* p. 107.

[123]Georg Lukács, 'The ideology of modernism', in *The Meaning of Contemporary Realism* (1957), trans. John and Necke Mander, London: Merlin Press, 1963, p. 40.

in the process of being resolved through transcendence into a form of material immanence, insentience, non-consciousness, even if, inevitably, it remains a performative declaration before the gates have been reached. How do we understand the hesitating form of this transcendence and movement towards the Absolute which never achieves any finality? Both of Fanon's plays could be said to perform Kierkegaard's basic position that 'true existence is achieved by intensity of feeling' – the intensity of which, paradoxically, puts the individual in contact with something outside of him or herself (*ekstasis*) which Kierkegaard calls 'the absolute Other'.[124] Following the French interpretation of Kierkegaard and Heidegger, transcendence has lost its religious or Hegelian character. It involves, rather, as in Heidegger, Sartre and Wahl, a perpetual movement towards the world and things, 'a transcendence in immanence', in which the absolute can be achieved momentarily in the instant through the individual act: 'I define myself as an absolute tension of opening.'[125] In a handwritten note tipped into Gaston Bachelard's *L'Air et les songes* (*Air and Dreams*) (1943) Fanon wrote:

Do not seek the Absolute through a relative. Totally illogical. A conversion must be undertaken and the Absolute must not be considered as a sort of End, [which] could not be conceived given the relativity of the means. I am thinking essentially of knowledge. The conversion therefore consists in transposing the absolute and in considering it a quality of things and in particular of acts (that would eliminate the pseudo-problem of failure, and even that of the *objective* failure). This is tantamount to return to Existence its character of unicity, metaphysical par excellence. Whence follows the notion of the absolute Other. But it would seem that thereby we rejoin the aesthetic level of Kierk[egaard]. But everything stems from a difference of interpretation of the *instant*, whether in considering the instant as something no longer lived on the aesthetic level but on the religious one, the conversion is made without [giving] primacy to that unique

---

[124]Jean Wahl, *Esquisse pour une histoire de 'l'existentialisme'*, Paris: L'Arche, 1947, p. 18 (*A Short History of Existentialism*, trans. Forrest Williams and Stanley Maron, New York, NY: The Philosophical Library, 1949, p. 6).
[125]Wahl, *Esquisse pour une histoire de 'l'existentialisme'*, p. 33, *A Short History*, p. 15. Fanon, *Black Skin*, p. 117 (translation modified).

instant in which the disciple receives the condition and which in fact appears as an essentialist infiltration that most heavily strains the metaphysical future of man. Every instant [must] count as much as possible.[126]

Fanon's play moves between two interrelated conceptions of the Absolute articulated by Wahl, whereby it is momentarily experienced as at once both the truest experience of the self and of the non-self: 'Our thought of the absolute would be that it is not necessary to seek the absolute in the totality nor in eternity, but in the partial and in the ephemeral felt with intensity.... The thought of the absolute is the thought of this atmosphere and domain where I realize myself by destroying myself.'[127] Where I (the eye) realize myself by drowning myself.

Parallel Hands

Fanon's second play, *Parallel Hands*, is a longer four-act tragedy set in a classical Greek idiom. He wrote it in 1949, immediately after completing *The Drowning Eye*. Joby recounts that Fanon, who was still finishing his studies, came to stay with him in July of that year in Dunkerque, where Joby was working as a customs officer. The new play was in the process of being written. Fanon arrived 'feverish, agitated',[128] and asked Joby to find him a typist. The wife of a colleague having duly volunteered, Fanon then spent three days dictating Acts III and IV to her. He was however stuck ('bloqué') with regard to the development of the last act. He did not know whether the heroine Audaline should survive the hero Épithalos (in the version printed

---

[126]Page 174 in this edition. Cf. Louis Lavelle, *De l'acte*, Paris: Montaigne, 1946, 'This is enough to show that philosophy and life itself only have a serious character on the conditions that the Absolute is not before me and outside of me as an inaccessible goal, but on the contrary in me and that in it I trace my furrow', p. 49, marked in Fanon's copy.
[127]Jean Wahl, *Existence humaine et trancendance*, Être et penser, Cahiers de philosophie 6, Neuchâtel: Éditions de la Baconnière, 1944, p. 62 (*Human Existence and Transcendence*, trans. William C. Hackett, Notre Dame, IN: University of Notre Dame Press, 2016, pp. 48-9). In *Black Skin, White Masks* Fanon footnotes his use of the word 'transcendence' with the comment 'in the sense meant by Jean Wahl, *Human Existence and Transcendence*', p. 117.
[128]Joby Fanon, *Frantz Fanon*, p. 133.

here, Audaline dies in Act III). Bizarrely, Fanon and his stenographer finally finished the play in the Dunkerque cemetery, 'the only place that seemed to him to be suitable for his concentration'.[129] As with *The Drowning Eye*, Joby interprets *Parallel Hands* as a personal statement by Fanon, and quotes freely from the play as if any lines from the dialogue comprise Fanon speaking directly about himself.[130]

Reality and illusion

Like Sartre's *Les Mouches*, *Parallel Hands* has a fictional Greek setting – the island of Lébos, the name evoking Lesbos but without denoting the island itself. The male characters have Greek (Polyxos), or Greek-sounding (Épithalos, perhaps from Épithalamus, 'the dorsal portion of the diencephalon', an appropriate enough name for a hero who represents the aspiring intellect), whilst the women characters have either French (Audaline) or Jewish names (Ménasha is Hebrew, a variant of Manasseh, whilst Dràhna is Bohemian Yiddish, meaning 'dear').[131] The cast is composed of the Chorus, Polyxos the King, Dràhna his wife, Épithalos their son, a proud young warrior, Ménasha, mother of Audaline, Audaline, her daughter and fiancée of Épithalos. The action takes place on the day planned for their wedding. In the opening scene, Polyxos has been disturbed by an ominous dream in which, as he puts it, 'merciless Épithalos absented me from this Earth'.[132] And indeed, instead of marrying Audaline, Épithalos, seeing himself as the superhuman agent who challenges society and destiny, chooses that day to kill Polyxos instead. From the feminist perspective that Dràhna consistently develops, one way of looking at the play would be that it involves a young warrior's choice to commit a political murder (his father) rather than submit himself to marriage on his wedding day, an act which would have involved Épithalos' submission to the status quo of conventional life (compare Fanon's letter to his *marraine de guerre*). In an echo of Hamlet's relation to Ophelia, Audaline subsequently dies ('I die and my death is unknown

---

[129]Joby Fanon, *Frantz Fanon*, p. 133. There are five cemeteries in Dunkerque, so the actual location of the composition of Act IV cannot be determined.
[130]Joby Fanon, *Frantz Fanon*, pp. 130–4, 139.
[131]Alexander Beider, *Origins of Yiddish Dialects*, Oxford: Oxford University Press, 2015, p. 423.
[132]Act I. 2, p. 115.

to me / I sink into the abyss').[133] Épithalos' murder of Polyxos unleashes an apocalyptic conflagration across the town in the course of which many people are killed; in an effort to contain the situation, the military commander announces that Épithalos must leave. In the final act, Épithalos confronts his own and then Audaline's mother, who tell him that what he thinks has been a heroic self-sacrifice in the name of humanity has been a failure and caused only chaos. His self-conviction begins to crumble and he accepts the return of what promises to be a new maternal order as inevitable.

As in Césaire's *Et les chiens se taisaient*, revolution is imagined as a Nietzschean Dionysian self-sacrifice, today we might say of martyrdom, which prompts the rebirth of the people and their political culture. The play portrays a rebellion against an old order that Épithalos condemns as complicit with the stifling hegemonic power of the gods, as well as being a play about revolution as such. *Parallel Hands* is not about a young man playing at revolution, as in Paul Nizan's 1938 novel *La Conspiration*, nor is it a play about revolutionaries, in the sense of a collective action taken against the dominant order. *Parallel Hands* is a play about a revolutionary hero who takes his own destiny upon himself and sacrifices himself in order to rid society of 2,000 years of complaisant rule, which at the same time involves an oedipal drama against his father. The drama of the play is less the murder of the ruler as such, which happens off-stage and is presented as inevitable, than a concern with the dynamics of *Oedipus Rex* rethought and refashioned as a play about revolutionary consciousness which shows the influence of Kojève's reading of Hegel's master/slave dialectic. It is thus also about a struggle for power, which means that, as in *Peau noire*, the oedipal struggle is overlaid and conflated with the fight to the death between master and slave.[134]

Invoking the obvious if unstated parallel between Lébos and Martinique, we can say from our historical knowledge of Fanon's situation that the killing of the King may also represent a struggle to the death with the white, colonizing father,[135] instantiated in Fanon's

---

[133]Act III. 3, p. 146.

[134]Compare Stuart Hall's prescient analysis of *Black Skin* in terms of an oedipal master-slave struggle, as well as his characterization of Fanon's theory of violence in terms of the wiping out of colonial culture, in his comments recorded in Isaac Julien's film, *Black Skin, White Mask* (1995).

[135]Cf. Fanon's repeated citations from Césaire about the rebel slave killing the master, footnote 17 above.

time by the notorious Admiral Georges Robert, whose Vichy regime in Martinique was in fact overthrown in 1943. Fanon's implicit, and wholly understated, oedipal re-reading of Hegel produces the energy for the unnamed force that drives Épithalos to commit his revolutionary act. In the play, however, the two men never actually meet on stage, and once the presumably white master is dead, the hero becomes not a triumphant Toussaint but reverts to his role as a semi-repentant Oedipus. Although Épithalos achieves the Sartrean authenticity of transforming his words into an act, his fierce resolution and self-confidence become more equivocal when he sees the consequences of his unleashing death and disorder in the city and is challenged by his mother and would-be mother-in-law. Fanon portrays Épithalos as a Dionysian revolutionary who pays the cost of his superhuman self-assertion according to the dynamics of the Oedipal trajectory described by Charles Andler:

> Oedipus penetrates beyond what the condition of man allows us to see. One only forces nature to deliver up its secret by resisting nature. The parricide and the incest of Oedipus symbolize this wisdom bought at the price of the overthrow of venerable things and the natural order. After which, no doubt, it only remains to suffer the punishment reserved by nature for those who have broken its laws.[136]

Some scenes are missing in the manuscript: Act II, scenes 3 and 4, and Act III, scenes 1 and 2. There is always the possibility that as Fanon's typists changed, or different drafts were put together, scenes were misnumbered.[137] Since most of the action happens off stage, according to the conventions of Greek drama, it is impossible to be certain that a gap in the narrative indicates a missing scene. However, Joby Fanon himself gives us evidence for the existence of lost material at the beginning of Act III. When he quotes extensively lines taken from the play, we can see that he is following the sequence of the manuscript. After lines taken from the end of Act II, he quotes the following which are not present in the manuscript (his quotations then resume with lines from Act III, Scene 3):

---

[136]Charles Andler, *Nietzsche, sa vie et sa pensée. Le pessimisme esthétique de Nietzsche: sa philosophie à l'époque wagnérienne*, vol. 3, Paris: Bossard, 1921, p. 59 (my translation). Fanon owned this book and marked up the early chapters in which Andler discusses Nietzsche's views on tragedy.

[137]All of the pages of the manuscript have been renumbered in red pen.

> And I, the lighter of worlds
> Words! Words! Words!
> I look for stars to 'wing' reason
> I'm inventing myself
> Surging up from the power of the act
> Me absolute contestation[138]

These pugnacious lines full of assertive abstractions are certainly characteristic of the language of the self-aggrandizing and self-heroizing main character, Épithalos.[139] Joby also cites the following argument for the play, which is also not present in the manuscript:

> Each of the consciousnesses on stage has made the leap.
> From nothingness to justified Being
> From unjustified being to Nothingness
> Whence the finite appearance of the expression.[140]

This philosophical statement, which seems to be invoking the leap of consciousness in Camus and its dualistic reversal, suggests that the play is concerned with Épithalos' leap from nothingness to justified being, to a 'higher consciousness',[141] just as Fanon announces at the beginning of *Peau noire* that: 'There is a zone of non-being, an extraordinarily sterile and arid region, a slope stripped bare of every essential, from which a genuine new upsurge can materialize.' The third and fourth lines, however, warn of the potential reversibility of this move: the dualism cannot be resolved or separated as Épithalos imagines.[142] In effecting self-transformation, Épithalos seeks to achieve the unfinished, god-like completion (*ens causa sui*) which, according to Sartre in *L'Être et le néant* (1943), haunts human

---

[138]Joby Fanon, *Frantz Fanon*, p. 131 (my translation).
[139]'Words! Words! Words!' recalls lines in *The Drowning Eye*, Césaire in the *Cahier*, 1947 (see footnote 31), as well as Hamlet's exclamation to Polonius in *Hamlet* in the translation of the Rosenberg article discussed above.
[140]Joby Fanon, *Frantz Fanon*, p. 130. This argument may have been typed on one of the missing three pages at the beginning of the manuscript.
[141]Act II. 2, p. 134.
[142]Fanon, *Black Skin*, p. xii (translation modified). Cf. Sartre 'it is difficult to explain the upsurge ex *nihilo* of the reflective consciousness …' (*Being and Nothingness*, p. 150), and Fanon's description of himself on his discovery of *négritude* as a form of recognition 'At last I had been recognized, I was no longer a nothingness', *Black Skin*, p. 108 (translation modified).

existence but which, according to him, is necessarily impossible.[143] His Promethean pursuit for self-realization, pursued through the killing of the father and the destruction of the social order, and transformed into Dionysian self-sacrifice as it becomes unsustainable, comprises the drama of the play.

The question of language and its relation to action

The intensity of the play's language means that its semantic continuity is nothing if not hard to follow. The best account of Fanon's language was given by Fanon himself to Francis Jeanson. Asked to explain a sentence in *Peau noire*, Fanon replied uncompromisingly:

> This sentence is inexplicable. I seek, when I write such things, to touch my reader with affect … that is to say irrationally, almost sensually.… Words have a charge for me. I feel myself incapable of escaping the bite of a word, the vertigo of a question mark.

Jeanson added that Fanon wanted his writing to flow like Césaire's, 'under the astounding lava of words the colour of feverish flesh'.[144] In *Parallel Hands*, though still much influenced by Césaire in its style, Fanon's language has become more opaque and less startlingly surreal, preoccupied with concepts and theoretical ideas. The 'lost' lines cited above ('Words! Words! Words!') suggest that a central focus of the play is placed upon the question of language itself and its relation to action. As in *The Drowning Eye*, there is a sense that language has become devalued, producing only abstractions with no purchase on the real. Language has become worn out and must be reconnected to action and the act: 'On the other side of the emaciated Word, / The initial Act is raised.'[145] Whilst the comprador Chorus suggests a corresponding antithesis between light and language, where language will not change anything beyond itself, 'speech is not distorted by any visions' (p. 107), Épithalos by contrast claims to Audaline that when pushed to extremes language can be made performative and erupt in action:

---

[143]Sartre, *Being and Nothingness*, pp. 150ff, 621ff.

[144]Francis Jeanson, 'Préface' to Fanon, *Peau noir, masques blanc*, Paris: Seuil, 1952, p. 12, *Œuvres complètes*, pp. 51–2 (my translation). Compare Fanon's language here to Lucien's evocation of the performativity of language in *The Drowning Eye*, Scene 3, p. 88.

[145]Act I. 4, p. 121.

> Audaline upon reaching the volcanic extremes speech makes
> itself act!
> A language haunted by exhilarating perception![146]

Even at the end, Épithalos exclaims: 'Language authorized by the ACT, raise the world.'[147] Whilst this articulates a desire for language to be intimately connected to and directly productive of human action with material consequences, in a different way the idea of language as an act also describes the strange language of the play itself, where characters, particularly Épithalos, speak words, phrases and sentences that work performatively so that meaning and semantic resonance are produced in the moment of their enunciation and directly felt on the pulses. Once again, language becomes an active agent in the play, at one level highly metaphorical and contorted, full of zeugma and catachresis, but typically grounding its metaphors in a literalism that intensifies the emotional resonance, as in phrases such as 'My forbidden blood bends its lucid nape' (p. 127) or 'lightning bolts of choleric majesties set the world's hair ablaze' (p. 120). Synaesthesia is commonly used ('I climb flaying my sonorous hands' [p. 133]), words are transformed by being put into different parts of speech, particularly in the past participle form ('essential nymphaea' [*essentielles nymphées*], 'Burnt floods', 'abyssal consciousnesses' [*consciences abîmées*], together with invented neologisms ('the *undivined Audaline*') (pp. 147–8). Even the stage directions become metaphorized in this literalizing way which would make them impossible to stage, for example in Act III, Scene 4: '*three harps wet the lips of a soul*' (p. 148). Such characteristics of the language mean that all speech in the play is performed in its own instance as an event, it erupts palpably as an act the moment it is spoken rather than leaving us with a paraphrasable or narrativizable meaning. Transformation of the self begins with turning speech into a creative self-defining speech-act.

As with *The Drowning Eye*, there is no title page in the manuscript of *Parallel Hands* – it starts at page 4 – but once again both Josie and Joby Fanon independently cite the same title. It makes an obvious allusion to Sartre's play *Les Mains sales* (*Dirty*

---

[146]Act II. 2, p. 131.
[147]Act IV. 3, p. 166.

Hands), which was performed in Lyon in May 1949.[148] Associated with work, action, the dirty hands in Sartre's play are linked to the pursuit of liberty during the Second World War: the play raises the question of the purity of motives with respect to the political assassination carried out by the central character, Hugo Barine. However, Hugo in turn discovers that he has been betrayed by the party who ordered him to carry it out and who now want to kill him. The play's mix of existentialism with a critical view of leftist politics has always been controversial. Fanon's play shares with Sartre's a focus on the physical hands of the assassin and a questioning of the value of the assassination: in *Parallel Hands* the killing involves an act of parricide which Épithalos sees as a revolutionary act but which his mother tries to persuade him was a delusion: although very different in execution, the fundamental narratives of the two plays have certain similarities.

Beyond the connection with *Les Mains sales*, literary sources for *Parallel Hands* include *Oedipus Rex*, *Hamlet* and Sartre's *Les Mouches* (which in turn draws on the *Oresteia*). Whilst in the last two of these, the heroes commit murder as revenge for the death of their fathers, *Parallel Hands* echoes the narrative of *Oedipus Rex*: the central event of the play is the killing of the King Polyxos by his son Épithalos. Unlike Oedipus, however, Épithalos commits the act deliberately in order to overturn the presiding order, just as Orestes kills Aegisthus (and Clytemnestra) in *Les Mouches*. Fanon's own father had died in January 1947, two years before he wrote the play. However, it is noticeable that whilst *Hamlet* and *Oedipus* focus on the feelings of guilt produced by the death of the father, this is not a significant concern in *Parallel Hands*.[149] Épithalos ends by expressing a certain regret, but guilt as such seems to be no more of an issue than social justice. Rather than the anguished self-blinding of Oedipus, he ends the play with the assertion 'I SEE'. The play is certainly preoccupied with death however (versions of the word 'death' occur

---

[148]Fanon first read the play in *Les Temps modernes*, where he marked up some passages. Josie Fanon's copy of the play, dated July 1948, is in the collection of Fanon's library.
[149]For Fanon's reaction to his father's death in 1947, see Joby Fanon, *Frantz Fanon*, pp. 91–7, and Macey, *Frantz Fanon*, p. 122. Joby's account tellingly quickly shifts to Fanon's relation with his mother. We might compare Dràhna's reactions to Épithalos' plans and subsequent actions with Mme Fanon's complaints when Fanon absconded from Martinique, on his brother's wedding day, to try to join the Free French army (see Joby Fanon, *Frantz Fanon*, p. 60; Macey, *Frantz Fanon*, p. 88).

in *The Drowning Eye* fourteen times, thirty in *Parallel Hands*), and as in *The Drowning Eye*, it interweaves complex antithetical punning relations between death, love and the word (*la mort, l'amour* and *le mot*: 'Death blocks my way / But the word must find life there').[150] Fanon, Joby claims, was obsessed with death at the time he wrote his plays. In this connection, he cites the following previously unpublished fragment:

> What is death? There is a contradiction between the heroic and the tragic, between the beings who seek death in order to show independence paid at the highest price. In death, the heroic man denies death, raises above death an invincible part of himself.[151]

Parallel Hands pits the drama of its tragedy against its staging of Épithalos' heroic, creative but necessarily destructive act of self-assertion, and therefore could be said to develop a contradiction of this kind as we see Épithalos apparently about to pay the ultimate price in the final scene. Whereas François is described as being inhabited by death ('Death is what inhabits François. /Death guides him'),[152] Épithalos' will-to-power seeks to go beyond death and raise an invincible part of himself above it in a gesture of the sort of Nietzschean prometheanism that Fanon found articulated in Michel Carrouges' *La Mystique du surhomme (The Mystique of the Superman)*: 'And it is here that man affirms his original destiny: that of a being on the march towards his own deification.'[153]

What, though, does Fanon's title mean: what are the *parallel* hands to which it refers? Like the eye of *The Drowning Eye*, they are invoked only once in the text, in this case in the course of the meeting between Épithalos and Audaline on the morning of their wedding. Épithalos exclaims:

---

[150]Act IV. 1, p. 157.
[151]Joby Fanon, *Frantz Fanon*, p. 138.
[152]Scene 3, p. 89.
[153]Michel Carrouges, *La Mystique du surhomme*, Paris: Gallimard, 1948, p. 23; the sentence is underlined in Fanon's copy.

> Stop threatened and horizontal crowds that tell me the powerless
> causality of my existence.
> An act! I want to spatter this pregnant sky with a vertiginous act!
> Parallel hands make the starchy world ring out with a new act![154]

Épithalos here announces his desire to transform the ossified horizontal world with his 'vertiginous' act, a world conceptualized as operating passively through structural causality rather than as the effect of human will. We can compare this with Fanon's remark in *Peau noire* where he describes the act of taking destiny in one's own hands: 'Man is what brings society into being. The prognosis is in the hands of those who are prepared to shake the worm-eaten foundations of the edifice',[155] an act comparable to his account of the necessary revolutionary destruction of a sclerotic bourgeois society: 'For me bourgeois society is a closed society where it's not good to be alive, where the air is rotten, the ideas and people are putrefying. And I believe that a man who takes a stand against this [living] death is in a way a revolutionary.'[156] The emphasis on hands is clearly related to the labour of revolutionary action rather than passive contemplation – the condition in which the island has stagnated for two millennia. For hands as the active basis of political resistance and revolution, we may compare Césaire's poem 'Transmutation', in *Soleil cou coupé*, where:

---

[154]Act II. 2, p. 128. The idea of parallel hands is set up in the opening lines of the play, spoken by the Chorus in a characteristically oblique fashion: 'The prismatic faces of my anxious hands walk their images into the heart of the obscure. Slivers of faces move about in parallel, and genuflexion, the centre of human nature's gravity, calms.' Act I. 1, p. 108. Épithalos also remarks to Audaline a little earlier in Act II, Scene 2, 'O refused intoxications! Will I revive who welcomes me as an unfulfilled sigh, when our parallel lives, captive of my hands, already face one another?' (Act II. 2, p. 126).

[155]Fanon, *Black Skin*, p. xv. Cf. also p. xiv: 'Man's misfortune, Nietzsche said, was that he was once a child. Nevertheless, we can never forget, as Charles Odier implies, that the fate of the neurotic lies in his own hands.' Matthieu Renault has pointed out that this observation, which Fanon attributes to Nietzsche, is in fact taken from Simone de Beauvoir who attributes it to Descartes in *Pour une morale de l'ambiguïté*: 'Man's unhappiness, says Descartes, is due to his having first been a child' (*The Ethics of Ambiguity*, trans. Bernard Frechtman, New York, NY: Citadel Press, 1948, p. 35). Matthieu Renault, 'Le genre de la race: Fanon, lecteur de Beauvoir', *Actuel Marx*, vol. 55, no. 1, 2014, p. 36.

[156]Fanon, *Black Skin*, p. 199 (translation modified). This follows the quotation from Marx's *Eighteenth Brumaire* on social revolution drawing its poetry from the future.

> in the absence of any objective reference ...
> *defense* a storm screams at me incessantly
> always foretold always deferred nourishing the unconscious of
> our crowds
> with all the peripeteia of nightmare
> Happily they did not notice that I noticed that I have my hands to
> keep me company I have my monkey tail hands I have my booby-
> trap hands I have my assassin hands....[157]

The poem then continues to elaborate the many further kind of hands that the poet possesses to defend himself and effect a violent transmutation.[158]

But if Épithalos takes destiny into his own hands, why do they specifically have to be *parallel* hands? The parallel hands in *Parallel Hands* relate specifically to the question of objective reference, as in Césaire. Épithalos sees himself as cutting through illusion to objectivity, which he describes in material, scientific, mathematical terms that are contrasted to the arbitrary interpretations and accommodating syntheses of Polyxos:

> Lébos that obstinately spurns spiritual resonances, I fragment the hypotenuse that redoubles the World. Polyxos, angular intimacy, the accepted syntheses abandon their scrawny horizons, arbitrary interpretations distort the purity of objectivity.
> Yes Épithalos, fundamental apparition
> Is braced by the unfinished.[159]

Just as in *The Drowning Eye*, where most see an illusory reality (the *schein* of the spectacle) and only François the primordial reality behind, so here the people of Lébos do not recognize the gap between the true or inherent meaning of signs, between what is objectively there and what they judge to be there. Whereas the earlier contrast was drawn from Nietzsche's account in *The Birth of Tragedy*, here Fanon seems to be recalling a comparable though very different kind of distinction from

---

[157]Césaire, 'Transmutation', *Œuvres*, p. 393, *The Complete Poetry*, p. 343.
[158]Compare Dràhna in Act I: 'Sire, protect us from misfortune! / Stop the blinding hatching of a metamorphosis. / Avert the transmutation of shuddering Épithalos' (Act I. 3, p. 117).
[159]Act II. 2, p. 127.

Maurice Merleau-Ponty's *Phénoménologie de la perception* (1945), which begins by analysing dissimilar kinds of perceptual illusion:

> The phenomenon of true perception offers, therefore, a meaning inherent in the signs, and of which judgement is merely the optional expression. Intellectualism can make comprehensible neither this phenomenon nor the imitation which illusion gives of it. More generally it is blind to the mode of existence and co-existence of perceived objects, to the life which steals across the visual field and secretly binds its parts together. In Zöllner's optical illusion, I 'see' the main lines converging. Intellectualism simply reduces the phenomenon to a mistake, saying that it all comes of my bringing in the auxiliary lines and their relation to the main ones, instead of comparing their main lines themselves. Basically I mistake the task given to me, and I compare the two wholes instead of comparing the principal elements.[160]

Zöllner's illusion, discovered in 1860, consists of a pattern in which parallel lines are interleaved. Instead of recognizing this pattern of interleaved parallel lines, however, the eye sees converging diagonals.

---

[160]Maurice Merleau-Ponty, *Phénoménologie de la perception*, Paris: Gallimard, 1945, p. 44 (*Phenomenology of Perception* (1945), trans. Colin Smith, London: Routledge, 2002, pp. 40–1). Fanon cites this book in the Conclusion to *Black Skin*, p. 200, though in fact his quotation actually comes from *La Structure du comportement* (1942), which had initiated the discussion of parallelism and convergence, and which was one of the two books by Merleau-Ponty in Fanon's library (Maurice-Merleau Ponty, *La Structure du comportement*, Paris: Presses Universitaires de Paris, 1942, p. 277; *The Structure of Behavior*, trans. Alden F. Fisher, Boston, MA: Beacon Press, 1963, p. 204). According to Cherki, one reason why Fanon moved to Lyon in 1947 was to attend Merleau-Ponty's lectures there (Cherki, *Frantz Fanon*, p. 15; Macey, *Frantz Fanon*, p. 126); the latter's analysis of consciousness, perception and embodiment and its relation to experience was of obvious interest to Fanon, whilst the emphasis on the perceptual structure of the event and its relation to the act, with absolute knowledge an endless movement forward of consciousness, evokes central concerns of *Parallel Hands*. Convergence in *Phenomenology of Perception* is similarly the eventual end towards which perception moves, not something obvious in the prereflexive everyday. On the question of convergence in a social context, compare Fanon's remark in *Our Journal*, 29 November 1956: 'To do so, would be to run the risk of creating autonomous societies with no point of convergence' (*The Psychiatric Writings from Alienation and Freedom*, p. 185).

'Immunized I direct my striated antennas against diagonal atmospheres'[161] Épithalos declares: only he can perceive the parallel lines, the other characters simply see deceptive diagonals. The threat, from their point of view, is that he is going to destroy their comfortable illusions, of seeing 'the perfect convergence':

Ménasha   A man, a single man, shifts the sun from its place and sticks it to his lips.

The Chorus   The main thing is to prevent the spectacle.

Ménasha   Tragedy, this palpitating possibility of humans, demands to be confirmed in its hesitation. Peoples, in hexagonal rows, refuse the stage.

The underwater expositions [explosions] pour out their boiling atmospheres into the crucible of the immutable.

Majesty, wisdom sometimes gives birth to sinister decisions. Let us go, SIRE, let us head for the ramparts of the Gesture and may the reckless torch that wants to abolish man's perfect convergence be extinguished.[162]

---

[161]Act II, 2, p. 133. Cf. *Black Skin*, 'I slip into corners, my long antennae encountering the various axioms on the surface of things' (p. 96). On language as antennae, see Sartre, p. 210 below.
[162]Act I, 4, p. 121.

At the end of the play, as Épithalos' confidence declines, Ménasha repeats this last phrase. Épithalos' act has created chaos, but he nevertheless continues to affirm his objective consciousness – a perspective reinforced by the large number of scientific and medical words utilized in the play.[163] His parallel hands are what allow him to effect an intervention that will overturn the ideological fabric by means of which society exists in its complacent subservience to the will of the gods, a perfect convergence of sorts, and enable him to assert human will and self-determination over any form of god-given 'destiny'.

Épithalos' emphasis on seeing through the illusions of common perception to a scientific objectivity is comparable to Lucien's desire to see behind the aestheticized spectacle of the world. Though for Nietzsche the Socratic scientific world view is the very perspective that destroyed the Apollonian-Dionysian world of the Greeks, here Fanon seems to have followed Césaire by merging the Dionysian with the Socratic and pitting both against the illusions of the spectacle,[164] which represents the Apollonian regime of indifference and repression against which Épithalos asserts the volcanic force of his own revolt. The conceptual structure could be interpreted as an attempt to break through the social illusion of ideology, in a Marxist sense, and it is certainly the case that Épithalos sees the people of Lébos accepting uncritically the terms of the lifeless world into which they have been born. Though couched in terms of revolutionary violence, the kind of transformation that Épithalos seeks is not however broached at any point in terms of socialism or communist ideals: his revolution is a Blanquist end in itself. No more than the word 'freedom', no word such as 'justice' or 'equality' is ever spoken in the play. Fanon's plays may both be anti-bourgeois, but there is no hint of a need to replace capitalist bourgeois society

---

[163]E.g. afferent, apertognathia, cavitary, colloid, epithelial, fumarole, gravid, haemorrhagic, lucule, serous [membrane], solstitial.

[164]'And above all my body as well as my soul, be careful not to cross your arms in the sterile attitude of the spectator, for life is not a spectacle, for a sea of troubles is not a proscenium, for a screaming man is not a dancing bear ...' Césaire, *Cahier*, 1947, *Œuvres complètes*, p. 157, *The Complete Poetry*, p. 27 (translation modified).

with socialism, concepts that are never broached.[165] For Fanon, the bourgeois world is simply the oppressive (white) world that his heroes either seek to go beyond or to destroy. His concept of freedom in the plays is existentialist, constituting the individual act of existence itself as a universal and absolute end: 'freedom is the act through which I come to myself'.[166]

Revolution and the will to power

The play's Promethean theme has much in common with Césaire's *Cahier*, though, as before, Fanon's indebtedness to Césaire operates without invoking his central themes of race, slavery or colonialism. Their absence once again signals the rejection of anything explicitly associated with *négritude*. There are links, however, not only to the *Cahier*, but also to Césaire's play *Et les chiens se taisaient* in *Les Armes miraculeuses*. Published in 1948, the centenary of the 1848 revolution, Césaire's own 'Greek' drama offers an abstracted narrative of a black rebel's revolt against white power, alluding to, though in the 1948 version not specifically representing, the revolt of Toussaint l'Ouverture against slavery and French rule in St Domingue. The Rebel's capture, torture and death are presented as a heroic assertion of the will-to-resistance against the oppressive and unjust status quo. The two narratives of revolt also bring out the differences between Fanon and Césaire: however much he may have been influenced by Nietzsche's concepts of the will-to-power and the *surhomme* (superman, overman), Césaire's play reads primarily as an evocative poetic text that brims with specific historical, geographical and cultural references and resonances. The Rebel may be a symbolic figure, but it is clear in what context he is situated and what he is rebelling against. Fanon's play, on the other hand, remains altogether abstract and contextually unsituated.

Having said that, the dismal portrait of the stifling bourgeois society of Lébos in the opening prologue and scene of *Parallel Hands*

---

[165]By contrast, Marx and Marxism are mentioned five times in *Black Skin*, most notably the quotation from *The Eighteenth Brumaire* on social revolution drawing its poetry from the future, which serves as an epigraph to the final chapter.
[166]'La liberté existentielle', in Mikel Dufrenne and Paul Ricoeur (eds.), *Karl Jaspers et la philosophie de l'existence*, Paris: Seuil, 1947, p. 144 (my translation). The whole first page of this section is marked in the margin of Fanon's copy.

nevertheless evokes the repeated descriptions of the oppressed and oppressive state of Fort de France and the people who live there portrayed in the opening of the *Cahier*:

> At the end of the small hours, this town sprawled – flat, toppled from its common sense, inert, winded under its geometric weight of an eternally renewed cross, indocile to its fate, mute, vexed no matter what, incapable of growing according to the juice of this earth, encumbered, clipped, reduced, in breach of its fauna and flora.[167]

Fanon echoes Césaire's evocation of the unnamed Fort-de-France as the Chorus and Polyxos describe the slumbering city of Lébos, dwelling in platitudes, blind numbness, obscurity and night. There are also resonances of the guilt-ridden inhabitants of *Les Mouches*: 'Guilty cities, lamentable sinners, deliver their resounding souls', encouraging the idea that the mythical island of Lébos may represent a proxy Martinique just as Argos stands for war-time France in Sartre's play.[168] And just as Orestes takes on the qualities of Nietzsche's *surhomme*, killing the King and Queen in order to rid the city of its oppressive political regime in order to institute a new just state, so Épithalos can be also seen as an alienated, revolutionary figure, seeking to institute a new political order in Lébos by his murder of Polyxos.[169] As in Césaire's *Et les chiens se taisaient*, the issue is not the question of the morality of the act, but the necessity for the destructive cleansing of the old order.[170] The act remains essentially individualistic: Polyxos' murder creates chaos on Lébos, but Épithalos seems to have no plan to take over power himself or the least idea of how a new society, just or otherwise, should be created. Any contemporary reference for Fanon's political theme remains

---

[167]Césaire, *Cahier*, 1947, *Œuvres complètes*, p. 151, *The Complete Poetry*, p. 13.
[168]Act I, 4, p. 120.
[169]In 1943, the Pétainist ruler of Martinique, Admiral Georges Robert, was overthrown by the Gaullist Henri Tourtet.
[170]Compare Nietzsche's comment on Oedipus in *The Birth of Tragedy*: 'The profound poet [Sophocles] tells us that a man who is truly noble is incapable of sin. Every law, all natural order, the moral world itself, may be destroyed by his acts; precisely those actions themselves will generate a magical circle of higher consequences, which, on the ruins of the old collapsed world, come to found a new world', *The Birth of Tragedy*, p. 60, English translation modified to correspond to the French translation.

submerged – there are no explicit suggestions or allusions for readers or a potential audience to pick up on.[171]

In comparison with *The Drowning Eye*, it is noticeable that in *Parallel Hands* the Kierkegaardian structure of alternatives has been reversed.[172] Whereas in both plays, the central question concerns the question of submission to an order of the social-political that is reinforced by the will of the gods, the choices that the characters make differ significantly: François rebels by allying himself to the world beyond the human, Épithalos revolts against a human world too closely bound to a demiurgical inhuman will. Following from this, the same opposition, of a nocturnal and somewhat inert consciousness as against a sunny active one, is reversed. In the first play, Lucien is correlated with light, day and action, whilst the passive François disdains any engagement with human affairs and associates himself with shadows, rain, the stars and night, an image structure that resembles the inverted cosmology of Césaire's *Cahier*, where the blood-red sun emerges as a force of oppression. In *Parallel Hands*, the hero Épithalos is the worldly man of action, a parricidal anti-Christ figure beyond good and evil, who makes a Dionysian voluntary sacrifice of himself so that, as he argues, the people of Lébos may be released from their insentient subservience. He is duly associated with sun and light ('"Mother", he said, "my eyes are thirsty for light"'), whilst Polyxos his father and his ally the Chorus shelter in shadows and darkness ('Blessed be the Darkness/For the light is terrible').[173] So although the two plays share the imagery of the sun and the moon, light and darkness, they invoke them in antithetical ways: Césaire's reversal of the norm is itself now reversed.

In both cases, the drive of the play involves a refusal of the status quo and a quest for the absolute, but whereas in the first the alternative involves a rejection of mundane human existence in the world in favour of access to a state of immanence, in the second it comprises the destruction of the social and political status quo through the killing of the King which enables the creative self-

---

[171]In that respect, the play compares to Jean Anouilh's *Antigone* (1944), where the rebellion of Antigone against the conformist power of Creon could easily be interpreted in the context of the German occupation of France, but nothing is said explicitly to suggest it.

[172]Kierkegaard also figures as a presence in *Parallel Hands*, e.g. Polyxos in Scene 1, 'My obsessed senses grow irritated with fear and I tremble' (Act I. 1, p. 109).

[173]Act I. 3, p. 110; Prologue pp. 107–8, and repeated seven times throughout the play.

realization and transmutation of the hero. Épithalos' revolutionary intervention is not merely one that challenges the contemporary political order, however, or even that of what might be historically interpreted as European dominance. According to the Chorus' approving opening description, the appeasing, placating and placated island has rested obediently and placidly for 2,000 years, a time frame that is re-emphasized by Épithalos at the end of the play: 'Two thousand years and the world sleeps / Two thousand years that men have forgotten themselves within a / Life in abeyance! / Two thousand years and days subjugate consciousness.'[174] Épithalos' act of will-to-power is directed against the destiny of a world that has lasted for two millennia: as opposed to the three hundred years of colonialism in the *Cahier*, here Fanon suggests the Christian era and, implicitly, its Nietzschean critique.[175]

With its strong emphasis upon the will of the super or overman (*surhomme*), and an explosive intervention that will return order to a primal chaos, *Parallel Hands* is certainly more overtly Nietzschean in its themes than *The Drowning Eye*. Whereas the spectacle in *The Drowning Eye* was the aestheticized world that Lucien wished to see through and beyond, the spectacle in this play becomes the event of the primordial act which the Chorus seeks to prevent and which Épithalos is determined to commit by turning his words into deeds in a violent act of destruction. Here Fanon was working in the context of contemporary promethean revolutionary ideas such as he would have encountered in Nicolas Calas' surrealist Rankian-Trotskyist *Foyers d'incendie* (*Hearths of Fire*), where shock is theorized as a spark that will ignite revolutionary fervour among the people:

> there is nothing to prevent us, using the initial shock that triggered the movement, from leading the whole of humanity onto the revolutionary path. We must not hesitate, we have no time to lose, once the spark has arisen, one must take advantage of it, seize the opportunity, and, with a promethean audacity, spread the fire. The hatred of the gods matters little, they will always be against us! Let us snatch the fire from the hands of the vestal virgin, let us

---

[174]Act IV. 1, pp. 157–8.

[175]In this context, recall Fanon's reading of Karl Jaspers, *Nietzsche et le christianisme*, Paris: Minuit, 1949. In *Black Skin* Fanon mentions two millennia in the context of his belonging to a race that two thousand years ago was already working in gold and silver (*Black Skin*, p. 109).

give back fire to the male so that it may transport him through this mad race that goes from revolution to revolution.[176]

Épithalos claims that his revolutionary act will produce renewal of the political order of Lébos by enabling the inhabitants actively to create their own meaning, whilst he is also confident that he can raise his consciousness, and his very being, to the level of the absolute through the recognition of his act. We have seen how Épithalos' superhuman striving to go beyond the ordinary, to produce and define himself, can be compared to Césaire's Nietzschean rebel. In Césaire the hero draws on a cosmic and political consciousness to refuse the master-slave relationship, leading to his sacrificial death: following Nietzsche's analysis of *Oedipus Rex* in the *Birth of Tragedy*, his suffering and grief become the force of renewal for society in the future.[177] Though Épithalos sees himself as renewing society through destruction, and could be described as an agonistic hero who pursues his path in the name of the transformation or transmutation of a present that he finds intolerable, he does not move straightforwardly into the tragic mode of suffering and grief of the Rebel: there is no catharsis as such in *Parallel Hands*. Épithalos appears from the first with his consciousness and aspirations already self-created, 'his eyes bathed in infinity' (p. 117), confident in the possibility of the affirmation of his 'dazzling superhumanity' (p. 127), pursuing the event that will raise him out of antagonistic dualism of human existence to the heights of the absolute. It is Polyxos who then suffers the ritual sacrificial death, which precipitates the death of others – Audaline, and the inhabitants of the city – in a convulsive, cataclysmic event. After he has committed his act and brought destruction on the city, the physical and social transformation that he achieves does not translate to his own condition: Épithalos lives on with a troubled and more and more tortured consciousness, speaking in an increasing mode of irresolution that creates a particular interpretive opacity, as the proud and self-obsessed hero vacillates, caught between conscience

---

[176]Nicolas Calas, *Foyers d'incendie*, Paris: Denoël, 1938, p. 106; a marked-up copy is in Fanon's library. Cf. p. 107: 'Every artist, as an artist, is revolutionary, because without the possibility of overturning an established order, a normal state and unsurprising state of things, it is impossible for him to create an emotional shock and associate elements in a surprising way' (my translation).

[177]Césaire himself stated that he drew on Nietzsche's *Birth of Tragedy* in his attempt at a 'Greek' tragedy. See Arnold, *Modernism and Négritude*, p. 118.

and consciousness, the burnt offering as sacrifice[178] and the too great intensity of perceiving a Nietzschean 'primordial spectacle':

> Disappear you inventions of my new consciousness!
> the holocaust specifies the sacrifice
> Primordial spectacle I drink from inner riches
> To see no more
>> To see death no more
>> the chasm[179]

When talking to Audaline, Épithalos focuses on the possibility of achieving his apocalyptic act of self- and social-transformation, but once realized and acted out he remains caught in the same state of inbetweenness, the 'painful production of schism' as Ménasha puts it, with which he began, that is, left with the fundamentally dualist human condition, the irresolvable paradox of the embodied intellect aspiring to transcendence, which can be viewed either as tragic (in his case) or absurd.[180] The now irresolute Épithalos remains caught within the Manichaean split that he has sought to go beyond,[181] seeming to succeed unconvincingly and to fail hesitantly at the same time. The perfect convergence can only be sustained by maintaining the paradox of the parallel dualism of humanity in its relation to the gods. Épithalos cannot achieve the absolute by himself. His Nietzschean aspirations have failed, along with his dazzling superhumanity.

Épithalos has nevertheless shown a fierce courage in his unwavering determination to carry out his decisive, destructive act against all comforts of the known, a revolutionary assertion of will against the status quo that would remain central to Fanon's understanding of any process of self-transformation and disalienation. Having announced to Audaline that his word can reach volcanic extremes by being

---

[178]In 1949 the term 'holocaust' was not yet generally used in the modern sense of the Holocaust, that is, the mass murder of the Jews by the Nazis. Fanon is here using the word in its historical sense of a sacrificial offering burnt on an altar. See Jon Petrie, 'The secular word "Holocaust": Scholarly myths, history, and twentieth century meanings', *Journal of Genocide Research*, vol. 2, no. 1, 2000, pp. 31–63.

[179]Act IV. 1, p. 155.

[180]Act II. 4, p. 134. Fanon thus aligns himself here with Kierkegaard's existentialist critique of Hegel whilst also invoking Camus' paradox of the absurd.

[181]Cf. *The Wretched*: 'The challenge to the colonial world by the colonized is not a rational confrontation of points of view. It is not a discourse on the universal, but the impassioned affirmation of their difference posed as an absolute. The colonial world is a Manichean world' (p. 6, translation modified).

transformed into an act, and driven by his sheer assertive will power, Épithalos enacts an explosion similar to that which would haunt Fanon's consciousness in *Peau noire*. Whilst he begins that book by saying that 'the explosion will not take place today – it is too early, or too late', he himself explodes later in reaction to a racist incident – 'I explode. Here are the fragments put together by another me.'[182] Unlike Fanon at the start of *Peau noire*, Épithalos is absolutely certain that the time for explosion is now: 'The rock I instituted defines the explosions', he declares, announcing to Audaline that:

> I force the frameworks with my still
> Depth and I explode
> Such final certainty. (Acts IV. 2, p. 163; III. 2, p. 133)

Whilst its narrative is at once Oedipal and revolutionary, the subject of the play could therefore also be described as Épithalos' staging of an explosive, surrealist shock, his acting out of an explosion of the self which overturns society, a total shock of a kind of which Fanon can only dream in *Peau noire*.

Revolution and the 'annihilation method' in psychiatry and in politics

Joby Fanon reports that after he had completed Act III Fanon did not know how to end the play. The point is that, in some sense, it does not matter how it ends once the explosive, surrealistic shock has been administered to society. The revolution in *Parallel Hands* turns out to be a social and political form of convulsive therapy. Épithalos has administered a total shock to the society of Lébos by killing the king – and here we see a strong connection with Fanon's enthusiasm for electric shock and other related forms of treatment for his patients that would be evidenced in the psychiatric writings.

As will be described in detail below in the Introduction to Fanon's psychiatric writings, Fanon thought that the administration of shock would move his patients out of the pathological mentality which they had developed within their particular familial and social framework to cope with disruptive neurological impulses. Electric or other forms of shock would wipe the slate clean so that the patient could start again

---

[182]Fanon, *Black Skin*, p. xi (translation modified), 89. Cf. also p. 119: 'The black man is a toy in the hands of the white man. So in order to break the vicious circle, he explodes.'

from an uncorrupted and undistorted tabula rasa and allow the work of reconstruction in a more sympathetic, understanding and constructive environment. The medical technical term for this was 'la technique de l'anéantissement', or, somewhat chillingly in English, the annihilation method. Fanon's therapeutic practice, as a psychiatrist, involved a two-part process: first, the use of shock treatment, electric, or insulin-induced coma, to erase the warped forms of social adaptation that constituted the form taken by the mental illness, and then, second, the process of reconstructing the patient's consciousness and personality through psychotherapeutic work and social therapy: to put it in other terms, we could say that it was a process of violent deconstruction, restructuration and reconstruction.

Fanon's later understanding of political violence ran exactly parallel to his psychiatric method – in both the object was to wipe the slate clean, in the case of Algeria to allow colonized population to begin again with a tabula rasa.[183] What we see here is that however alien the FLN doctrine of violence may have been to Fanon as a human being, conceptually it corresponded perfectly with his own practice of how to cure his patients in a colonial society: disalienation through violence, the annihilation method, followed by reconstruction in a normative social context (or common political struggle). Working in Algeria with colonizing and colonized people, with torturers and torture victims, Fanon came to equate the effects of colonialism with the causes of mental illness, with a society which was producing a sickness that could only be eradicated by removing the as-it-were neurological cause of the disease – colonialism – not by treating its symptoms. Those neurological impulses that created the disturbance correspond to the originary and continuing violence of colonial rule and its ideology of racial and cultural superiority. Fanon understood colonial society through homology: it was like a mental patient, and the revolution was the necessary form of shock that would enable the reconstruction of the colonized society. This dialectical connection between the two sides of Fanon, Fanon the doctor and Fanon the revolutionary, allows us to see the underlying continuity of his thought and the fundamental correlation between his psychiatric

---

[183]Already in *Black Skin* Fanon announces that: 'As a man, I undertake to risk annihilation so that two or three truths can cast their essential light on the world' (p. 202); in *The Wretched*, 'On Violence' begins with Fanon's announcement that 'we have decided to describe the kind of tabula rasa which from the outset defines any decolonization' (p. 1).

and therapeutic and political practices. Fanon used his psychiatric understanding as the basis for his understanding of all social and political phenomena: anticolonial violence was the equivalent of the annihilation of shock therapy, whilst anticolonial struggle and the new culture that it prompted formed the basis of a social reconstructive therapy. Fanon's politics of freedom, in other words, were closely modelled on, and derived from, his therapeutic practice.

Much of this is anticipated in *Parallel Hands*: the killing of Polyxos seems designed to give a similar kind of shock to the society of Lébos as that which Fanon would give to his patients or the FLN to colonial Algeria. Once the primordial act of the killing of the white, colonizing father has been committed, and the consequent shock administered to the complaisant society colonized by the gods, the work of reconstruction would be able to start, initiated importantly not by Épithalos but by his mother Dràhna. *Parallel Hands* combines the political determination of *Les Damnés de la terre* with the anger, self-doubt and painful self-consciousness of *Peau noire*. The power of Épithalos' will is turned into an explosive act that overthrows the father's regime that he regards as oppressive, but with its destruction the oedipal drama comes into play, and his own violent gladiatorial masculinity becomes insupportable. The focus turns on him rather than the second part of the process, the renewal, and for Épithalos, as for Césaire's rebel in *Et les chiens se taisaient*, his self-sacrifice ends in a tragic, isolated defeat.

Feminist critique of masculinity

The social dynamics of renewal however are clearly indicated. Although the play may appear at first to be focused on its histrionic Nietzschean main character, its structure is more dialectical and involves constant critique of his sentiments and behaviour. Whilst from the point of view of its dramatic action, the play is concerned with Épithalos' assertion of self-determined will, as in *The Drowning Eye* a feature of the play is that much of the dialogue is concerned with arguing against the intellectual position of the anti-social hero or anti-hero, offering a critique of his Promethean 'overman' sentiments, and to that degree begins to spell out possible terms for renewal and reconstruction in other terms. Épithalos does not enter until Act II, and only returns to claim and justify the heroism of his act in Act IV. The bulk of the play is taken up with most of the other characters lamenting his violent intentions and then, subsequently, their effects. Whilst Polyxos is understandably largely concerned for himself, and Audaline is in part persuaded, it is the other women, Dràhna in particular, who take a strong and critical view of Épithalos' ideas and actions. Ménasha, though Audaline's mother, plays something of the traditional wifely consoling role to Polyxos; Dràhna is far more independent. She does not blame the gods or destiny: for her the problem lies squarely with the alpha-male whose psychic lack drives the need to surpass himself. For her, the main issue amounts to a contestation of masculine and feminine values, and we can here detect the strong influence on the play of the work of Simone de Beauvoir, whom Fanon had read very carefully.[184] In her first appearance in Act I, having heard of Épithalos' plans, Dràhna immediately criticizes men's violent, Promethean aspirations and pretensions, forever unsatisfied, from a strong feminist, perspective:

> To what summits will you lead me, dissatisfied men? What else is there to discover but what we give you? …
> Vainglorious males, stop with the powerless edifice of your agitation. Your darkening acts hurt and the dreams animating you, hopelessly unachievable, flay our lips.
> I am tired. Tired of living for men. Tired of waiting, anxious, for the splendour of their feats.
> Men who barely listen, pity for your female companions![185]

When Polyxos and Ménasha join her, she continues her criticisms of the disruptive, violent effects of men's obstinate egotistical pretensions:

> Alas Sire! Will we ever know from which unconveyed sources man brings back the tenacious fevers with which he annihilates cities?
> Strewn at the whim of the world's hot breaths, women strive to defend a shred of root. We are the ones from whom the universe is organized, but the men, ridiculous creatures torn from ourselves, whip our faces with their homicidal hands.[186]

---

[184]See Renault, 'Le Genre de la race'. De Beauvoir's *Le Deuxième sexe* (*The Second Sex*), vol. 1, 1949, is in Fanon's library.
[185]Act I. 3, p. 116.
[186]Act I. 3, p. 118.

Dràhna provides the only critical evaluation of Épithalos in the play other than that of the perspective of the vested interests of the status quo. Through her, women here become the Apollonian figures of order, men the violent, homicidal Dionysian destroyers of society: whilst at one level the play concerns an oedipal revolt against an oppressive father figure, at another it dramatizes the self-obsessions of the over-reaching male ego against the more measured and social behaviour of practical, socializing women and pits them dialectically and disdainfully against each other.

Dràhna's meeting with Épithalos at the end of the play is reminiscent of the reunion of the Rebel and his mother in Act II of *Et les chiens se taisaient* when she reproaches her son for his revolutionary actions. But whereas she collapses and dies when the Rebel dismisses her objections, Fanon's Dràhna is a survivor. In the opening scene of the final act, we find Épithalos ambivalent and vacillating, still in part managing to convince himself that his act has been liberating and transformative ('See the EXTRAORDINARY has righted the obliquity of darkness and the ACT's assailing force invents sublime metamorphoses')[187] but sensing also that the forces of the larger world are closing round him whilst his consciousness has failed to be transformed in the way he had hoped for. When he meets his mother in the following scene, it is the first time that they have been on the stage together: this is the moment of dramatic denouement in the play when he finally faces resistance from another human being. He greets her equivocally, claiming some form of triumph by offering her day over night ('Mother, accept the day that I bring you …').[188] But her revelation of Audaline's death, and her extended critique of the brutal narcissism of his Promethean enterprise, her direct challenge with regard to the intellectual claims behind his act and her characterization of his hands now as radial rather than parallel – 'What have you done with your radial hands?'[189] – soon deflate his pretensions so that he begins the final scene by asking Ménasha, Audaline and Dràhna for their forgiveness. As the scene progresses, he wavers on the cusp between the old assertions ('Language authorized by the ACT, raise the world / It is by feeding off the spectacle that you will create absolute demands') and an increasingly more tentative and uncertain

---

[187]Act IV. 1, p. 158.
[188]Act IV. 2, p. 161.
[189]Act IV. 2, p. 160.

sense of the failure of his power ('But the world crushes me in its black irresponsibility').[190] The hero's downfall at the end does not form an example of catharsis or tragic suffering in which he gains insight into his own humanity, it rather comprises a gradual awareness of the consequences of his own overreaching. Seeking to achieve a form of sacrificial death at the gates of the absolute in sentiments that recall the ending of *The Drowning Eye* ('Alone I want to go to the bold abyss into which consciousness sinks'),[191] the play ends with a resigned Épithalos becoming aware of the human advantages of the encroaching forces around him as he begs the night to return:

> Night germination that legitimates the sleep of men
> Come back
> Limit the world's perspective ...
> To see no more.[192]

Épithalos' attempt to destroy the power of the night has ended in failure. Germination and night are now accepted. In Césaire germination characterized *négritude* and the magnificent 'tongue of the night' closed the *Cahier*: the rest of Fanon's work would be a continuing attempt to get over the fascination of night and sleep. Épithalos' aspirations melt into the conditional tense of 'If I could', a phrase which echoes Orestes declaration towards the beginning of Sartre's *Les Mouches*[193] though spoken here in the different context of a tragic defeat.

Having sought to effect revolutionary transformation and renewal, Épithalos now accepts the inevitability of the return of an Apollonian structure of human society; his final uncompleted 'I SEE', pronounced 'like flesh torn apart by a hail of bullets', leaves what he sees unsaid, now no more than the words of a solitary, defeated, dying Dionysus. If he was unsure how to finish the play, it seems that in the Dunkerque cemetery Fanon himself had come

---

[190] Act IV. 3, p. 166.
[191] Act IV. 3, p. 165.
[192] Act IV. 3, p. 167.
[193] 'Ah! If it was an act, you see. An act which gave me the right of being one of them; *if I could* seize, even by a crime, their memories, their terror, and their hopes to fill the void of my heart, even if I had to kill my own mother.' Jean-Paul Sartre, *Les Mouches* (1943), Paris: Gallimard, 2000, Act I, Scene 2, p. 126 (my translation and emphasis).

to accept the Sartrean critique of Hegel and implicitly Nietzsche: in the final Act, the 'surhomme' and his philosophical pretensions to the absolute are shown to be unachievable, even at the level of the act.[194] Épithalos cannot realize his vision concretely but has to acknowledge instead the force of the Chorus' repeated aphorisms set in the double negative, announcing that the word become act only achieves knowledge of its own limits:

> Reaching its maximum limits, human thought can only transmute …
> For speech is not distorted by any visions.[195] …
>   on reaching the eruptive peak the ACT can only be absorbed![196]

With Épithalos' homicidal and now radial hands left blood-stained and empty, Ménasha quietly announces Lébos' return to order:

> Épithalos, the night is done
> my eyes clutch the divine things
> Lébos becomes organized once again
> Blessed is darkness.[197]

Et les chiens se taisaient ends with the idea that the collectivity has been reborn and renewed as a result of the self-sacrifice of the Rebel and the convulsion that he has precipitated.[198] In *Parallel Hands* the convulsion has been destructive but reconstructive in an unexpected way: the play ends with the hero's tragic defeat as he reaches the

---

[194]Sartre, *Being and Nothingness*, pp. 150ff. For Sartre, only freedom is absolute, though Fanon points out that it is hardly so for the black man. On Sartre's relation to Nietzsche, see Christine Daigle, *Le Nihilisme est-il un humanisme? Étude sur Nietzsche et Sartre*, Paris: Les Presses de l'université Laval, 2006. Though, as suggested above, for Fanon the absolute always takes the form of an act rather than an end.

[195]Prologue p. 108, and repeated by the Chorus through the earlier part of the play. Compare Hegel: 'But consciousness is for itself its own concept, so it immediately becomes the act of going beyond the limit, and, when this limit has been incorporated into it, the act of surpassing itself' ('Préface', G.W.F. Hegel, *La phénoménologie de l'esprit*, 2 vols., trans. Jean Hyppolite (Paris: Aubier-Montaigne, 1941), I, 71; cited in Maurice Merleau-Ponty, *Sens et non-sens* (Paris: Nagel, 1948), p. 114 (my translation).

[196]Act IV. 1, p. 155.

[197]Act IV. 3, pp. 167–8.

[198]Arnold, *Modernism and Négritude*, pp. 124–6.

limits of the human but with the promise that, inadvertently, he has transformed the gender politics of his society. Women, it seems, will be directing the new social order of the future.

Épithalos' emphasis on the necessity of self-assertion through the act of violence in order to achieve political renewal has obvious and suggestive links to Fanon's political writings a decade later and shows the extent to which he had already explored and anticipated the moral and philosophical issues involved in any revolutionary consciousness predicated on violence. Both Fanon's plays are concerned with young men who react against the political, social and familial order. The first rejects it, the second seeks to overturn it. Both plays present these projects ambivalently. Both plays offer extended dialectical critiques of the positions that their heroes advocate; in both cases the 'hero' is presented as the least attractive character in the play: in their acts of creative self-assertion, destruction and self-transformation, the two men are both, in different ways, anti-heroes. The overall implication of Fanon's theatre seems to be that whilst it presents examples of heroic refusals and revolutionary empowerment, the self-transformation of consciousness and the achievement of disalienation must be effected in another, more human way, one that is forcibly articulated by the women characters in the second play, rather than the transcendental or apocalyptic paths that the male anti-heroes of the plays present: that would be the concern of the books to come.

Wifredo Lam, *Rêve d'une nature morte* (*Dream of a Still Life*), oil on canvas, 1944. Exhibited in Paris in 1946 (UNESCO, Galerie Pierre, *Les Peintres de Paris*). *Wifredo Lam Prints: Catalogue Raisonné* (Paris HC éditions, p. 366, *fig.* 44.87) © ADAGP, Paris and DACS, London 2020.

1

The Drowning Eye

A room. A window. A door.
The door opens onto a dark hallway. The window opens out onto
a garden in which flowers amuse themselves in short dresses. A
thick velvet curtain. A sofa. An armchair. A table. In a corner, a
painting by Wifredo Lam.
On a cushion, a blind black cat.
François is seated at Ginette's feet. As the curtain rises, he looks
at her intensely.

THE CHARACTERS

François: Ginette's lover.
Ginette
Lucien: François' elder brother.
A blind servant.

The lighting has to be metallic. If possible, an intelligent play of
lights must render:
Lucien *aiming at* (we never know at what, Ginette perhaps):
pewter colour;
Ginette *absorbed* (her face must lose all human heaviness): rain-
drop colour;

François *absorbing*: new blotting paper colour.

Scene 1

As the curtain rises, a voice: 'The rain that chaps the overly essential clarity of the night, yesterday, in full grip, surprised the confession-less rivers.'

François   Do you love me?

Ginette   I love you.

François   Say it.

Ginette   I love you.

François   Again.

Ginette   I love you.

François   Wait. You mustn't reply so quickly. You mustn't be in a rush. Swear to me that you will never be in a rush!

Ginette   I swear it to you!

François   Swear to me that you will not look at the time whenever you are with me.

Ginette   Yes!

François   That you will not move unless the moon has brought down the murderous hordes of the day.

Ginette   Yes!

François   Look at me straight in the eyes. Immerse yourself in me, gently, very gently, and say to me that never will you laugh as they do!

Ginette   Yes!

François   That never will you cry as they do.

Ginette   Yes!

François   You see, it's easy! That lot, they say that everything is difficult, that living is such a complicated business. I didn't want to leave yet. I was waiting. Now that you're here, we can go. *(A moment passes.)* Do you love me?

Ginette   I love you!

(Silence. François gets up and walks very slowly. He reflects. He would like to talk. Ginette, satisfied, looks as though she's passed an exam.)

François   Since when do you love me?

Ginette   I don't know. I adore you.

François   It happened just like that?

Ginette   Yes! I looked at you through my cigarette smoke and I knew that I was soon bound to love you. I saw your eyes seeking my lips, your tormented lips that twisted with expectation and I knew that I would have to love you.

François   Why?

Ginette   I don't know anymore. I love you!

François   Yes, I know that you love me, or at least you say you do. But do you get it, I want to know.

Ginette   What?

François   The beginning.

Ginette   What beginning?

François   I would like you to explain to me how, why and at what moment you started to love me.

Ginette   Why? I love you!

François   *(He stops walking.)* That's not enough for me! I do not want to be loved in their way. I do not want the germ of their decay coming to live alongside me …

Some things happen to you and you know neither why nor how. I was born and no one explained it to me. When I got it, I was told that I had to be serious, so I fought. I have struggled every day, and I've had it tough, very tough. Minute after minute, *I refused to grow up*: I refused to wear their ties, their big shoes that hurt your toes. Minute after minute, I clung to my childhood, to my old short-trousers, to my pockets with holes in them. When small, I was given tonics that I then spat out. I saw the adults with their large strangling hands roaming freely and I was afraid, very afraid! Minute after minute, always tense, tired, *I fought those who wanted me to believe in hate, in blood, in tears.*

I preferred dogs to the boys of my age and their ball games. *Do you know what it means to fight people?*

I was proposed a certain kind of man. That man set fear into me … *Oh those sustained struggles against others' joy, against others' misery, against others' indifference.* There is something despicable about what they call their feelings. Everywhere that impression of the unaccomplished, that impurity weighing down the most marvellous subtleties. The Evening was my glory. I climbed onto the rooftops and spoke to the stars. They alone understood me. They spoke among themselves and debated a lot. But when one spoke to me, the others hushed up. Once, the night was buzzing, I clambered up a tree, and wanted to reply to a question that one of the biggest stars had asked me. I shouted very loudly so I would be heard. Then all the stars began trembling and I saw their hearts panic. My father made me come back in. I cried a lot because I had surely saddened my friends. The next day, I climbed up again, totally fearful. When they saw me, they smiled at me a long while. They were all there, young, new, armed with their first teeth. They just didn't stop playing around. One was rubbing its eyes still swollen with sleep, another hastened to get back to its corner …

I went back down happy and fell sound asleep like a star.

Ginette   And then?

François   And then they shook me like they shake the beasts on the day of their first communion. *They told me that there were books, emotions, struggle, a role to play, a life to contest …*

Ginette   And then?

François   And then I got to know men. True, hard, strong men!

Those who harmed me because they loved me, those who harmed me because they hated me. Those who harmed me because, they said, something must be done.

But even so I have sought to understand! I told myself that there was perhaps a word to be known. A word of the sort that opens doors and forces the smiles of mean men …

You, you really do not know what it's like not to understand. Not to understand what's happening to you! You're in your big white bed, as light as if flying in a dream, you get a knock at the door, men enter. You see them dimly, very dimly. They speak, you hear them faintly, very faintly, and then they start hitting and lynching you, and you get hurt, badly hurt. They leave and you've understood nothing, and you are beaten down by blows.

Later they return, you get up, you want to talk to them and you think you will understand. Then you are told that you are also a tough guy and they leave you alone with a medal and you are beaten down by blows.

Ginette   I love you!

François   No Ginette, this time I want to understand, just this once.

Ginette   I love you!

François   Yes Ginette, but I'm not tough like they are, not in a hurry like they are, not learned like they are.

Ginette   I love you and if you love me, I will smile at you like stars with mad hearts. I love you and if you love me, I will tell you why those men beat you down with blows and medals. I love you and I want to repeat to you what the manchineel tree confided in me one evening when, naked, I scattered grains of love on the riverbank. *(She stands up and moves close to him.)*

I love you, oh my God, and I want to tell you why your body has the audacity of the coconut tree and the muted brutality of a negro tom-tom.

I love you, oh my king, and I want to tell you why my breasts possess the turbulence of the stars and my thighs the docility of the night.

François   No Ginette, we must not rush things. *We must not hurry to live like a remedy swallowed too quickly.* They, they always start out like that.

They come. They speak. They must speak.

I love you.

I detest you.

I adore you.

I hate you

They could not care less so long as you answer them with: 'Me too.'

You love me?

I hate you!

I loathe you!

Scoundrel!

Glutton!

Darling!

My love!

And there you go. They are good. Two. A couple. A couple of human beings living fully immersed in life for love and for hate. That tires me Ginette! I want to be alone!

Why do you love me? Is it really me that you saw through the smoke of your cigarette? There were plenty of people at that hour! A man, a man whomsoever, smiled at you and you felt as if you ought to love him. Why? Because he smiled at you?

But there you have it, since you were all young you've been told that a man would come and smile at you. And you are everywhere lying in wait for him, watching out for him, calling for him, beseeching him. From a young age you learnt the ways of smiles, curtsies, small shows of resistance, games, the hands that you surrender at the bottom of the path. No, Ginette, that tires me!

Ginette   I love you! Let me love you.

François   No Ginette, *I don't want you to have waited for me as one waits for the postman.* You were waiting for me, Ginette! You've always waited for me! You shifted a little and made some space on your right. For he who would come. No matter whom, he was to come, you were promised. Your mother told you: never fear, you will get your darling. So when you saw me, you smiled at me and you loved me!

No Ginette, you ought not to have smiled. *(A moment passes.)*

I would have wanted not to find a place! I would have wanted to enter into you in spite of yourself. I would have moved aside your arms folded over your breast and I would have said to you:

You, who has never been hungry, swallow me!

You, who has never been thirsty, drink me!

And then I will say to you again that never must a place be at your side, but you must open yourself up so that I can create a home in the heart of you … but you shouldn't have waited for me! You shouldn't have pushed yourself but rather split yourself!

Ginette   I love you!

François   No Ginette, no.

Ginette   I love you and you ought not to question me like farmers do the clouds during Lent.

I love you and I am small in your hand,

I love you, my adored one.

I love you and I will laugh when you hurt me,

I love you and …

François   *(Collapsing on the armchair.)* No, no, Ginette you don't love me, you never have!

Ginette   Yes, I love you!

François   *(Silently.)* Then it's I who doesn't love you.

Scene 2

Enter Lucien, François' elder brother. Sporty. Blond. Nice squirrel-yellow, triple-soled brogues.

Lucien   Hello.

(François looks at him without responding.)

Ginette   Hello Lucien.

Lucien   I beg you, don't be so pale. For eight hours the Sun has slapped the face of the world with its fan and you remain still mute and drained.

(He goes to the window.)

Look: outside it flowers enough to split rocks.

The young shoots snigger in the face of the bees.

The jostling leaves climb up the trees.

Listen: a corner of the globe rises. The earth trembles …

(A voice.) 'The rain bathes in the lunar pulp and invents eternal stria.'

Listen, the earth groans and creaks

A hot wind rises without hurting the fragile envelope of cold covering the world.

The sun shakes creation with its midwife's hands …

Scream to show the heavens that life is

no more untameable than you.

Springtime, frenzied victor, alarms our blood.

Our clutched heart staggers and grows heavy.

(François rises and gets ready to leave.)

What is the matter? Have you been quarrelling again?

When will you understand that living and sleeping are two different things? Let's go Ginette, a smile for your gladiator; kiss me. *(He kisses her on the cheek.)*

(To François.)

And you, still sullen. Still dulled with bile. Still with slow death in your eyes?

By the way, do you know who I met this morning?

(François turns around without responding.)

Bussières. Georges Bussières.

(François keeps looking at him.)

You know, he still does not understand why you just ditched everything. At first, he thought it was because of a relationship, weariness, a bit of depression. But now, he says that you should get busy, do anything at all, but not remain seated there in your corner, brewing over some prayer. François, you must live, my young man. You must consent to life, François. You must get up, shake your body, be a party to things. There is a bad moment to get past as the water hits the bottom of your gut. After that, it's over; it can only repeat itself. And then there's habit. The skin toughens, the water becomes less hostile, moister.

At the end of the tether, it even seems to become a game.

(François does not respond.)

What are you thinking about? Why don't you respond?
Why do you adopt that idiotic air when one speaks to you?

Ginette   Lucien!

Lucien   Oh no, enough, you! What do you want me to do, to be silent, not to say anything to him? For me to leave him alone? But tell him that it won't last. Tell him, since you love him, that it must end. I myself have had enough of his crêpe shoes, of his 'Shush no noise, an angel is passing.' Thus far, he has been lucky, okay.

But, good God, he must decide!

Ginette   Lucien, shut up.

Lucien   No!

(To François.)

He was nice though, Bussières. He let you get away with so many things. All the dirty tricks you played on him, all the pranks you pulled on him, he forgave you for them all!

Respond François, respond because I'm talking to you. Bussières, the boy who got three-months school detention because you had broken the windowpanes 'in order to see the night better'.

Bussières the idiot who occupied your bed when you ran atop the high school's roofs at night!

(François does not respond. He looks into the distance.)

Ginette   Leave him alone, you're hurting him.

Lucien   That's it, let's go, you're trotting out that song, too! He must be left alone, humans weary him, noise gets on his nerves, silence around him! You believe all that, do you?

(To François.)

Respond: Bussières, the one who cried because you were being punished, who refused his prizes because you didn't have any, who got detention because you had it! Bussières, the man who lived in your place. You remember him?

(Yelling.)

Smash your face in, that's what ought to be done! No one has yet dared. No one has grabbed you by the scruff of the neck!

Yet … Perhaps that would fix things!

Do you think that he did not sometimes want to rock you with blows, your little 'me I'm so pure' mug?

That Normale Supérieure College matter, do you think that he came to grips with it?

You forgot to bring the letters. That's it. It doesn't matter. A forgotten act. A simple act.

But life precisely is the accomplishment of all the small stupid, childish, little acts. Only Monsieur has decided not to perform any acts. There are fearless men, shameless men, men without honour, but he will be a man without acts. Above all do not think that he has any remorse. He doesn't play such games.

Ginette   Lucien, be quiet! See how he suffers.

Lucien   Who? Him? You don't know what you are talking about.

Suffer, him? But since I'm telling you that he is 'PURE'.

Regrets, tears because one has a sore stomach, nails in your shoes, measles that destroy your mouth, none of that is for Monsieur. A velvet sky protects him.

Does he suffer? Ask him to repeat my words. Go on.

François, who is Bussières? He wanders, wanders, wanders …

Throat-gripping pain, dazing fever, that's for you and me! You understand, to suffer one must be somewhere, for something and not for something else. He, he is nowhere.

François, do you want some bread? 'Bread, good god, and what for?'

François, go to bed, it's late. 'Sleep, what is that again?'

Since he ditched everything, Monsieur doesn't talk to anyone. Of an evening, an old blind servant comes and they talk till dawn. My father used to say: 'This young man lives his life on the back foot.' But that's not true, there is only one foot from which to attack, and it's the front foot. Those who prefer the other one are bastards, cowards, yes, that's what they are!

No matter the price, François wants to avoid living. He accepts everything, everything, everything! But let no one force him to live and he believes that this will last! Idiot!

*During this time François leaves; the light imposes itself
increasingly harshly. Ginette looks at Lucien.*

Scene 3

Ginette   Lucien, you're dreadful, as dreadful as a gladiator.

Lucien   And yet, if only he wanted to understand a tiny little bit?

Just what must be done to get the motor going.

If he could just get cracking and say no to the shadow that anchors him …

If he could grasp a vase in his own two hands …

(The voice.) 'Silence! The gutter barks out its groove and weaves a door …'

Ginette   Who is Bussières?

Lucien, that Bussières, who is he?

Lucien   I don't know any more.

One day he entered into François' life. For twelve years he tried to understand him.

One word, he would say. One word would be enough for me.

But François did not open his mouth.

Ginette   So?

Lucien   So he left without having understood anything.

He went away, saying:

When words scratch each other's eyes out, the only remaining resource is action.

But when acts slip through one's fingers, all one can do is to lie down.[1]

Ginette   What's that about?

Lucien   I don't know.

---

[1]Editor's note: In the original typescript, this line and the preceding one are underlined with a wavy line and marked with two strokes in the margin.

Ginette   That's all?

(The voice.) *'Silence! The snatched white gesticulates and sharpens pencils of rain.'*

Lucien   He added that François was consistent … as he had also put a foot forward.

Ginette   What does that mean?

Lucien   I don't know.

Ginette   Did he love François?

Lucien   Of course he loved him! Everyone loves him. That's where I see the problem. He is not like you and you love him. You like to cry, sing, run, dance; you like noise.

You love day, the [sun-smiling] pewter-sheet sea …

And you love him, he who is the contrary of all that.

As far back as I can recall, I've seen him alone and silent.

He would stay put in one place for entire mornings. Never did he play with me. Everything that wrought cries of joy from me left him cold.

One day we were taken to the circus. He cried at it as if at a funeral. He seemed to have found 'something' he didn't ever want to lose. The slightest movement risked being fatal. He was riveted to the 'thing' and wouldn't let go.

From time to time we discussed things. I liked listening to him. He would speak as though his words were right before his eyes.

And then there was that star that interfered with it all …

Ginette   What star?

Lucien   *(Suddenly serious.)* It had rained all day. I couldn't meet up with my friends at the park. The lamp was lit as night was already falling. *(Indicating the dark corner.)* François was patting his dog there. Suddenly a great clamour resounded in the air. The house was rocked with sobbing and the light went out.

I let out a cry, because up there, just up above the painting, I had seen a star.

(Very agitated, he stands up and takes Ginette by the shoulders.)

I swear to you that I saw it, Ginette. It was green with fire. To François I said, look at the star. He stared for a long time at the spot I showed him but the star had disappeared. He then looked at me with wet eyes.

He cried for a long time. He stayed in his room for three days.

He has not spoken to me since.

Ginette   Did he see the star?

Lucien   I don't know.

Ginette   Did you love him?

Lucien   Yes I loved him! As never before a brother has loved. I loved his eyes.

Some morsel of our being is both source and mouth, he would say.

One day he confided to me that he would like to be blind.

Ginette   Why?

Lucien   The eye, he answered, must be worthy of the spectacle, but the spectator himself must have a certain dignity. And he went away saying: 'What a waste!'

Ginette   What did he mean by that?

Lucien   I don't know. Besides, even he wouldn't have known what to answer. He's never been able to say exactly what he thinks.

Be pure, do not do as they do. That was his motto.

He didn't say banal things, he wanted to live at the level of the fantastic.

No expressions such as:

It's cold.

I'm hungry.

I'm sleepy.

Sometimes, he would stand up and express himself. He wouldn't speak, he would express.

The day tastes like unpurified salt.

After ten months of modest caresses, the leaves emigrate to the depths of the soil so they can make love properly.

He thinks that as the stars do during the day, the leaves thus take up their winter quarters.

I've always thought that he tried at all costs to believe in all those things.

He always refused to see things as they are.

One day in philosophy class we were given an assignment: 'What possible reasons does a human have to exist?'

It was awful. Some other time …

Ginette   No!

Lucien   What do you mean, no?

Ginette   I want to know.

Lucien   What?

Ginette   The assignment. What did he answer?

(The voice.) 'A man with scissors between his teeth [eats] his share of comedy.'

Lucien   He said that flowers don't need anything, not even the tree that supports them.

That they tirelessly reproduce a unique flower that cries flower drops; people, though, need flowers in order to believe that life is made for them.

Ginette   And then?

Lucien   Things are beautiful between themselves and for themselves, not for humans.

And he added that no man on Earth believes entirely in his own existence.

Ginette   And then?

Lucien   Only the idiot, that is indeed the word he used, only the idiot can hope for such joy.

Ginette   *(In a muffled voice.)* He was right!

Lucien   *(Looking at her abruptly.)* What?

Ginette   What he said, Lucien. He was right.

Lucien   He was right! What do you know about it? What does that mean: he was right?

Were he here, he would tell you that no one is right. He would send you to the other side. Far away from himself. Far away from his strange world in which the humans that we are demand supports. He loves no one. You believe he loves you and it is you that loves him.

He scorns all those who think like him; all those who want to think like him. He fixes on you that gaze borrowed from other skies that he has some days and says to you: 'Pity, reason is on the side of the stars and flowers!'

Ginette   He's right.

Lucien   No, he is not right! You think he's right, do you?

Do you also say that life is absurd?

Your lips like wine, your hair likes flowers, your body likes clean water and your eyes want to see everything.

You clearly see that he isn't right and that you do not think like him.

(He takes Ginette by the hand. They go to the window.)

So, look here.

White death, slain, wrested from its shroud rises up dripping and disappears.

A new shiver travels along the earth's spine, a sky blue joy sweeps away our boring evenings, our pores open up to the point of hurting: distended, gaping, bleeding from everywhere.

I become a vast fairground and you dance Ginette in a white dress with violet flowers.

The clown is there wresting the first ray of sun from our breast, the waltz that asks to be swept along in a lively red waltz, you are there Ginette standing alone against me and my body envelops you, loves you and calls to you …

You are there and I tell you the blue prayer that ascends from the earth.

You and I are there, and we sleep on a bed of wild flowers …

(The voice.) 'Behind the barren hills, a man, two drops of water between his fingers, builds a new world …'

Ginette   He's right, Lucien.

Lucien   No, Ginette, he is not right. Life is not this absurd exercise in punishment that forces François to bow down.

Take your gladiator by the hand and let's go.

I will teach you to bite into the mammaries of life, to caress the lips of the world.

Come Ginette and perhaps …

(The voice.) 'Silence! Two captive stars commit suicide at the bottom of orbits.'

Ginette   He is right, Lucien, you know that he's right.

Lucien   But I'm telling you that this and saying nothing are the same thing!

We are all right!

Besides, being right is not the main thing.

(The voice.) 'A man, his teeth broken by shards of white water, sucks on his share of comedy.'

You see, I've thought hard about all that: I think ultimately that a man will always have to choose between life and death.

It is said that man is great because he accepts to die. But dying is nothing. The greatness of man lies perhaps in his acceptance of life.

Life, with its hard blows, its shames to bear, its under-the-table blows dealt without a word, its cowardice, its compromises, above all its compromises.

A man is perhaps only a compromise between life and death.

But even though he may be only that, he must live on.

He must live, for nothing, because he is there;

He must seize life with both hands, head-on like a gladiator.

He must be a constant insult to destiny.

Ginette   Mere words, Lucien. He's right.

Lucien   Then death is right against life.

Hearts must stop beating.

The spring must cease its wedding march.

Then, the smile must desert and give way to the hideous tenseness of anxiety and death.

Mere words, you say?

But words the colour of pulsating flesh.

Words the colour of mountains on heat.

Of cities on fire.

Of the resurrected dead.

Words, yes, but battle flag words.

Words like swords.

The love that makes you live to the power of two.

A word,

but a word strangled by life,

bristling with life.

A thirsty,

hungry,

screaming word that,

    cries,

        calls out,

            is engrossed

              and gets

                lost.

Ginette   What you say isn't true.

He's the one in the right.

Lucien   You as well! How you love him! What have you discovered in him?

What secrets have you pried from him?

What did he do to you?

As a young boy, faces turned toward him. It was said that he had a secret. One day, a priest came to the house. He stayed in his room for an entire afternoon.

When he came out, he said to the boy's mother: 'That child has seen something that has marked him for life.'

But that is wrong. Death is what inhabits François. Death guides him.

François does not want to live, that's the secret.

There is nothing to see on this earth.

Nothing! Nothing but red and white suns that make the days tumble.

It's easy to clench your fists pinch your lips

bow your bounced-cheque of a head

and say no!

It's easy to stay up on a roof for a whole night in mid-winter, because, it would seem, you have a date with a star!

It's easy to stay motionless and repeat tirelessly: 'Life is death's antechamber.'

Ginette   But that's not easy either.

Lucien   But it's more difficult to believe in life and in love.

It's more wearying to open up your hands and seize life fiercely, humanly, that is to say, frighteningly.

It's more difficult to fight, to shout, not to scream for death but for life!

Ginette   *(Breathless.)* He's right, because he chose.

Lucien   I've also chosen.

Ginette   No! You know that you did not choose; that we did not choose.

We want to live, but we want to know why *he* wants to die.

Lucien   So?

Ginette   So, he will have to tell us.

We can no longer let him go,

We can no longer forget him,

We can no longer separate ourselves from him.

(In a distant voice as if frightened by what she seems to discover as she speaks.)

Does it not bother you to live swigging beside that dead but still warm man?

When you return of an evening after a very heavy man's day

still moist with the dew of the world

does it not hurt you to find him as solid as before? Say Lucien, do you not sometimes desire to see him dissolve like the wall of ice that imprisons the sap awaiting the spring? …

Sometimes, do you not want to kill him all of a sudden?

(Lucien stares at her.)

Have you seen on waking where he goes to fetch his gaze?

A wall.

A thick and heavy wall, that's what he is.

(Now she's right next to Lucien.)

Do you know why you would like him to die?

Lucien, Lucien, it feels that he has been put here before us on purpose,

As if to hide something from us.

I do not see what he sees.

I do not hear the noises that caress his ears.

I've had enough of standing on my heels.

I've had enough of opening my eyes wide.

Enough of seeing the sun disappear with him.

Enough of hearing my blood hiccupping.

Enough, enough, enough!

(Lucien shrugs his shoulders and goes to the other side of the room where the light is harsh and heavy. Ginette on the contrary recedes further and further into the darkness. At her feet a blind cat sleeps or plays. It's the same thing. When it's pitch black, Ginette, now calm, starts to talk.)

Ginette   It's night time.

The waves invited to the seabed return late,

Quickly abandon their foam outfits and retire bare-footed,

their cold lips in the throat of the conch.

Lucien   Why do you say that?

Ginette   *(Without hearing.)* It is night and the crabs draw their eyes from the fire.

The fire of the sky

this skyful of eyes pounding on the doors of my flesh.

The lips of the world

gashed

ripped

crushed

the sucking of my blood!

And my eyes a back door that one has not closed

and my old joy, an abode that babbles in rubbing its stomach!

The night that forces the night to get out of bed!

Lucien   Why do you say that Ginette?

(Little by little the light that shined on Lucien begins to cover its eyes.)

Ginette   *(Without hearing.)* It is night and François' reign has come.

Things will rise up.

The table surrounded by its chairs will come to bow down before us.

The hour hand, so timid during the day, will mischievously pull the tail of the cuckoo.

The teasing ivy will repeat without blushing the secrets that it has heard.

It is night and François' kingdom gets stirred up.

This kingdom is missing a queen!

Lucien   You dreamt that you were to be that queen?

Ginette   I am the queen of the night!

Lucien   It's not true, that kingdom needs no queen!

You are the one who needs a kingdom!

You are the one who needs a nice little corner where everything shall be in its place!

Ginette   It is night and the tears …

(From this moment on, the light alternates between veiled and bright, respectively, depending on whether Ginette or Lucien is talking.)

Lucien   It's midday and the Sun explodes to the four corners of the world.

It's midday and things have lost their mystery.

The small bit that they put in front of or behind them disappeared.

The mirage is over!

A dog is meant to guard the house.

And the house is meant to shelter the family.

It's midday!

Once again, and this time definitively, things recapture their true weight.

A weight in kilogrammes and in tonnes.

Ginette   It's night.

From tree to tree a movement begins to murmur.

My blood puts on its venules papered with white gold.

Already …

Lucien   No, I tell you!

Besides, you don't believe in all that!

You yourself are not a thing.

You are a true girl and your blood asks to put on boots of wild leather.

Ginette, look at me

Look at how much I am like you!

You have also had dreams,

Dreams of limbs of enraged flesh.

When I dreamt that I was rich, famous, loved,

You, you dreamt that you were beautiful, rich, happy.

He, the other, has never dreamt.

He is good as he is.

He, he's one thing.

He's from the other side, but you and I, what do we care about the murmur of the broken chair,

the hysterical cry of the macawflower?

We need docile chairs.

Doors that close.

Ceilings that do not move.

(Ginette takes her head in her hands. Little by little the darkness disappears. The light rings Ginette. Like a flaming torch Lucien enters into the luminous circle.)

Ginette   François, François to the rescue! François …

Lucien   You must not call out, Ginette.

You must gently let life enter into you.

Ginette if you are hurting, be happy,

it is life that inhabits you.

Ginette   François, I beg you, come!

Lucien   No Ginette, he can do nothing against the Sun.

You've already stopped loving him.

Ginette   No, I love him.

François, you hear me, I love you!

The first day you smiled at me for a long time.

I was confident and pretentious like a new book, do you remember?

His hand on my left breast, and it's the birth of the world.

His lips whet themselves at the source of my eyes, and it's the friendly deluge.

And when his loins, grenades exploded mid-air, listen to the buzzing of my love,

I see Adam pardoned,

the Moon encircles the tousled head of the Sun and

I hear the noise of my blood hurtle down the avenues of his heart.

Lucien   And then?

Ginette   Then? Then he goes leaving my body open like a novel that one will finish later.

Lucien   And if he doesn't love you?

Ginette   It isn't true, you know that he loves me.

Say, answer me Lucien,

does he not love me?

(She grabs his arm.)

Answer me, answer me.

(Sobbing.)

Oh. I've had enough of this,

Since he touched me I no longer know who I am!

He came, smashed me in, leaving me gaping without Sun and without Moon.

He left and I am here, speechless and disconcerted before this hole that he dug in me.

He touched my body and I began spattering.

His hands laid on me and scattered my flesh over things

Lucien save me!

Lucien   Don't tremble Ginette, I'm here.

Come lean on my shoulder,

I will protect you.

(Ginette nestles against him.)

Ginette   I'm hurting Lucien, I'm hurting, defend me!

François I'm calling you, answer me!

Lucien   No Ginette you must not call him anymore.

You clearly see that he's abandoning you.

Ginette   *(Extricating herself.)* Let me go you, let me go!

(Lucien withdraws into his corner. The light that had begun to impose itself moves back after a moment's hesitation, regretfully.)

The night caresses the milky paws of the moon.

The Great Bear has signalled silence to the babbling stars.

Tears of night light up the armpit of my body.

Flowers dazed by the sun, old feverish mercenary, whet their lips lovingly.

Glory to you firefly!

Glory to you processions of the Night!

Fiancées brown and paling

Greetings to you all!

Lucien   *(Oppressed.)*

Intoxicated earth!

Smashed earth!

Ginette   It's over Lucien, humans have lost.

The shadow slips from grass to grass.

The asystolic heart of the world becomes congested.

In a suit the mountain whistler[2] welcomes the jealous oyster and the violated red anemones cry in their corner again.

It's over Lucien, humans have lost.

The mocking sun drowned itself after the cry of blood just now.

Lucien it's over humans did not win

Arrogant things,

Magnanimous things

that bear no grudges against humans for their stupidity, smile at this intruder and make a place for him among us.

Lucien   Sun proclaim your name! And wring the guts of the earth's stomach!

Ginette   Moon oily as my docile brow,

stay and console me.

Moon, plate on which I forged my body

Shall your reign be eternal!

Shall your moan be praised!

O you who awaken things and send humans to sleep

O love-struck Moon, salute!

It's over Lucien humans have lost.

---

[2]Editor's note: A bird found in Martinique near the volcano of Mount Pelée, and Dominica, the *siffleur de montagne* (lit. mountain whistler) is known in English as the rufous-throated solitaire.

Lucien   Sun! You who comb the world's hair

Sun who dresses the cold wounds of humans

For you hosanna!

(Lucien moves toward Ginette.)

The trees have taken each other's hands and are dancing.

Sun humans have opened their lives.

Look at them offer themselves to you as an impatient mare.

(Ginette moves away again slightly troubled. The light returns more confidently, a smile in the corner of the mouth.)

(The voice.) 'The world's toes latch onto the cement of water ... A man moves forward up to the flint and falls down.'

Things are speaking among themselves, love one another.

It is a strong family, well seated, with a past, a coat of arms, a tradition, martyrs, a visitors' book.

Things, they're not for humans.

Humans ought never to make them their business.

Do you know why François loves no one?

(Frenzied.)

Ginette a mad man beats the swell of existence with his naked fists.

Ginette a child cries, cries for not having understood anything.

Ginette we are upright on the picture rail of the world and interrogate impossible dreams.

(The voice.) 'Water is metamorphosing in all street corners.'

Ginette …

Ginette   A wall hides its face …

The thirsty earth inhales the sweating fogs.

François harrowing vertigo I hoist my frenzy up to the audacious limit of your refusal.

François o heaviness …

Lucien   *(Interrupting her.)* François o unfathomable death your eyes break upon contact

with the avalanche.

Ginette the stiffened silhouette of existence releases its first broadsides.

Ginette the flame clutches open throats

Ginette …

Ginette   *(Yelling.)* Enough … Enough …

(The voice.) 'A drawer opens out and the rain, old alcoholic millipede, stumbles[3] *on the stomach of the earth.'*

Stay where you are Lucien, the sun hurts me.

Lucien   No Ginette, stand up straight.

The sun gilds the vitelline membrane that separates humans from things.

Ginette   I'm in pain,

my body cries,

my nails break in the arid soil,

I'm thirsty.

Pity for my naked skin!

Pity for my fleshy teeth!

Lucien   The day enters into us like the sugar cane cutter with his daily labour of piecework.[4]

The Sun rubs us with its head nurse's large paw.

Come Sun,

may your sperm turn the world upside down!

---

[3]Editor's note: Handwritten addition.
[4]Editor's note: *'le coupeur dans sa tâche de cannes'*. System of remuneration per 'tâche' or task, the quantity of average work that a sugarcane worker is supposed to provide in one day.

Salvation and glory to the deluge of seed-sowing!

Ginette   I'm in pain and my head is swaying.

I'm in pain and my whole body in suspense would like to rest!

(The light has almost entirely returned.)

Lucien   Sun,

red robin from disaster escaped,

don't lean toward the mirror of the sea anymore …

Dwell at the Centre of the universe

so that the brain of humans melts in your warmth.

Ginette   I'm in pain, stop, away with you!

(She has fallen to the ground and cries trembling. The light strikes heavy blows on her nape. Lucien picks her up.)

Lucien   Stand up Ginette, the sacrifice is consummate!

Life climbs on the sky's back.

The stars, their gaze extinguished, sign their testament

and their eyes and their mouths and their bodies say:

Borax summer day, salute!

The stars kiss the shameless crosses of the cemetery one last time and their eyes and their mouths and their bodies say:

lipothymic[5] Night

White night

Black night,

the male Sun perforates your uterus.

Virginal night

Prepubescent night,

farewell.

---

[5]Editor's note: Lipothymia (or presyncope) is a benign light-headedness, generally short lived, comprising a feeling of faintness able to arise during intense emotions.

(The voice, very far away.) '*The mutilated waters of winter undo their violences ...*'

Ginette words absorb all germinations

Ginette two wanderings fall as psalms ...

Ginette   *(Troubled.)* No, no, Lucien I'm in pain,

the light wrests me from myself,

I'm in pain, leave me alone.

Lucien   Come Ginette,

I love you and I will protect you,

I will teach you to live and to love.

Ginette   Love?

Lucien   Yes Ginette, love!

(Ginette's voice is defeated. Sparkling Lucien speaks as a conqueror.)

To live is to live with the other.

Ginette   In the other.

Lucien   For the other.

Ginette   By the other.

Lucien   To love is to get drunk with distress when the other forgets that you no longer like black grapes.

Ginette   It is to get heavy with tenderness for the harvest of kisses.

Lucien   To love o adorable bee is to dilate like a plain of grey sky.

Ginette   It is to exhaust yourself o brutal hornet until you fall

Wings folded up in the crucible where my ardent soul burns.

Lucien   To live is to see your face in the clouds on their way to elsewhere

to kiss your lips in the bitter stream

to cherish your eyes in the crystal of the sonorous morning.

To love, to love you

is to hear you with my hands

to drink you with my hands

to taste you with my hands.

Ginette   It is to split myself in two when you bite my teeth.

Lucien   It is with my needle and your thread to stitch the world's wound.

Ginette   It is to stop the haemorrhaging that drains me.

Lucien   It is to die in you.

Ginette   It is to live in you.

(Lucien takes her by the waist. They speak gently.)

Lucien   I love you Ginette, almond forgotten by the night.

Ginette   I love you Lucien, Sun drop.

Lucien   The stomach of the world moves.

The arms of the world move.

The eyes of the world move

and the sex of the world assaulted by the sky's barrage rubs its hands sniggering

Sun, old scoundrel!

The sources of [philtre waters]

The course of hourglass eyelids

Cry of horror turns and blows inside my perverse wound.

Ginette   O feverish overwhelming of my being!

A geyser hollowed out in the worship of the fire,

Day, vertical sex

insatiable stars ruminate at the doors of my blood

there is the course.

Nubile mauve gardens

the famished moon throws a wing-beat and scratches

the menstruated sky

there is the course.

Glaucous feelings

a red robin smile taking root at the blurry limits of my teeth.

Lucien   O Ginette

Draped in my love

move forward alone

move forward to the uncertain signs where language ponders itself

and having moved forward

living at last

Set the world's heart to the rhythm of your desire.

Ginette   Lucien arm me with your love

Lucien cure me of the lunar leprosy

Lucien mark me

light me

I implore you

increase me!

Lucien   The chafing morning waters have hardened me with hope

and the hands spread

on contact with your body.

Lively Noon stone,

tangled stupefaction whence my soul has precipitated.

Ginette   Let me kiss my lips with your lips that so weigh upon me.

Lucien   Come Ginette

Come overwhelmed moon

timid moon bathe in the solar cancer

Come Ginette

Come.

Ginette   Yes.

The light bubbles up as the last phrases are spoken. At this moment, Lucien and Ginette get ready to leave. Darkness again. They leave.

[Scene 4 is missing from the original typescript.]

Scene 5

Ginette appears at the door. The light bats its eyelids. She advances slowly: to François who wants to go to her.

Ginette   No, François, do not move!

I am so drawn toward you that with a word you could make me sing and cry out my love higher and clearer than a hymn,

more brutal and madder than the string of the wind

that lashes the stars.

I love you marvellously and I live and I tremble at once.

It's true I was gone! But this open wound that your hands made in me had to be stitched.

I implore you, restart me.

I implore you, complete me.

I love you marvellously and I live and I tremble at once.

And for me this is a new thing, but new in the way of the first damp leaves fallen in my hair.

New, like the first stone of cold against my breast,

like your hands,

like your body.

I love you marvellously and I live and I tremble at once.

I implore you, finish me.

I am at the edge of the red clearing where our love explodes and blazes but I know that as soon as I shall place my lips on the magic circle it will open and close upon me …

And once again this shall be the beginning.

I love you and each moment must be unique.

It is neither a sequel

nor a preface …

And I do not love you each time like the first time,

but like a first time always new.

Oh! May it always be like just now, when

in leaving you all was lost for me,

like now when my whole body crackles and vibrates in thinking of your body.

I want to hold you in my two hands

just like red embers are murderous.

I implore you, envelop me like a proud flame clear and blue.

(Further and further away, the voice.) 'I call ...'

It's true I left you! ...

But you mustn't scold me, I didn't know that the wait was like desire and that it brought pain.

I imagined it white and calm like snow,

but I had forgotten that white snow also burns

the hands and the lips.

I await you my love,

and I no longer know how to be sad

I know only how to howl with pain,

and I no longer know how to be cheerful

I know only how to howl with joy.

(The voice, almost imperceptible.) 'I call the first poetry.'

It's true that I had left!

But this abyss sustained within myself

I had to fill it.

I implore you François,

Fashion me frighteningly!

François   *(Takes her hand and gets ready to go.)*

O Return, exuberance not yet torn

My foaming nudity takes you, broken with horror and I want to lead you to the ABSOLUTE gates

where life is seized.

Curtain.

Wifredo Lam, *Le Sombre Malembo, Dieu du carrefour* (*The Sombre Malembo, God of the Crossroads*), 1943. Exhibited in Paris in 1947 (Galerie Maeght, *Le Surréalisme en 1947*). *Wifredo Lam Prints: Catalogue Raisonné* (Paris HC éditions, p. 328, fig. 43.06) © ADAGP, Paris and DACS, London 2020.

2

Parallel Hands

Prologue[1]

The curtains are closed. The chorus appears

The prismatic faces of my anxious hands walk their images into the heart of the obscure. Slivers of faces move about in parallel, and genuflexion, the centre of human nature's gravity, calms. Lébos, from time immemorial, implacable darkness, has consolidated spirits.

I come deluged in man's sweat to rest on the foothills of this city. Weary.

Yet the spectacle is born from darkness! Reaching its maximum limits, human thought can only transmute.

The essential thing is to prevent the spectacle. Two thousand years since the sun disappeared. City of Polyxos, blind for two thousand years, I stop in your walls.

Light, dissolving source, gives way to speech. For speech is not distorted by any visions.

Deluged in man's sweat, sated with circumflex faces, I spread a coat with no hole over the drowsy world.

O Polyxos, you were wise the day when upon your order the lights were extinguished.

Held in this non-spectacle, the sleeping man speaks and forgets himself.

The strange, a gaze's first claim, is abolished at the gates of the expressible and the sea caresses the skeleton of adventure.

Sleep, city of propitiousness to me.

Blessed be the Darkness

---

[1] Joby Fanon, *Frantz Fanon*, cites an 'Argument' for the play, presumably from a manuscript now lost, which would have preceded the opening:

'Each of the consciousnesses on stage has made the leap.

From nothingness to justified Being

From unjustified being to Nothingness

Whence the finite turn of the expression.' (p. 130)

For the light is terrible.[2]

The gloomy day's brushed out hair [*peignures*] have vanished and the world rediscovers its original contingency. Beyond improper categories, consciousness lies, happy, in its black density.

Light, dissolving source, gives way to speech.

Blessed be the Darkness

For speech is not distorted by any visions.

(Claps of thunder, lightning bolts glide their red eyes over the stage. The chorus, with hands, protect its eyes.)

What! Does the sun dare violate its pledge? Was its promise not to bother us no longer?

Polyxos, stand! The day star, in fury, pounds on city's docile head.

(The lightning flashes grow in number. Slowly, the curtain rises and the helpless chorus retreats.)

No, no, to see no more, to see no more!

Polyxos, get up! The rent of a world is brewing.

Polyxos, Polyxos, stand up!

Forestall the EVENT!

---

[2]See the opening of Césaire's *Cahier*, where the bleakness of dawn on the island is abolished by darkness (Césaire, *Œuvres complètes*, pp. 74-5; Arnold and Eshleman, *The Complete Poetry of Aimé Césaire*, p. 13-15).

Act I

The curtain rises. Palace room; darkness made lighter by discrete lighting. The ambiance in which the tragedy unfolds depends upon the luminosity. Where Épithalos is concerned, furtive lightning bolts go to confirm the fears of the actors on stage.
Épithalos haunts the stage. He burns to come on.

Scene 1

The Chorus, Polyxos.
(Polyxos, distraught, rubs his eyes.)

Polyxos   O dreadful Dream! Hallucinatory thoughts! My obsessed senses grow irritated with fear and I tremble. My name resounds all around. In my marmoreal soul doubt is sown.

Gods of the city, Polyxos at your knees implores your clemency; deign to remove the illusory clarity from our brows. May we never be possessed by anfractuous desire!

Gods, makers of men, you know that we thirst for peace and likeness above all.

Total darkness! Absolute silence! Man reveals his perfect facticity.

Calm and indistinct, passions fall into their weighty forms! But what, what nascent movements in my innermost depths? Strange night! This buzzing in my ears!

(The Chorus from a corner of the room.)

The Chorus to Polyxos – Beware, woe betides you!

Polyxos   Who is calling me? *(Very loud.)* Who's calling me?

(Claps of thunder, in the distance a bell wails for a long time.)

Stop, choruses of criminal children, drops of clotted blood in the trough of orbits, set out to storm the firmament. Stop, the rediscovered man, inhabiting his consciousness of icy imminence, inhale the false fogs.

Man, stupefying illusion, absurd gratuity, seizes, limited by serene darkness, the incontestable secret.

Stop, man must feed on lies. Admire Lébos's tranquil platitude. Men and women, the ones stuck to the others, turn their happy brows toward my august face.

(More thunder claps.)

The Chorus   Polyxos, beware, woe betide you!

Polyxos   Polyxos, yes it is I the day's assassin! Who is calling me?

It is I the man of darkness.

The Chorus   *(Very distant.)* Blessed be the Darkness
For the light is terrible …

Polyxos   *(Not hearing.)* A breeze caresses the harmful daybreak, docile flowers collapse in tears, Gardens of dead water shelter trembling hearts, yes, it is I, Polyxos, the architect of Destiny! Destiny, with a steady hand, demands control.

The diverse effusions of avenues break at my touch.

(Thunder claps.)

Stop! Cease the lateral emission of noises, stop! Speech must not be distorted by any vision.

The Chorus   Polyxos, Polyxos, beware, woe betide you!

Polyxos   Why try to shake my unfathomable knowledge
with vain terrors? I am hardly, you know, in search of massive argumentations. The fate that I dispense to men lengthens and reduces linearly. The strangled sun lies, inert in the hollow of its desire. For two thousand years the world has been thickening with extreme complacency! Yet what turmoil inhabits me? What already anarchical effusions wound the uniformity of my permanence? There is a point of the globe that moves, stop!

Why today? Why such a long wait? Two thousand years! So close to the end.

Audaline is promised to Épithalos. Soon, with my kingdom's posterity assured, I will be able to admire the incomparable achievement.

What sudden confusions besiege me?

Hallucinatory thoughts, dreadful dream?

Épithalos, in executioner's tunic, appeared to me this night. Strange visions! Why the want to bother me in this way?

The Chorus   *(Very distant.)* Polyxos, Polyxos, beware!

Terrible is the light.

Polyxos   What! Which! Misfortune is gone from the earth of men.

No more sparkling days to feed audacious dreams … Horrible portent! With his face flayed by fires, with his naked sword, Épithalos advanced, threatening. I moved back, unable to shout, motionless, and he, brandishing his weapon, plunged it into my breast … The exhausted sun has lowered its hands for two thousand years. A parcel of the globe shakes convulsively. A beginning mobilizes forces, stop! Peace and silence on the earth of men! Lébos in diastole organizes darkness. Newly arisen breaths die out, vague desires are amputated.

The Chorus   Polyxos, the spectacle is born from darkness.

Reaching its maximum limits, human thought can only transmute.

Polyxos beware, misfortune pierces the universe's cloak.

Polyxos   Again! Treacherous shudderings, slidings of sticky instruments insinuating themselves into my narrow coincidence. Stop! Speech must not be distorted by any visions. Guards, to me! *(Frenzied.)* Yes, it is I, Polyxos, the day's assassin, the artisan of human rest!

(A noise is heard.)

Guards, help me, stop him! Here! Guards, guards!

(Enter Ménasha panic-stricken.)

Ah! It is you Ménasha.

Scene 2

Polyxos, Ménasha, the Chorus.

Ménasha   Already up, Sire! Yes, Your Majesty, it is I. What noises suddenly shake those hardest of hearing? Torn from my bed I cross the palace running, and the sound of my steps on the amnesiac paving stones excites my spirit. In the deserted rooms the air hardens with hostility as I head toward your apartments. Whence comes the sudden agitation moving the atmosphere? What is it? I do not find my daughter in her room and anxiety, an awful anxiety, overcomes me. Why these minor notes that cling to the verso of our souls? Why this heaviness at the dawn of the fecund day? Let us lend an attentive ear to nature's manifestations. The secret of problems, of all the problems that alert men's hearts, lies dormant somewhere in the pit of a vale or in the murmur of icy winds. Each perfume is a message and the sense of smell must get used to interpreting it. Pitch of sounds, incomparable splendours, I return your ancient coats of arms. Let us deign, Sire, to rejoice at the first palpitations of morning. Is Audaline not to be given to Épithalos today? Flappings of heavy wings protect our thoughts. Let us rejoice!

Virgin garlands, come in farandoles wiping the concerns from our brow. Épithalos, the fierce warrior, gets ready to pluck Audaline the White … Substantial fountains, water our furrows with tears of joy. Come in groups mad girls and boys and intone the most beautiful hymns … But what, Sire, are you unwell? Why this trembling? I can hardly make you out so heavy is the darkness, but the blood that usually animates your face seems to have deserted it. What woes have cut into the flesh of your serenity? Sire, pray, will you tell me?

(A noise is heard. Polyxos starts.)

Polyxos   Listen, do you hear?

Ménasha   Yes Sire, the doors were opened.

The air rushes in in heavy bunches laden with rosemary. Pregnant with kisses from the wallflower, jubilatory nature sends us its peace messengers.

Polyxos   No Ménasha, the air in nonchalant ribbons has nothing to do in this palace. These are the first chords of the useless walk. He's coming to life.

The Chorus   Polyxos, beware!

Polyxos Listen, he's coming!

(Ménasha, a hand on the sword, hearkens.)

(Polyxos prey to an intense fright.)

Come, look, over there: stop him!

Ménasha   *(After a few steps in the direction indicated by Polyxos.)*
I don't see anything, Sire.

Nothing bar the walls that turn toward us their shimmering
hands, pensive columns that for many long years have carried the
impermeable vault. Hasn't Lébos chosen a destiny of eternal calm?
Let us rejoice, the vainglorious Épithalos welcomes Audaline
exhaled.

The Chorus   *(Intoning.)* Polyxos, Polyxos, beware,

Woe betide you.

Polyxos   You heard. This voice, this buzzing, this essential
vibration; smokestacks are attempting the sky's escalation. Stop,
move no further! Stop the terrible preparation of your mission.
Never enlarge the circle where man's destiny is caught. Listen
to me. Today, after two thousand years, I have the right to speak.
I discovered the point of equilibrium where consciousness is
immobilized. Elementary reasons replace ineffective intention;
the Word encloses the World, expressed presence. Stop, move no
further! I keep on telling you that you must listen to me. Stop; the
cantors of churches wail and place their voices on my icy brow. The
coffin insulates me from all alternation, the church resounds with
unknown chords, Ménasha tell them to stop!

Ménasha   *(Going toward the exit.)* Listen, Guards! Lébos is in
danger! Guards!

Polyxos   No, no, do not call

the guards!

It is over. It is too late.

The Gods sometimes warn us of events due to overwhelm our
lives. Wisdom advocates giving them credence … Ménasha, I
want to relate a dream that shook me. Each of its joints unlinks the

chain of my days. And I am afraid. A falling note! And nothing is able to suspend its vibrations.

Ménasha   The more violent they are to human reason, the more necessary it is to decompose nascent dreams. Intuition, vertiginous wealth of the soul, goes in anticipation of the accident and warns us of it.[3] The sensitive fountains whose source despairs, gives the distant sketch of the gesture. But Sire, what, a dream, a rapid cloud, let go …

Let us be avid for feasts, for laughter, for ornamental gems. Let us rejoice, Épithalos is ready to pluck Audaline the flower with trembling thighs.

Total waters are preserved on the rhythm of an eternally repeated cadence.

Sire, Sire, why make such an anxious face?

Polyxos   Keep quiet. Listen instead.

It was day. A day as fleshy, as thick as this one. I was readying to descend to the council when a dark premonition made me turn back.

Wounding the night's hermeticism, the aura of Adventure hurled towards me its denuded effluvium. A noise of wings hit my astonished ears. I was frightened, Ménasha, I was frightened and wanted to shout; from my parched throat no sound came out. I closed my eyes. Arms break when faced with such threats. In this motionless position, forewarned of the increasing imminence of the danger by the bird's breathing, my impatient eyelids rose … O Gods, the unforgettable spectacle! …

Ménasha   Pray, Sire, continue!

Polyxos   Yes, I will finish. Lend an ear. The day had lost its unfathomable neutrality. Objects, lightened, exalted the power of the sacrilegious gaze. And the universe, shaking its numb limbs, suddenly set off.

---

[3]Editor's note: In the original typescript this phrase is marked in the margin with two oblique lines.

(Pointing at a part of the stage.) There, covered with red embroideries, seeming no longer to have to carry his body, the weapon in his hand … Him.

Ménasha   Who? Finish!

Polyxos   Épithalos!

Ménasha   Heavens!

Polyxos   Impregnated with a thousand fires, vibrating with blinding waves, yet undeniable excrescence of my flesh, merciless Épithalos absented me from this Earth.

Ménasha   Dreadful and horrible omen!

O Gods, sources of bitternesses, eternal and indifferent, you condemn us to unceasing returns! You panic our hearts of flesh and overwhelm our brains. Painful visions! Desist from taunting us, indisputable divinities. On your council, we have suffocated all of this city's hopes. Why these bitter visions? Has Polyxos released himself from his pledge? Has he not darkened, at leisure, Lébos's horizons? Are the limits that you assigned to the human adventure not being respected? Gods …

Polyxos   *(Interrupts her.)* Ménasha, listen.

Ménasha   Yes Sire, someone is approaching from that room.

Polyxos   Let us be on our guard.

They hide. Enter Dràhna.

Scene 3

Polyxos, Ménasha, Dràhna, the Chorus.

Dràhna enters very restless; she is to be clothed in a long dark blue dress, without jewellery, her hair falling on her shoulders.

Dràhna   The clear morning waters hide terrible tidal waves. In inspiration, they are waiting …

And when the hour tolls, they demolish the most resilient jetties – red atoms, isolated in days gone by, attempt a precipitate junction.

Pure world, you can shake your small head …

But we women, do we have the right to forget?

To what summits will you lead me, dissatisfied men? What else is there to discover but what we give you? Can the umbilical cord not be cut, once and for all? I am tired! Tired of struggling, of moaning! Excessively resounding men, for each one of your intoxications we are made to pay. So when, full of scorn for impossible glories, will you hang from maternal havens? Where do we find the words? How are we to make man understand that the calls that he perceives at decisive hours emanate only from us? Gods, toward whom our ravaged faces turn, inspire me and give me the strength to convince! Listen, frenetic males, the source is nowhere if not in us.

Vainglorious males, stop with the powerless edifice of your agitation. Your darkening acts hurt and the dreams animating you, hopelessly unachievable, flay our lips.

I am tired. Tired of living for men. Tired of waiting, anxious, for the splendour of their feats.

Men who barely listen, pity for your female companions! Pity!

(Polyxos and Ménasha see each other.)

Polyxos   Madam!

Dràhna   Sire, Sire, I was looking for you. Appease an anxious mother's spirit!

Polyxos   What is it, Madam, and what is at stake?

Dràhna   *(Having calmed down.)* The wolves, upon returning to the den, fall asleep. But the she-wolves, old trembling witches, know how to interpret the slightest growling from the motionless surroundings. They know the forest's safest retreats. Well, the forest, like the soul, stirs in the lightest winds.

Polyxos   Speak, Madam.

Dràhna   When the point of intersection has been reached, man stops talking, Sire.

Ménasha   Give us the reasons for so lively a commotion.

Dràhna   The reasons, do I know why it is they assassinate me …

And did I know what impieties would arise on this day? Did I know the torments with which my soul was to be besieged?

(Turning toward Polyxos.)

Sire, I tremble. I'm afraid.

Children, when able to walk with assurance, want to plunge into the earth or rise into the air.

Sire, protect us from misfortune!

Stop the blinding hatching of a metamorphosis.

Of shuddering Épithalos, avert the transmutation.

Polyxos   *(Grabbing her arms.)* But well, Madam, speak.

Dràhna   *(drawing back slightly. A moment passes.)* The black gold of the day moistened its lips and the paths of the night, evocative nostalgias, streamed.

I rose, shivering, from the chasms of Dream and went to prostrate myself at the altars.

I moved forward, restless with renewed joy.

Our son was there, his eyes bathed in infinity. His face, with a new architecture, seemed to be the original hypothesis.

Dressed in red …

Ménasha   *(Interrupting her.)* O abysses.

Dràhna   What is it?

Polyxos   Go on!

Dràhna   … He aroused strange harmonies.

I moved forward, happy to be the first to embrace him and when I wanted to place my lips on his forehead, I saw that he had not noticed me.

I called him. He stared at me a while and taking my hands: 'Mother', he said, 'my eyes are thirsty for light.'

(A moment passes. A clock descends from the sky on tiptoes. Like a flight of startled larks.)

The Chorus   Polyxos, beware! Speech must not be distorted by any visions.

Reaching its maximum limits, human thought can only transmute.

Polyxos   My heart, cease weighing me down with cumbersome obsessive fears.

Light! What light?

Dràhna   Alas Sire! Will we ever know from which unconveyed sources man brings back the tenacious fevers with which he annihilates cities?

Strewn at the whim of the world's hot breaths, women strive to defend a shred of root. We are the ones from whom the universe is organized, but the men, ridiculous creatures torn from ourselves, whip our faces with their homicidal hands. Yesterday, women, eternally powerless, tilted combustible eyes toward the noons in act.

Yesterday, submerged by avid sun, voracious with life, we threw our raw calls at the dazzling days.

Upon contacting my memory, I rediscovered, pulsating, the wishes my particularity shaped. But the men, our transparent idols, came and, again, dispersed us with the cadence of their acts. Since then, our wet heads cry drops of night. Of such cancerous darkness, we have known the pearliest shells.

We, voluptuous spouses of the pubescent sun, we entrusted our bodies to the night. And Lébos found the secret in mourning of calm destiny. Monotonous days strung out to the rhythm of this city oblivious to living! Agile spirits, to which unexplored regions do you take me in the evening, at the engorged hour when the blood in my arteries stands still. With heavy walls, Lébos, unable to contain the symmetrical explosion of multiple calls, trembles in its bowels.

The world already awaits the necessary splashing of a new event. What will happen on the earth of men?

What obscure designs is Épithalos taking on? What surprising thoughts at my soul's awakening!

What will happen on the earth of men?

Daughters of the flesh, when a corner of the earth bleeds, it is the most mobile of our arteries that collapses. Side by side with the earth's, this kneaded earth's secret, we moan perpetually furrowed routes at the bottom of our damp jails. Prisoners of our drenched jails, we dwelled upon life's uncertain detours.

The storm punctures the sky scattering on the backs of houses. Likewise, each act develops new harmonies. Allow, Sire, that I should go to the altars to pray to the Gods to remove the Strange, whose morning modulations I already detect, from Lébos.

She exits.

Scene 4

Polyxos, Ménasha, the Chorus.

Polyxos   *(Overwhelmed.)* The light!

The Chorus   Be careful o Polyxos, be careful! Speech must not be distorted by any visions.

Polyxos   *(Still overwhelmed.)* The light!

The Chorus   Blessed be darkness,

For the light is terrible.

Polyxos   *(Gently.)* Strange manifestations in men's hearts! From time to time, for no apparent reason, one of them rises up and demands the Unknown.

The light!

For two thousand years Lébos, numb, has been sleeping. Here the days flow into essential fluidity. The people give me graces for the tightened immobility in which it is reflected. Why shake the structure of the Indivisible?

For no apparent reason, defying time, one of them rises up and tries to inscribe the curve of his triumphant message upon the forbidden sky. And who makes men if not TIME.

Catching fire at movement's sources, one of them develops its multiple dimensions to the utmost and wrests God from his lethargy … Then, lightning bolts of choleric majesties set the world's hair ablaze. Guilty cities, lamentable sinners, deliver their resounding souls.

Tortuous catastrophes toil to uncover the houses, stunned heads, smashed in chests, precipitated legs and arms, cracked walls. Agile epidemics. Mouths …

Repentance, bled out, sows new constitutions. From time to time, one of them rises up and demands.

The Chorus   *(Interrupting him.)* The essential thing is to prevent the spectacle. Be careful Polyxos!

Polyxos   *(Starting.)* But serene Lébos will refuse the adventure!

Two thousand years! A falling note and nothing is able to suspend its vibrations!

Ménasha   Sire, in the open hours, the forces in presence stop measuring each other up. Yes, for no apparent reason, new speeds shake the blossoming worlds. A man, a single man, shifts the sun from its place and sticks it to his lips.

The Chorus   The main thing is to prevent the spectacle.

Ménasha   Tragedy, this palpitating possibility of humans, demands to be confirmed in its hesitation. Peoples, in hexagonal rows, refuse the stage.

The underwater expositions[4] pour out their boiling atmospheres into the crucible of the immutable.

Majesty, wisdom sometimes gives birth to sinister decisions. Let us go, SIRE, let us head for the ramparts of the Gesture and may the reckless torch that wants to abolish man's perfect convergence be extinguished.

(They exit. [While] the curtain slowly falls.)

The Chorus   *(With a voice returned by a distant echo.)* Polyxos, prince of Lébos,

On the other side of the emaciated Word,

The initial Act is raised.

On reaching its maximum limits, human thought can only transmute.

---

[4]Editor's note: Explosions?

Act II

Scene 1

Same settings.

The Chorus   Audaline, delicately murmured dewdrop, enters …

Audaline   World, keep your velvet eyes shut!

Don't move any, the anemic stars have fallen quiet.

Intimate paginations, thoughtless borders, desperate parentheses …

The blue of day sucks the mauve of night and both of them, equally trembling, hesitate.

O insubstantial Minutes in which two trails can quarrel with each other! Clever showers of the Spirit, closely arrange the oily relations. Thought's petals form an overcoat of shadows … let the stirring era begin.

Affectionate flowers with untouched napes, take my hand and let's smile,

Ivy, giddy Audaline comes

A new thing hatched with the day

Blessed.

Nubile world do not blush, the diffuse daylight surrounds its head with absolute knowledge.

Germs hardened gently in the hollow of august oblivions.

Profound and lamellate, regained consciousnesses are sending necessities to sleep.

Clever waves of the Spirit, closely arrange oily relations. This morning in the barren countryside I went to meet the crystal. It was only a small virginal star, imperfectly distilled, but I pressed it against my breast and took it to Épithalos.

I lay down against the earth…. The earth was calm. Our breathing gently commingled.

Warm proximities disarming unknown spaces.

Borne from flower to flower

Yes I come, created by the breath of the world

To place the breathing of sleeping prairies on the altars.

The walls of Lébos in perpetual thesis struck their desires with all prohibitions. I went, taken, to kiss the daffodil's astonished lips. The last twigs of the night scattered, nonchalant on the ground and my hair, moistened with the fogs' hesitant milk, fell on my face.

Circuits of obedient waters meditate at my gaze's sources while the prattling riverbanks clean their teeth.

I am the waiting one, whose open hands no longer know how to close around anything.

The rose algae, secretly hatched, wound themselves around my body.

And they cradled it.

My throat, half-opened soul, conquered the wild flowers.

Which tamed it.

May panic now come!

The hymeneal kindling brushed against me and the marvellous

and harrowing blood of tenderness exhaled into my heart.

I am the waiting one, torch not yet aflame, taken in the inaugural wind … and the lace of my young arteries catches light in blushing …

(Moved and blood-stained, bells palpitate.)

The body's gentle curves, startled grasses.

The tree broken by the storm cries and

Unity disperses its possibilities.

Over there a bell calls me

Feasts, calvaries, impermeable slabs

Yes germinated Audaline responds

The vigorous Alleluia torments me

Too quickly proclaimed, the harshness of the embrace pervades me

Épithalos, o exhilarating minstrel, I come by the rhythm of bells

Moulded, to sing the hopes of my soul in turmoil.

The bells superimpose their definitive calls

Put down their regrets

Forget the violation …

Slowly divined aerial bells

Shelter me!

Enter Épithalos.

Scene 2

The Chorus, Audaline, Épithalos.

Épithalos appears with a sword in his belt. He is clothed in red satin, a large, dazzling coat on his shoulders. As soon as he appears, the spotlights seize hold of him. Audaline, frightened, draws back.

Épithalos   Stay Audaline frightened source stay, it is I Épithalos, son of Polyxos.

(One by one the bells fall silent. Audaline stretches toward Épithalos.)

Audaline   Oh my beloved with lime-blossom eyelids and soft shadow!

Épithalos   What! What unexpected generosities debase my entreaties!

At the peak of high herbs sleeps the last systole of the night …

Love's tears wound my feverish hands,

My bowed soul rediscovers the significance of its nudity for a moment and the light, enchantment detected within BEING, sets my destiny.

Audaline, weightless forms that surround me, all remain.

Audaline   My beloved with the silver-shield and scented-flower breast to rest my head!

Épithalos   Alas! Creations devoid of all participations!

Digging until total emergence, grappling with the invariant I stop my journey and lock into my identity.

EVENT! Stamping about the other side of life, at the doors of the Gaze I raise myself Absolute!

Audaline   My beloved with hay-cut hair dried in the moonlight.

Épithalos   Audaline, echo leaning against the night's wings!

Audaline   Épithalos, I give you my hair bathed in the mountain stream and my hands perfumed with hanging flowers …

Épithalos   Yes, Audaline, essential quaking.

Audaline   … my eyes bathed in the confused flame of gestating corollas.

Épithalos   Shreds of darkness isolate me from myself, clouds entwined delay the inevitable becoming of my own creation, what sudden movements silently renew me?

Low down, very low down, I looked for the causes of Worlds!

Tenaciously I interrogated crystallized beliefs!

The earth's lips inhaled the secrets and today my head stamps with impatience.

Privileged prisons, my aroused consciousness contemplates the fatal wound.

Audaline   Épithalos the immediate presses! Now my expectation is consumed and I am filled with calm and trust in you.

Épithalos   O refused intoxications! Will I revive who welcomes me as an unfulfilled sigh, when our parallel lives, captive of my hands, already face one another?

EVENT! A day, a single day! Cries of winter birds bristle my brains,

The applause of wild and weary crowds tells me the powerless causality of my existence, whereas

Traversed by silent shadow

One vision obsesses me …

The sun sleeping in a corner anxiously watches blood beat the amber walls of its rays.

Audaline   Épithalos, son of Polyxos! …

Épithalos   Again the superb trace of a yet to be summoned youth

Ah may the accursed avowals in which my voluptuous waves were resorbed leave me!

Audaline, adventure of green enamel, I cry with my vainglorious hands that refuse to touch each other

Aggressive notes whirl at the limits of my eyes …

Audaline   My beloved, the sown lands bathe their inner hypotheses.

The first lava burns the sea's eyelids …

Épithalos, sublime offer of my wait, see how weak and destitute I am before you.

I am no more than a smile drop trembling in the hollow of your hands.

Épithalos   Lébos that obstinately spurns spiritual resonances, I fragment the hypotenuse that redoubles the World. Polyxos, angular intimacy, the accepted syntheses abandon their scrawny horizons, arbitrary interpretations distort the purity of objectivity.

Yes Épithalos, fundamental apparition

Is braced by the unfinished.

Audaline   Épithalos …

Épithalos   Audaline, my gold-strewn dreams stagger when, hailed, you appear to me

Beginning with a deployment, my hands captured the conjugations evoked.

(Épithalos has approached Audaline. He takes her by the arm.)

Audaline!

Audaline   Lord I swoon!

My veins isolate themselves

My forbidden blood bends its lucid nape …

Épithalos   Audaline, astonished root of my being catch the dazzling superhumanity of my Gaze!

Audaline   O formidable Cults! Temperatures too unequal! Intellectual ecstacies finished upright at life's temples, will you ever know how to proclaim the unverifiable affirmation?

May imprudently solicited negations go under and crumble!

Épithalos, the undergrowth rests its eyes

The reasonable mountains stretch out

The barked water falls back epithelial

Deign beloved to drink at my source …

Épithalos   I claim dunes of sun to shelter my soul of stone.

I want days of fire

red

green days …

Audaline   Épithalos, I brought you the gentleness of the earth, but your gaze changed it to fever

See that my heart is surprised and suspends its steps

And that my hands now know only to tend toward you.

(Épithalos, who has not let go of Audaline, looks at her.)

Épithalos   It is true one day and it is you.

One day and it is death

One day and my life is torn from this gravity

One day and old age's wise darkness is obliterated

One day and life exhausts in signifying.

(A moment passes. He separates himself from Audaline and steps backwards.)

Stop threatened and horizontal crowds that tell me the powerless causality of my existence.

An act! I want to spatter this pregnant sky with a vertiginous act!

Parallel hands make the starchy world ring out with a new act!

Audaline   What dramatic pantings already transfigure my expressed destiny?

What excessively acute contributions?

Blue rocks, the morning's eyes mourn nights of violated waters.

Am I not able, subtle immediacy, to confound the successive effects?

Épithalos–   A day, a single day!

Man has a day to live

In a day his existence must end

A day

A single day and it's death

Audaline, a day and it's love

A day, a single day!

Audaline   Épithalos, imperturbable events shake up individual consciousnesses.

Lébos a created fidelity to oneself develops its ties

Épithalos the fateful conflagration …

Épithalos   Audaline, what are History and the Future to me

The Eucharistic beauty of the Past

Ancestral virtues[5]

Future elevation?

What matters to me the temporal proliferation of humans?

I want not to be of any centuries!

At the heart of my existence is where I shall find

The cry of rage my love hymn!

Audaline   Distant and pensive circulations interrupt the unused depths of chaos.

Polyxos tutelary reasons vertiginously supposed consequences

More drunk with forms

More repeated

---

[5]Editor's note: From the first edition of *Cahier d'un retour au pays natal*, published in 1939, when he at last tackles the theme of *négritude*, Aimé Césaire celebrates it in these terms: 'Tiède petit matin de vertus ancestrales' (*Œuvres*, p. 86. In their translation of the *Cahiers* Arnold and Eshleman render this phrase as 'Tepid small hours of ancestral virtues'. Césaire, *Œuvres complètes*, p. 170, *The Complete Poetry*, p. 45). Here we already see then, in the mouth of Épithalos, the rejection of a return to the past of a mythical identity that is capable of reviving the sleepy island – this would become a fundamental theme of *Peau noire, masques blancs*.

Pale and uncertain

May the unchanged illuminate me

May the prepared vertigo

Die useless!

Épithalos   Daughter of Ménasha

Absorbed nymph

The coalescent approaches

   buried

   the other evening

reappear

Fecund and axial

The ineffable Uranogée[6] authorized

Set up its unexpected spiral

Polyxos non-resounding, obese consciousness

I want to make you shudder with peace and infinity!

Father of Épithalos

Happy thought

I climb the portcullis

Fragments of sun in my hands!

Audaline   Voluntarily arid voyages, mortally affected souls, anticipated tears,

Épithalos, pretext of infallible incidences, my wait enveloped me in a cloak of glory and now you have denuded me of it.

Illegitimate openings propose sustained intervals

Densified profusions absorb mediations

---

[6]The sky made earth and the earth made sky in alchemy. In *La Psychanalyse du feu* (1938, chapter 4 'Le feu sexualisé', section 3, on alchemy) Gaston Bachelard links this material marriage of earth and sky, to sexual sublimation.

On the threshold of the supreme flight, Épithalos

Audaline

Circular

NAMES you!

Épithalos   TO NAME!

O impenetrable wound!

But Audaline, anxious chord of my being

Language is formed but slowly

Speech stemming from the Spectacle feeds off new essences.

Emotional affirmations

Recaptured brought closer

Bound.

Reiterated unifications, worried, are undone …

And speech is no longer the world's rest

The sentence returns to the gestural origins and disarms the prolixity of observation.

Audaline   To speak! Abysses enclosed

Such inclemencies started up again!

To speak! Unelucidated presence no innocences bend

Language's light constellation.

Intelligible motivations absent the indecisive soul

Love improvises the necessary

Occultly

Your hand in my hair

My lips …

Épithalos   Audaline on reaching the volcanic extremes speech makes itself act!

A language haunted by exhilarating perception!

To look at the sun head-on

To integrate the world's beat into my existence

To take the breathing of cursorial clouds with tireless feet in my hands …

Perpendicularly I make my way!

A rhythm of rupture bathes my thoughts

Abruptly I compose incendiary scales

On a single theme I want to develop

The streaming chords of my ascent.

I demand thunderbolts to stick into my hands

Nights before the world

Fall

The abyssal mouths of the earth

Albeit inconceivable

Withdraw

Organs shake this town's sterile air

A day!

And at the first flutterings of this day's wings

I demand of myself to be the audacious architect of a tireless contempt.

The strains of my will cut into the undifferentiated ramparts

Of the human edifice.

I want to be the promoter of an absolute loss

Convinced water hesitates to get its feet wet while my burning fingers scatter shivering stars.

A day. A single day and it is too late

A day.

An act and man opens the circle where consciousness rests

Immunized I direct my striated antennas against diagonal atmospheres[7]

I Épithalos

Indistinct adventure

I climb flaying my sonorous hands

And I burst onto the stage.

EVENT! Absolute precipice in which dissociation is forged.

World coldly erased consciousness

Which believes in History

World awaiting which postulates Destiny

I force the frameworks with my still

Depth and I explode

Such final certainty.

Fortuitous offerings

Repressive matrices

Hands mine on this day

Swollen with revelrous promises

With sighed stalactites

Question rescinded rememberings.

Audaline   *(Discouraged.)* The serous membrance of the world, repudiated, mediates itself like a

Confidential shroud.

What is to be done?

What imperfectly discovered rival habits?

(A noise is heard.)

What new clashes hit my dishevelled convulsion?

---

[7]Cf. *Peau noire, masques blancs*, 'I slip into corners, my long antennae encountering the various axioms on the surface of things' (*Black Skin, White Masks*, p. 96).

Épithalos the anvil of events activates

The fallout of illusion

Lébos armed for the Adventure readies to confound the first solemnities!

(The noise gets closer.)

Épithalos sacramental smoke

Wipes the recommended ground.

(Épithalos draws his sword.)

Épithalos   I, higher consciousness

Powerful reality frenzying the armpit of the cosmos

I, Épithalos …

(Audaline, interrupting him, goes to him.)

Audaline   Lord

Beloved

The first gaze

exploded

fervour

Distorts the determinate.

[*Four pages (out of forty-nine) are missing from the original typescript, including scenes 3 and 4.*]

Ménasha   To know and to keep quiet! …

To await the rallied similitudes …

Facing the powers of the Spirit

The human condition? Paradoxical Peruvian woman!

Épithalos rival and magnificent mistake

Do not yell

Cease the painful production of schism!

Enter the Stronghold's Commander.

Scene 5

The Chorus, Ménasha, Stronghold's Commander.

The Commander enters helpless.

Ménasha   What is happening, Sir, and what is the meaning of this extreme agitation I see you in?

The Commander   A misfortune Your Excellency!

A misfortune, for Lébos prepares its collapse!

Thick with sleep I climbed up to the day's bluish shores

When upon them inexplicable noises were heavily cast.

Unknown accents fluttered about vigorous …

Milky white clouds hushed with arrows

I awoke questioning the shaken surroundings.

An officer came in search of me and at the headquarters I went to alarm had reigned for two hours.

There I was given the reasons for this terror.

The Sun is moving toward Lébos

Covered with murderous flames!

Ménasha   O excessively essential relation!

How are we to find out the first causes?

Avid to know, the men

Interrogated the vagabond planets in their nascent livery.

They read their geometrical destinies on the flank of thick stars.

Calm ordered years!

The moon, prey to some cancer, strove to rediscover

An eternally distorted unity …

And the necessary evolution of this reborn gestation

Rhythmed the human adventure.

Calm years in which, in primary relation, men and things gently imprinted each other.

Moistened from all quarters fatal amazement lost its dazzling aridity.

Calm destinies whispered!

(The bells that have been discussing since the third scene clarify their remarks.)

What is to be done? Now man is initiated in demiurgic pathos!

The upset stars bow their heads and rethink their fate

Might it be Épithalos again?

Mistake, exasperated mistake

What fatal separations drive him?

Peace to men of good will!

Peace to beings of reason!

The fierce multitude keeps silent un-spined

    contested

    ignorant

What demands illuminate the desperate space?

What unthinkable precariousnesses absorb the nothingness of all decisions? Equally weighed down plebeian consciousnesses

    quenched indistinctly

    arranged themselves

    as univocal effigies.

The golds ringed with waters, outpoured existences …

Silences embedded in proximal immanence.

Pollarded, fracturing boldnesses

    impalpable amassing

        were reaped …

    Eloquences drunk again

        with abstractly sonated hyperboles.

(The impatient bells, furious at not being understood, set fire to the stage with their exclamations. At that moment, claps of thunder, lightning, satisfied tongues, take place in laughing. Ménasha and the Commander shield their eyes.)

Inner excitations devoid of reciprocity

simplified constituents take each other's hands

Separated spaces beam with aborted syntheses.

Infinite destructions unintelligible rotations adolescent discoveries

What is that? What melodic unknowns marble the voices of the Spirit?

Lébos, star-harped city, weigh on your coherence!

A moment passes.

(The rushed light opens the palace doors. It proclaims original effervescence.)

(Ménasha has drawn her sword.) Stop the earth's hand raised against the face of the sky!

Enter Dràhna.

Scene 6

*The Chorus, Ménasha, the Stronghold's Commander, Dràhna.
    Dràhna seems overcome ...*

Dràhna   The tortured Sky bemoans bygone dissension!

O supreme Mercies

Oppressed sanctifications

The Sun's unfurled satin bows the shadowy brows ...

I shall speak the distorted dimensions

I shall speak the hatched resonances

I shall speak the expiatory oil!

Men subjected violence

I shall speak tragic bearings ...

Ménasha   Madam ...

Dràhna   Men abusive adventures

The stained-glass windows of a chapel abandoned hands lift me up ...

Polyxos function of itself

emerged

dims

Ménasha   Madam the lucules wound Lébos's veins like disastrous bites!

Dràhna   Let them bleed!

With blood we will wash our eyes!

Ménasha   What sudden despairs irritate you?

Dràhna   Irritate me?

O arched virulence

City slowly noised

City of overheated adjacencies

The garden's wooden planks collapse

Polyxos blood-stunned definitive absence

I shall speak the masterly finds

(A pause.)

Lébos's veins bleed …

Polyxos's ruptured arteries run dry …

Épithalos parricidal adventure LOOK …

Ménasha   Polyxos …

Dràhna   His Majesty, with his throat pierced in many places, rests his face on the burgeoning paving stones.

Ménasha   O Gods!

Dràhna   Peace to useless gods!

It is with blood that we shall wash our dead!

I shall speak!

I shall speak the continued baptism

the existential ablution

   the liturgical fire …

I shall speak the fundamental mistake

I shall speak the overturned twilight …

Men eternally vanquished glories

I shall speak the opulence of your defeats.

Once again the pitilessly lacerated intimacies …

The streets outlined handcuffs

close again …

Our star-rained heads commit suicide …

Men spectacular discordances

I will speak

your unreasoning your ardors expatriated at dawn

What do you seek in the Sun's eyes?

What do you seek in the Sky's wrinkles?

To where will the now resumed fervour of Épithalos lead us?

Reeds deformed beech trees

Twin banks detained leaves

Winds

Short circuits ousted in a day …

Ménasha   Thus Polyxos is dead!

Épithalos in the Palace

LOOK at the volcanic illusions.

(Coming from far away choirs of irresponsible children lean toward the ground. Despairing bells lament …)

The gates of disjunct Lébos gape …

Your Majesty must we? …

Dràhna   The irrigated world silts up

Daily flowers spray the clutched temples …

What is to be done?

Amputate the unfruitful harmonies?

Declare the fountain disruption?

Prune the arid consciousnesses?

What is to be done?

What is to be done?

The emptied imminence of Épithalos

   Curves

(Frenzied.)

From everywhere condemned attacks return to me!

The tearful openings hollow out with abysses

O Creatures intrigued with yourself

My icy soul

Sets down its blood-streaked

limits

She collapses.

Curtain. End of Act II.

[Act III[8]]

Scene 3

The Chorus, Audaline, Dràhna.

Dràhna, after a few steps on the stage, sees Audaline.

Dràhna   Audaline!

Audaline

Dràhna   Audaline marvellously iridescent crystal!

Audaline

Dràhna   It is true the crystal has drowned itself with distress; the folds of pulverized shadows are crossed with schistose perceptions.

Audaline

Dràhna   O events too unjust! Is it our fault if the Suns set ablaze, existence impalpably puked?

Is it our fault if in a movement of their brains men seize hold of frenzied possibilities?

Audaline

Dràhna   Audaline mirror in which the Day devours itself!

Audaline fiancée of Épithalos see how the air hesitates see

How instaurations shudder …

The curve of absence stamps on the threshold

See how the wake wonders!

Audaline

Dràhna   It is true rebel efforts broke juvenile hopes.

---

[8]Editor's note: Scenes 1 and 2 of Act III are missing from the original typescript. In his book, (p. 131), Joby Fanon cites the following lines, which are clearly taken from this missing passage: 'And me, the igniter of world / Words! Words! Words! / I see stars to "wing" reason / I develop myself / Arisen from the power of the act / I absolute contestation.'

The autonomous tragic stage today arranges its first fumaroles

Polyxos blood-drunk consciousness

closes up …

Épithalos …

Audaline   Madam …

Dràhna   Yes I know … Death … already defective sketches …
Matched origins.

O intellectual juxtapositions …

(A pause.)

Audaline diversities abolish themselves on contact with the inclusive
fact!

necessities move at the whim of reflection …

Audaline   *(Dreaming.)* Vanished ivy Audaline comes

New thing hatched with the Day

Blessed …

Dràhna   The world's structuration …

Reality, tortured a moment with negation,[9] isolates

accidental meanings

tangential appearings

saturated hues …

Audaline   *(Dreaming.)* I am one who waits, a torch not yet
burning, taken in the inaugural wind … and the lace of my young
arteries lights up blushing.

Dràhna   Men merciless transfixing pains see the irreducible crack
of our smiles!

Polar correlations abandon the represented

---

[9]In these words of Dràhna, Fanon, who was familiar with Hegel's *Phenomenology
of Spirit* (1807), as well as with Kojève's, Sartre's and Wahl's discussion of Hegel,
follows Kierkegaard in rejecting Hegelian negation, and by implication any pursuit of
the Absolute through the transcendence of the *Aufhebung*.

harassed spaces lament immobile faculties

Audaline sails uncertain

is it our fault if the inventoryings confound sensible evidences?

The drooping dream

the broken sheaves

dazzled alterities kill one another

Audaline inherent suffering feeds off our blood ....

(In the distance men cut up by Sun-blades scream.)

Outside inordinately smashed drunk heads

are fulfilled

The palace central core throws distended concepts into meaningless skies.

Lébos ashed city

the requiem falls in heavy clamours

I don't know anymore!

Audaline morsel of history

I don't know anymore!

I don't know the Causes anymore!

Yes death once again

   hell once again

   enthusiasm once again

   fevers once again

      heavinesses

      rapidities

Torn flowers of intermingled organs once again ...

Once again intolerable speeds

irrepressible flights

Audaline   Épithalos o thrilling minstrel I come shaped by the rhythm of bells to sing your infinite glories.

The bells superpose their definitive calls

    lay down their regrets

    forget the violation …

Aerial bells slowly divined

shelter me!

Dràhna   Audaline …

Audaline   *(Waking up.)* Madam all sleeps in my soul

The tumultuous prows split our sworded chests

Madam all sleeps in my soul and I cry

O already exhausted immortal transposition

my soul staggers

The tomb is open and the rediscovered source saddens

Anxious flutes

Infernal oboes

resound!

Wrenched hands

Orphan hands tremble

the tomb has opened up!

Madam I sleep and I traverse the world with closed eyes, my hand

clenched on something that I do not want to see die.[10]

Dràhna   Audaline …

Audaline   *(She staggers.)* The fiery sand burns the eyes

I die ignorant of everything

---

[10]Editor's note: Handwritten addition in the margin of the original typescript: 'O lie! Mockeries.'

I die and my death is unknown to me

I sink into the abyss

and the theme settles in definitively

come down angels foamy with refusal

strike me

your barbed wings will find the path of my misfortunes

Clouds

bludgeons of Thought

throw disarray into my dishevelled soul

I sink into the abyss

Dràhna   Daughter of Ménasha …

Audaline   Listen,

Sleep returns

Listen blood makes me rebel

Listen world that loses me

the earth tears itself apart

Listen to the depth of my abyss

I sleep my hand clenched on something that will die with me

(Bells gently take her hand.)

Light curves of the body,

alarmed little herbs

the tree broken by the storm cries and

unity disperses its possibilities.

Calvary feasts impermeable paving stones

yes germinated Audaline responds …

She exits.

Scene 4

The Chorus, Dràhna, Ménasha.

Bells from the other side accompany Audaline.

Dràhna   Desperate voices,

embrace the final memory

A needle makes its way slowly

surround the original palpitation

the theme is annihilated.

(The bells shove the undivined Audaline.)

Voices that seek the opening

Cry

the estuaries sink into the abyss

Audaline

Unusual symphonies

essential nymphaea

kneel down

voices keep quiet.

*(She is unsteady on her feet. The choirs of aggressive children cut out
sections of peat.)*

O this heaviness

draped with Sun, I swoon

the converged white wounds my eyes

the explored incarnations are slaked

Burnt floods are repudiated

The Question gets martyred …

Suspended Voices

go to sleep

the oppressed wings of love

sink into the abyss!

(Far off the screams of assassinated men.)

Accumulated truths extinguish themselves

Pity murderous star!

May our resignation resuscitate us …

Lit water drops plant their teeth in my throat

Networks of abyssal consciousnesses attest

Thousands of abyssal smiles attest

Thousands of disarmed hands attest

Pity murderous star!

(Against the stage three harps wet the lips of a soul.)

Moistened wadding

pity!

Silence separated from itself

Hold back your ulcerating assaults.

May our upheaval resuscitate us

Murderous star

Pity!

(Ménasha enters.)

Ménasha   Unfortunate Life forsakes me;

Audaline is dead!

Dràhna   *(Unsteady.)* With blood will we wash our dead.

I will speak!

(Bells and harps keep quiet. The children with their innocent voices raise Audaline.)

Ménasha   Audaline white and beautiful …

Dràhna   With blood will we wash our dead!

I will speak!

Ménasha   All dark

Bare space sticks to innocent promises

All collapses

the atmosphere grey with flourished hostility strikes down innocent ardours

All gives way

the expiring lyre unjustly brushed against

gloves the hand of despair.

Condemned surfaces fall

come back engulfed notes

rivers …

Come back sad rope too abruptly withering

all is destroyed.

Dràhna   The drooping dream

the broken sprays

dazzled alterities kill one another …

Ménasha   Audaline first syllable

Dràhna   *(Unsteady.)* With blood will we wash our dead!
I shall speak!

Ménasha   Fatal erosions

equations dilate

O untranslatable lamentations

origins intrigue one another

Audaline watered poem

The impulsive deflagration immolates you

Audaline murmur at death's door

Circular fatalites rue …

Dràhna   Unleashing forces that assail me

Limitless scales that outrage me …

Event that shakes up my manes …

Eruptive world

Your rebellions are fatal to me!

(She staggers.)

But why this expressing of despair?

Why these words that kill me twice?

Why this pain seeking itself?

Silence within the silence!

Silence on this deserted earth!

Silence in the solar aridity!

Peace and death at the gates of gravid skies

eternally!

Death, death

Men irremediable absurdities!

Ménasha   Yes All keeps quiet

 Yesterday's vibrating exclamations proclaim

their final accents.

All crumbles

takes on waters

the world loses

All crumbles

Tragedy absolute insertion

fixes becoming

Our earth plunges into mourning …

Dràhna   *(Interrupting her.)* Our earth!

Rejected from the world will I create illusory conquests for myself?

Our earth!

Is it my fault if the consciousnesses scribble the flesh offered?

Is it my fault if negations dissolve categories?

Our earth!

What imprudently uttered

Ironic belongings?

Alone

Alone in this foreign world I divest

The essential phosphorescence.

(Some noise is heard.)

What unrelenting, imperfectly satisfied flames are moving towards us?
Enter the The Stronghold's Commander.

Scene 5

The Chorus, Dràhna, Ménasha, the Stronghold's Commander.

The Commander is very agitated. He addresses Dràhna.

The Commander   Your Majesty,

Crucified Lébos howls in pain

men in continual transformation

dissolve

Majesty Lébos bleeds …

Dràhna   Let her bleed, with this blood we will wash our dead!

The Commander   Majesty

I crossed the city drowned with dead

The Sun strikes the surrounding windows.

The fires terrify the skies.

The Chorus   Blessed be Darkness for the light is terrible

Ménasha   To know and to keep quiet

That is the question!

(Violins chase each other.)

The Commander   Majesty, vehement Lébos disowns

The disastrous wound.

Insensible Universal consciousness

rediscovers its ramparts.

The attributes recently sprung from the WHOLE

ask to be interrupted.

The light prohibits all ways out …

Dràhna   What is to be done?

Ménasha   Man is an embodied error

Diffluent approaches introduce multiple careers

But error

That colloid subordination

Annihilates solstitial perspectives …

Dràhna   Error! …

What constructions can we legitimate with the weight of this vengeance of REASON?

Error!

Is it my fault if the compact space of thought

is made of the Unknown?

What is to be done?

(She staggers.)

Murderous star, pity.

The Commander   Majesty

Weighty Lébos

Parricidal Lébos

Seeks the return of Equilibrium

Soon the Sun will sink on our heads …

Unless?

Dràhna and Ménasha together   Unless.

The Commander   Épithalos must leave the city within two hours

Then

consciousness, void from inchoative emissions

will rest.

Dràhna   DEATH once again

Frightful speeds once again

(She staggers.)

Definitive ruptures once again

The illusory ABSOLUTE once again

(She staggers. Ménasha, the Commander, try to support her.)

Back, Back

What to me now are the plains marked out with fraternal interruptions?

What to me are hopes

tendernesses

the children's fears?

Useless world defeated Dràhna

awaits the paradoxical repressions!

Curtain. End of Act III.

Act IV

Scene 1

The curtain is raised. A tripled incandescence. For a full minute, no one on stage.

Enter Épithalos. After a few steps.

Épithalos   O eviscerating trophies

Infrangible calls

Exuberant opposition coagulates …

The fighters of the swell dissect the energies

The sidereal revolution is engulfed

Wild swell

O eviscerating trophies!

Distended Lébos vibrates unfathomably

Hierarchy multiplies the intentions

The schism hurries the affinities …

O sumptuousness curb your motivity

To see no more

To see death no more

Severly broadened light

Measure the hydra of destruction.

The Chorus   Épithalos, heterogeneous spark

on reaching the eruptive peak the ACT can only be absorbed!

Épithalos   Disappear you inventions of my new consciousness!

the holocaust specifies the sacrifice

Primordial spectacle I drink from inner riches

To see no more

To see death no more

the chasm

The light successively precipitated

Evanescent objects throw against my gaze a heightened resistance!

Support my life across the span of my negation

Pulverizing the impudent habits

Yes I see

I see my life taken vertiginously

attached to the ACT

precipitated toward the ACT

My life created with this act

My hard

heavy life

I see the swept avenues

Narrowed sordid precautions

I see old ages lamentably authenticated

I, Épithalos, raised

joy fluttering about prohibited summits

LIFE

But words avoid me

The only tragedy, language beats my thought

Non-abstracting world at last

World that finds the existential bearing

Moan your sickly evenings

Moan your cavitary sleeps

Moan and creak

Old burnt out world

(A pause.)

To see no more

To feel now the shock of things

    their movements

    their horizons

    to touch their perspectives

O eviscerating trophies.

(A horn confronts the abundance of sun.)

Impardonable snows

humiliated liquids

See the dryness aureole my soul!

Multiplied creation sobs

The ivory of the known groans unaesthetically

Shame on the flank of thought!

The Chorus   Épithalos unfurled adventure

On reaching the eruptive peaks, the Act can only be ABSORBED!

Épithalos   At the gates of the torrent devouring perception stands timid!

Death blocks my way

But the word must find life there

Impractible paroxysms …

A day

A day and my life is wrested from that gravity

Reasons distributed to unexpected weakness!

Two thousand years and the world sleeps

Two thousand years that men have forgotten themselves within a

Life in abeyance!

Two thousand years and days subjugate consciousness

See the EXTRAORDINARY has righted the obliquity of

darkness and the ACT's assailing force invents sublime metamorphoses.

I scrunitize, Tyrant of an irremediably violated azure

Irremediably torn apart

Illusory futures!

Ah let temporal hopes be drowned!

The wide open hour gets jammed

grotesquely!

Man intoxicating adventure

proclaim the stiffness of your curve to the leafy times

(He staggers.)

Oh this intrusion

this flesh that slowly confounds!

I seek things!

adapted things

permanent phenomena

I seek your texture

To see the speechless white no more

DEATH

the terrifying VOID

To see the UNGRASPABLE no more.

Enter Dràhna.

Scene 2

The Chorus, Épithalos, Dràhna.

Dràhna enters, Épithalos doesn't see her.

Dràhna   Épithalos!

Épithalos   Who calls me? *(Seeing Dràhna.)* O Mother, wake up the flagellated summits are fringed with expectation!

Dràhna   Polyxos …

Épithalos   Look!

The sky's eyes are open. Mother life, required life shudders in the hollow of our hands.

O impulsive construction

Oscillating tension!

O exercise of my full interrogation!

See the brutality of our existence …

Dràhna   Halted Lébos crumbles …

Épithalos   Miserable gape!

Mother look

Mother look at the offer getting impatient

at the gates of my creation

consciousness chafes, universal unpityingly tracked down.

At the gates of the ACT is illuminated the absolute voice of the

GAZE

Mother, o flame equally unfixed

Look,

Existence true incarnation sprawls

Mother wake up, the flagellated summits are fringed with expectation!

Dràhna   My Son painful impetuousness

My powerless wait is imprisoned

the hermetic gates the impossible blindingly draw away

Ah! Épithalos trenchant exclamation

why have you stupefied us?

blood-smeared cliffs wash in the ebb of sterility

My son … What have you done?

(Épithalos takes her hands.)

Épithalos   Mother …

Dràhna   What have you done?

Épithalos burning cut

What have you done with your radial hands?

O horrifying action!

Where are we to go now?

The world's horizons rediscover the sense of their afference

what are we to hope for now?

Singular consciousness ends flanked with silence

O horrifying action

Épithalos what have you done?

(Screams flood the stage, Dràhna staggers.)

See the Universe demands forgiveness,

Men fantastic apparitions persist in paralysing their desires

Épithalos how have you not heard the voice of pure thought?

This breach in my sanctuary!

Immensity like an enlightened victim disperses your fury

Notes of fire shake up the mirror where language is rooted.

See the gulf of the inaccessible crack open

See the summit expose its ephemeral dwellings

Épithalos incisive origin

See, tragedy interrogates its prey

Épithalos   Mother the mirror is tarnished at the breath of the undifferentiated

The immobile contingency weighed down consciousnesses devoid of asperities

Mother, behind the useless and the darkness

Behind the silence

Behind the divine night …

And there, at the centre of the world,

our sacred night,

Our hands sublime cities

refusing sleep

forgetfulness

there, at the centre of ourselves, the irreducible instrument

that will rhythm the perfect lives of men

O Rhythm of hollowing out!

The literally deafened truth

splendours thunder and strike the World's bark with their scoriae.

Mother, accept the day that I bring you …

Dràhna   My son …

Épithalos   Mother, I fashion a frothing day with my anxiety-armed hands,

The vaulted, ghostly moon emits its last gasp

Harrassed mountains

Promontories

the steel of my words haunts your flint[11]

---

[11]In *Moi, laminaire*, 6 (1982), Aimé Césaire describes Fanon himself as a 'guerrier-silex' (flint-warrior) (Césaire, *Œuvres*, p. 624, *The Complete Poetry*, p. 665).

Mother I bring you

Damascened eruption

the fulgural day

Dràhna   Yes, dreadful battles

Agitations, sacrileges

Yes, the moon crashes at the gates of solar vivacity,

Lébos contemplates innumerable funerals

Already insensitive sepulchral memories prepare to regain the heath

But, my son, what are we to hope for from the overwhelming nudity?

What to hope for now, as the hostility of death assails us?

Polyxos, Audaline …[12]

Épithalos   Audaline?

Dràhna   The thorn of the named star froze the silver of her soul!

Épithalos   *(he staggers for the first time.)* O exhausting bruises

murderous glows with what unsteadinesses do you strike me?

Audaline marvellous side of my polarity

I brought you the depths of the day and, lo and behold, death wrests you from the magnificences of Love!

Audaline, adventure of green enamel, I cry with my vainglorious hands that refuse to touch each other!

O Melancholia!

(Dreaming.)

A day

A day and it's Love

A day and consciousness self-seized is legitimated.

(Dràhna gently interrupts him.)

---

[12]Editor's note: This page of the manuscript has not been revised by Fanon, Audaline here is written Andaline.

Dràhna   A day!

A day and it's death!

A day and the question falls back inert,

A day and seized consciousness commits suicide.

The Chorus   Blessed be darkness

For the light is terrible.

Épithalos, on reaching the eruptive peaks the ACT can only be absorbed.

Dràhna   A day and the world bares all!

(She staggers.)

A day and my eyes are veiled with bitterness!

My son, what have you done with your hands?

Tell me, essential movement, why have you stupefied us?

Épithalos   Mother, necessity reveals itself to our eyes

Constitutive appeals accuse the deplorable security

Mother methods disappear

Listen, life warmly invites us!

Dràhna   *(Staggering.)* Death …

Épithalos   Mother, listen

Dràhna   Death …

Épithalos   Life, Mother!

my illuminated denseness unfurls

Life, Mother

The rock I instituted defines the explosions.

Dràhna   All is lost my Son!

But the bloodiest loss is yours

O painful failure!

Enter Ménasha.

Scene 3

The Chorus, Dràhna, Épithalos, Ménasha.

Ménasha   Gesture, cries, lamentations, flanks ripped apart …

No tree trembles

The ACT must be taken back to its first night

What are we to hope of that cave in which trembling consciousnesses eye one another.

The glow-worm disappears with the day

Likewise Man with the ACT

Épithalos creation wrings its hands

To know and to keep quiet!

To speak …

To hope …

Sinister tragedy in which the bloodied brains of the tireless contradiction evict immobile REASON!

(Dràhna collapses. Épithalos leans over her and lifts her up.)

Épithalos   Mother

the requested life …

O Melancholy

I brought the day's scintillation and

Now death wrests you from the solemnities

of my definition.

(He puts his mother down. At this moment the spotlights leave Dràhna in the darkness.)

Stars who condemn me …

Audaline, Dràhna, pretexts of myself

I ask for your forgiveness …

The Chorus   Blessed is darkness.

Ménasha   May the bold torch be extinguished that wants to abolish the perfect convergence of man!

Épithalos   Alone

I will express!

Alone I want to go to the bold abyss into which consciousness sinks.

Day, enchanting light enveloping my reality

Ah! The path leading to the human is long!

Alone, I will go to the gates opening onto impossible certainty.

Fever

My heart

My fierce body collided with the flank of human history

My fever dissolving the comic banality.

My glory

I rise up

Sacrificial ACT I rise.

Oh! The mountains are absent

The far plains, far are lost

the squalid earth

my flesh

My dreadful finitude

my flesh

Ah! The path that leads to the human is barren

Tough is the path that leads me to myself,

The Chorus   Fire devours the nascent fire!

Épithalos   An uphill journey …

I rise

My chest heavy with exhilarating intoxication.

(An orchestra penetrated with screams frames the stage, the light shakes convulsively.)

Ménasha   What to hope …

Épithalos   *(interrupting her.)* Roll barren sources!

What to hope for?

My fever!

Oh! If I could …

If only I could no longer mark out the world but

anchor myself in its eternal vacuity

If I could …

Words wrested from myself

Words replete with my spilt blood

Murderous words

If I could …

Language authorized by the ACT, raise the world

It is by feeding off the spectacle that you will create absolute demands.

But the world crushes me in its black irresponsibility

Time,

mocking power enriching old ages

crouching

Men amused by yourselves

I will express the movements of your flaccid nerves!

(He staggers.)

If I could …

Ménasha   Laugh at one's heavy latitudes inexhaustible

Exuberance of knowledge!

Épithalos   If I could …

Haemorrhagic stars that condemn me

Stop!

Oh! To see no more

To see the silent white no more

To see death no more

Permanent things seize my gaze

rampant

The Void

The end

Night deprived brilliance

Night germination that legimates the sleep of men

Come back

Limit the world's perspective …

To see no more.

(Bells and orchestra try to infiltrate the stage.)

Night of the WHOLE come back to drown the flame of my consciousness

My body attracts me

This flesh

Me, Épithalos reality whipping the Cosmos into a fever

Night, I beseech you

Come back

To see no more

To see the VOID no more

Things, rediscover your texture …

(At this moment, the light settles in the auditorium. On stage, darkness returns as the curtain falls).

Ménasha   Épithalos, the night is done

my eyes clutch the divine things

Lébos becomes organized once again

Blessed is darkness.

Épithalos   *(Like flesh torn by a hail of bullets)* I SEE.

Curtain.

Frantz Fanon's Library

List established, presented and commented by Jean Khalfa

Presentation

This list of some four hundred works was drawn up on the basis of the catalogue made by F. Boulkroune and S. Khouider of the library that Olivier Fanon gave to the Centre national de recherches préhistoriques anthropologiques et historiques (CNRPAH) of Algiers.[1] This family library also contained Josie Fanon's books as well as several books published after Fanon's death in December 1961. In the following list only those titles published in his lifetime are given. A certain number of works that were manifestly not his were left out, but others that likely belonged to Josie were kept insofar as they had perhaps elicited their shared interest. It is well known in particular that Fanon read a lot of poetry and theatre.

During this period in France books and journals were not yet all trimmed. In several cases, only some of the pages are cut, and I have indicated which ones. Each volume has been verified. Many of them contain marks in the margins or under certain words or phrases. When they appear to be significant, in particular in relation to the rest of the œuvre, or when they are accompanied by annotation, I indicate them. While it is quite possible that some of these marks or inscriptions were made by other readers, in most of the cases Fanon's interests, style and writing are discernible. This library also contains a certain number of propaganda brochures or classic editions of Marxist works. It is highly likely that Fanon, as a journalist, and Josie, who was herself a journalist in Algiers, automatically received a large number of them, as was the case for a good proportion of the intelligentsia in Europe and in Africa up until the 1970s. Most of them do not seem to have been read. I have presented a separate list of them in the interests of clarity. But from that list Fanon has carefully read various works by Marx, Engels, Lenin and Plekhanov. Lastly, he read and contributed to several important journals of the period, in particular *Esprit*, *Les Temps modernes* and *Présence*

---

[1]The catalogue can be accessed on the site of the CNRPAH, http://www.cnrpah.org/images/catalogues/fanon.pdf.

africaine, all of which marked his generation, as well as the major Francophone journals on psychiatry and neurology.[2] I have drawn up a separate list of these journals, which are often abundantly annotated and moreover allow us to date his preoccupations at precise moments. The testimonies concur: Fanon read incessantly and very widely. Many books were probably lost during Fanon's various moves, but this library gives us an idea of the range of his interests. By no means are these works to be taken as 'sources' in the sense in which the œuvre might be reduced to them, but instead as encounters or as shocks,[3] or else as toolboxes that enable the work which unhesitatingly appropriates them to deepen its founding questions and intuitions.

In what follows the reader will find a good proportion of the books to which Fanon's published works, in particular *Peau noire, masques blancs*, refer. Naturally, we find among them a large medical and psychiatric literature, as well as classics of existentialist philosophy, including Jaspers, Kierkegaard, Merleau-Ponty and Sartre. However, one also notes Fanon's considerable interest in other thinkers: Nietzsche, of course, but also Bachelard, Kojève (for his reading of Hegel), Jean Wahl, Emmanuel Levinas, Simone Weil, Nicolas Calas and Michel Carrouges. In literature, theatre and poetry dominate; readers of Fanon's plays will not be surprised to find Aeschylus, Corneille, Racine and Claudel alongside Saint-John Perse and Césaire.

---

[2]Charles Geronimi remarks: 'Training the interns was also one of his preoccupations. He took care of the medical library and enriched it considerably. By 1956, it was notably better endowed with works of psychiatry and neurology than its university counterpart in Mustapha. Under his influence, the HPB [Blida Psychiatric Hospital] had subscriptions to all the Francophone journals of neurology and psychiatry' (*Fanon à Blida*, unpublished manuscript, kindly given us by the author). For this reason, though some collections in the personal library stop upon his arrival in Algeria, this does not imply that he had stopped reading these journals (in particular, *L'Évolution psychiatrique*, in which all the debates in that domain at the time were taking place). This is reflected in the editorials of *Our Journal* that were more specifically targeted at the hospital staff.

[3]Or 'dark precursors' in the sense of Gilles Deleuze in *Différence et répétition* (English translation: *Difference and Repetition*, trans. Paul Patton, New York, NY: Columbia University Press, p. 119). Fanon stages the shock of such an encounter in *Peau noire, masques blancs* concerning the revelation of negritude, Sartre's dialectical critique of it, and the communist critique of both of them (in Gabriel d'Arboussier's article, 'Une dangereuse mystification: la théorie de la négritude' ('A dangerous mystification: the theory of negritude'), cited in note 34 of the chapter on 'The Black Man and Psychopathology', p. 150).

In a text sent to René Hénane,[4] who kindly passed it on to us, Raymond Péju, the great bookseller of Lyon (Librairie La Proue), described Fanon's relation to books in the following terms:

I can still see that man, who, for some time, came more and more regularly to the bookstore. That was in 1948, I was a young bookseller and paid close attention to the clients, to the readers, who came back to the store regularly; he was one of them! I can see him entering again, a smile on his lips as he 'slipped' between the display stands with the elegance and suppleness that only he had. He was rather young (I think we were close in age), rather tall and thin, with a lively and penetrating gaze – he was immediately rather likeable, to me in any case!

He returned increasingly often, sometimes making only a whirlwind stop, at other times lingering more tranquilly, and then he would talk more readily. He didn't open up much and we spoke above all about literature; he was curious about everything, most especially about the human sciences and poetry, which was one of our favourite subjects. I don't have an accurate memory of the poems that I might have introduced him to, but what I do recall is that he allowed me truly to appreciate Aimé Césaire, about whom he spoke with intelligence and sensitivity. We were very quickly on friendly terms with one another and he started speaking to me of himself.

His name was Frantz Fanon, he was from Martinique, he had completed his studies in medicine, specialized in psychiatry; he talked about his country and his profession with the passion that was so characteristic of his personality; a passion that you felt was, beneath a calm and likeable exterior, wholly ready to ignite, to explode.

Our conversations became longer, more personal and, one day, I proposed to him that we continue them in a more comfortable setting at my place; he accepted enthusiastically! On the agreed evening, my wife Marie-Aimée and Fanon got to know each other and spontaneously sympathized with each other; it was a long and cordial evening and on that day a friendship emerged between the three of us that was to last for as long as he was alive.

---

[4] A French doctor who specialized in tropical medicine and authored several books on the poetry of Aimé Césaire, with whom he was friends.

He returned often; I think that he liked being in a friendly, almost familial atmosphere, with us, which he had probably been missing; and little by little he began to talk about himself in a more intimate way and more precisely about his suffering as an 'excluded man', as a man rejected owing to the colour of his skin! He told us about the rebuffs, the affronts that he had endured: he mentioned the woman who had advertised a room to rent and who, when he showed up, retorted: 'I asked for a student, not a negro!' And also of the man in the train who interpellated him: 'Hey negro, put my suitcase in the rack.' An imbecilic racism that came through at any given opportunity in the most anodine acts of everyday life. We were sickened, cut to the quick! ...

That must have been the time when he began to write *Peau noire, masques blancs*. He spoke with me about it sometimes in the course of our conversations. ... However, if this topic returned frequently to our conversations, it was nonetheless not the essential point ... Poetry, for example, always had pride of place; we always took the greatest pleasure in chatting about Césaire or Char, as well as Aragon, Breton and Éluard or Damas and Senghor.

One evening, he took us to a poetry reading of Aimé Césaire organized by his friend Achille.[5] He had chosen to recite 'Batouque', a poem that he liked and that he read with a remarkable accuracy of tone. Frantz was curious about all things and he could be extremely eloquent, he was a born storyteller!

---

[5]Louis-Thomas Achille (1909–1994), professor of English for the preparatory classes at the Lycée du Parc in Lyon from 1946 to 1974. He also hailed from Martinique and was a recognized specialist of African American sacred music, on which he published 'Negro Spirituals' in the May 1951 issue of *Esprit*, the same one in which Fanon published 'La plainte du Noir: l'expérience vécue du Noir', which was later to be incorporated into *Peau noire, masques blancs*, and Octave Mannoni, 'La plainte du Noir'. The author of several articles in French and American journals, Achille participated in the first International Congress of Black Writers and Artists held at the Sorbonne from 19 to 22 September 1956. He taught at Howard University in Washington from 1932 to 1943. There he met the African American intelligentsia. His entry in Sister Mary Anthony Scally's *Negro Catholic Writers 1900–1943 A Bio-Bibliography* (1945) describes him as a Catholic writer who had primarily written about racial problems and about the fate of French colonial subjects.

Books

In what follows I have cited some annotated passages (mostly in pencil) in Fanon's library. Underlined passages are indicated in italics, except when otherwise noted. The dates given are dates of publication of the volume in the library.

Abd-el-Ghani, *Le Problème algérien de l'émigration en France*, Paris: Cahiers algériens, 1951.

A. M. Paul Abély and Jean Delay, *L'Anxiété. Limites et bases, diagnostic, thérapeutique, considérations endocrinologiques*, Paris: Masson & Cie, 1947.

Albert Adès and Albert Josipovici, *Le Livre de Goha le simple*, Paris: Calmann-Lévy, 1921.

Alfred Adler, *Connaissance de l'homme. Étude de caractérologie individuelle*, Paris: Payot, 1949 (*Understanding Human Nature*, trans. Walter Béran Woolf, London: George Allen & Unwin, 1928).

[The chapter titled 'The feeling of inferiority and the striving for recognition', a theme that he tackled in *Peau noire, masques blancs*, is marked in the margins in several places. In particular, the following sentences: 'It is the feeling of inferiority, inadequacy, insecurity, which determines the goal of an individual's existence.' 'His goal is so constructed that its achievement promises the possibility either of a sentiment of superiority, or an elevation of the personality to such a degree that life seems worth living' (p. 72).]

Julian Ajuriaguerra and Henry Hécaen, *Le Cortex cérébral. Étude neuro-psycho-pathologique*, Paris: Masson, 1949.

Alain, *Système des Beaux-Arts*, Paris: Gallimard, 1926.

Alain, *Préliminaires à la mythologie*, Paris: P. Hartmann, 1951.

Théophile Alajouanine, *Les Grandes activités du lobe temporal*, Paris: Masson & Cie, 1955.

[In this volume, Warren S. McCulloch's article, 'L'organisation fonctionnelle du système nerveux central en vue du contrôle de la position et du mouvement', was carefully read and underlined in several places.]

Théophile Alajouanine, *La Douleur et les douleurs*, Paris: Masson & Cie, 1957.

Théophile Alajouanine, *Bases physiologiques et aspects cliniques de l'épilepsie*, Paris: Masson & Cie, 1958.

Théophile Alajouanine, *Les Grandes activités du lobe occipital*, Paris: Masson & Cie, 1960.

Jacques Stéphen Alexis, *L'Espace d'un cillement*, Paris: Gallimard, 1959.

Nelson Algren, *La Rue chaude*, Paris: Gallimard, 1960.

Georges Allègre and Robert Vigouroux, *Traitement chirurgical des anévrysmes intracrâniens du système carotidien: anévrysmes supraclinoïdiens*, Paris: Masson & Cie, 1957.

Ferdinand Alquié, *La Nostalgie de l'être*, Paris: PUF, 1950.

Alexis Amoussou, *Synergie vasodilatatrice, nicotinate de sodium, électrochoc dans les psychoses*, Paris: Impr. Bouchet et Lakara, 1951.

Charles Andler, *Nietzsche, sa vie et sa pensée. Le pessimisme esthétique de Nietzsche: sa philosophie à l'époque wagnérienne*, vol. 3, Paris: Bossard, 1921.

[Many passages are underlined. For example, the following sentences: 'The major novelty of Nietzschean thought is that it makes philosophy into a theory of civilization, that is to say of the superior life that men can live'; an annotation in the margin indicates: 'The criterion of progress would be that of relations between men' (p. 25). 'A civilization is a world of immaterial norms to which men submit because they find in them, in joy or in suffering, their purest blossoming. So who has the right to create these norms? In ancient intellectualism too, one asked: who, then, has the quality to constrain us to observe the law? And Fichte replied: "He who demonstrates by the fact that he can." In the immaterial order of norms, Nietzsche similarly affirms a de facto mastery' (p. 377).]

Joseph M. Angel, Francis Peillet and Pierre Wertheimer, *La Thérapeutique par le sommeil. Physiopathologie, technique, indications*, Paris: Masson & Cie, 1953.

Jean Anouilh, *La Valse des toréadors*, Paris: La Table ronde, 1952.

Aristophanes, *Comédies. Les Guêpes, La Paix*, vol. 2, Paris: Les Belles Lettres, 1948.

Aristotle, *Éthique de Nicomaque*, Text, translation, preface and notes by Jean Voilquin, Paris: Garnier frères, 1940.

Artemidore d'Ephèse, *La Clef des songes ou les cinq livres de l'interprétation des songes, rêves et visions*, Paris: Arcanes, 1953.

Miguel Angel Asturias, *Hommes de maïs*, Givors: Imprimerie A. Martel, 1953.

Maurice Aubert, *Vertiges et surdités d'origine vasculaire*, Paris: Masson & Cie, 1958.

André Aubin, *L'Appareil vestibulaire. Anatomie, physiologie, pathologie. Conférences et travaux pratiques publiés*, Paris: PUF, 1957.

Gaston Bachelard, *L'Intuition de l'instant. Étude sur le* Siloë *de Gaston Roupnel*, Paris: Stock/Delamain et Boutelleau, 1932. (*The Intuition of the Instant*, trans. Eileen Rizo-Patron, Evanston, IL: Northwestern University Press, 2013.)

Gaston Bachelard, *La Psychanalyse du feu*, Paris: Gallimard, 1938. (*The Psychoanalysis of Fire*, transl. Alan C.M. Ross, with an introduction by Northrop Frye, London : Routledge & Kegan Paul, 1964)

Gaston Bachelard, *L'Air et les Songes. Essai sur l'imagination du mouvement*, Paris: José Corti, 1943. (*Air and Dreams: An essay on the imagination of movement*, trans. Edith and Frederick Farell, Dallas, TX: Dallas Institute Publications, 2011).

[The following chapters contain numerous markings in the margins; here are some significant passages. The italics are Bachelard's:

'The Wind', p. 227: 'Through *anger*, the world is created as a provocation. *Anger* founds dynamic being. Anger is the commencing act. As prudent as an action may be, as insidious as it promises to be, it must first cross a small threshold of anger. Anger is that acid without which no impression is stamped on our being; it determines the active impression' (translation modified – SC).

'The Silent declamation', p. 245: 'Emerging in the silence and the solitude of being, untied from hearing or vision, so poetry appears to us as the primary phenomenon of the human aesthetic will. ... Before all action, the human being needs to say to himself, in the silence of his being, what he *wants* to become; he needs to *prove* and *to sing to himself* his own becoming. That is the voluntary function of poetry. The poetry of *will* must therefore be placed in relation with the tenacity and the courage of silent being.'

'Cinematic philosophy and dynamic philosophy', p. 295: 'We first need to give a value to our own being in order to gauge the value of other beings. And that is why the image of the weigher is so important in Nietzsche's philosophy. *Je pense* (I think) therefore *je pèse* (I weigh) are not for no reason linked by a profound etymology. The ponderal *cogito* is the first dynamic *cogito*. It is to this ponderal *cogito* that all our dynamic values must be referred' (translation modified – SC).

In an unfinished note written on a sheet of paper inserted into the end of this volume, which joins up with Fanon's reflections and readings on existence and time (Jaspers, Lachièze-Rey, Blondel perhaps, Wahl probably, and of course Kierkegaard and Sartre), we see the outline of a fundamental immanentism and skepticism in relation to both religious and dialectical thinking. It has echoes in what is said about

Hegel in *Peau noire, masques blancs* and even of Sartre as regards 'Orphée noir': 'Do not seek the Absolute through a relative. Totally illogical. A conversion must be undertaken and the Absolute must not be considered as a sort of End, [which] could not be conceived given the relativity of the means. I am thinking essentially of knowledge. The conversion therefore consists in transposing the absolute and in considering it a quality of things and in particular of acts (that would eliminate the pseudo-problem of failure, and even that of the *objective* failure). This is tantamount to return to Existence its character of unicity, metaphysical par excellence. Whence follows the notion of the absolute Other. But it would seem that thereby we rejoin the aesthetic level of Kierk[egaard]. But everything stems from a difference of interpretation of the *instant*, whether in considering the instant as something no longer lived on the aesthetic level but on the religious one, the conversion is made without [giving] primacy to that unique instant in which the disciple receives the condition and which in fact appears as an essentialist infiltration that most heavily strains the metaphysical future of man. Every instant [must] as much as possible ...'.]

Gaston Bachelard, *Le Nouvel esprit scientifique*, Paris: PUF, 1949. (*The New Scientific Spirit*, trans. Arthur Goldhammer, Boston, MA: Beacon Press, 1984.)

[Here there are a few marks in the margins, for example at this sentence in the introduction, p. 7: 'As Nietzsche says: everything decisive comes into being *in spite of*. This is as true of the sphere of thought as of the sphere of action. Every new truth comes into being in spite of the evidence; every new experience is acquired in spite of immediate experience.' Bachelard's italics; translation modified – SC.]

Georges Balandier, *Sociologie actuelle de l'Afrique noire*, Paris: PUF, 1955.
Gustave Bardy, *Saint Augustin. L'homme et l'œuvre*, Paris: Desclée de Brouwer, 1940.
Maurice Bariéty and George Brouet, *Phtisiologie du médecin praticien*, Paris: Masson & Cie, 1953.
Philippe Barrès, *Charles de Gaulle*, New York, NY: Brentano's, 1941.
Georges Bataille, *La Haine de la poésie*, Paris: Minuit, 1947.
Georges Bataille, *L'Érotisme*, Paris: Minuit, 1957.
Pierre Bayle, *Pensées diverses sur la comète*, Paris: Librairie E. Droz, 1939.
Simone de Beauvoir, *Le Deuxième sexe*. vol. 1, *Les Faits et les Mythes*, Paris: Gallimard, 1949.

Simone de Beauvoir, *Les Mandarins*, Paris: Gallimard, 1954.

Nicolas Berdiaeff, *L'Esprit de Dostoïevski*, Paris: Stock, 1946.

André Berge, *Le Facteur psychique dans l'énurésie*, Paris: Seuil, 1946.

François Berge et al., *Le Destin de l'individu dans le monde actuel. Enquête internationale auprès des étudiants*, Paris: Éditions de Clermont, 1947.

Henri Bergson, *Essai sur les données immédiates de la conscience*, Paris: Félix Alcan, 1929.

Henri Bergson, *L'Évolution créatrice*, Paris: PUF, 1948.

Paul Bernard, *Psychiatrie pratique. Formation, spécialisation et selection des auxiliaires médico-sociaux du psychiatre. Formation psychiatrique générale*, vol. 1, Paris: Desclée de Brouwer, 1947.

[Some sentences are marked in this volume, for instance: 'Behavioural disorders, which are the object of psychiatry, in general have more complex causes than the organic disorders that are studied in the other branches of medicine. Indeed we know that *behaviour is the reaction of the organism as a whole engaged in its effort to adapt to its milieu*, with incessant exchanges occurring between the milieu and the organism' (p. 60).]

Jacques Berque, *Les Arabes d'hier à demain*, Paris: Seuil, 1960.

Auguste Blanqui, *Textes choisis*, Paris: Éditions sociales, 1955.

Jean Bobon, *Introduction historique à l'étude des néologismes et des glossolalies en psychopathologie*, Paris: Masson & Cie, 1952.

Gerhardt V. Bonin, *Essai sur le cortex cérébral*, Paris: Masson & Cie, 1955.

[This volume bears the stamp of Blida-Joinville Psychiatric Hospital (arrival date 24 February 1955).]

Joël Bonnal et al., *Les Abcès encéphaliques à l'ère des antibiotiques. Étude statistique de 547 observations*, Paris: Masson & Cie, 1960.

Jacques Borel, *Le Déséquilibre psychique. Ses psychoses, sa morale*, Paris: PUF, 1947.

Jorge Luis Borges, *Fictions*, Paris: Gallimard, 1956.

Georges Boudin and Bernard Pépin, *Dégénérescence hépato-lenticulaire*, Paris: Masson & Cie, 1959.

L. Bourrat et al., *L'Enfance irrégulière. Psychologie clinique*, Paris: PUF, 1946.

Olivier Brachfeld, *Les Sentiments d'infériorité*, Genève and Annemasse: Éditions du Mont Blanc, 1945.

Bertolt Brecht, *Théâtre complet. Le Cercle de craie caucasien. Homme pour homme. L'Exception et la Règle*, vol. 1, Paris: L'Arche, 1956.

Albert Burloud, *Le Caractère*, Paris: PUF, 1948.

J.J. Frederik Buytendijk, *Attitudes et mouvements. Étude fonctionnelle du mouvement humain*, Paris: Desclée de Brouwer, 1957.

Roland Caillois et al., *L'Homme. Le monde. L'histoire*, Grenoble: Arthaud, 1948.

[The margins of several pages in this small volume are marked. The following passages, for instance, some of whose phrases are underlined with pencil: 'I have chosen this topic "The lived world and history," because it seemed to me that, in the times in which we live, we have an increasingly acute awareness of the historical depth of the world such as it is lived, and also, correlatively, an awareness of participating in history, of making history. … As a result, while being one philosophy among others, a disinterested philosophy in search of the true, *it has, as it were, a revolutionary pretention, since becoming aware of the situation must at the same time be an act*' (pp. 8–9). 'Marx said: "Reason is not lived as reason," reason has its foundations in a lived historical reality' (p. 12). '[P]henomenological also means historical since the history of consciousness contains in its depth the history of the entire world. If Hegel can rediscover in man, such as he describes him, the stages of the world, it is because man really does contain them, because he lives them in some manner. If there was no lived history – and this history extends endlessly into the past – there would be no reflected history' (p. 47).]

Nicolas Calas, *Foyers d'incendie*, Paris: Denoël, 1938.

[Several passages are marked here, in particular in a section on the inferiority complex, but also on evolution and culture. Thus: 'Henceforth, man's adaptation to his milieu is performed in two times, the first proceeds as with all living beings, by a movement of organic adaptation, and the second produces a transformation of the elements of matter into objects of value, which becomes a form of specifically human assimilation and which is, as we have seen, the fundamental principle of civilization' (p. 241).]

Albert Camus, *Les Justes. Pièce en cinq actes*, Paris: Gallimard, 1950.

Mayotte Capécia, *Je suis martiniquaise*, Paris: Corrêa, 1948.

Mayotte Capécia, *La Négresse blanche*, Paris: Corrêa, 1950.

[Two passages are marked in the margin: 'No drop of white blood. With her slave mentality, she [Lucia, who "was the purest type of African"] was devoted heart and soul to Isaure' (p. 36). 'But you are not black, Isaure, you are scarcely mixed blood [*métisse*]; your skin is nearly white. In a few years, when you've earned millions with your bar, you will have a house built on the Didier plateau and pose as creole' (p. 44).]

Fernand Caridroit, *Psychophysiologie des glandes endocrines et du système neuro-végétatif*, Paris: PUF, 1946.

John C. Carothers, *Psychologie normale et pathologique de l'Africain. Étude ethnopsychiatrique* (English title: *The African Mind in Health and Disease: A Study in Ethnopsychiatry*) Geneva: World Health Organization, 1954.

Pierre Carpentier-Fialip and René Lamar, *Les États-Unis. Civilisation*, Paris: Hachette, 1948.

Michel Carrouges, *La Mystique du surhomme*, Paris: Gallimard, 1948.

[Numerous markings and 'yes's' of approval from Fanon's hand in the section on 'The Overman and the Death of God'.]

John Cassels et al., *The Sterling Area. An American Analysis*, London: Economic Cooperation Administration, Special Mission to the United Kingdom, 1951.

Jean Cathala and Pierre Mollaret, *Manuel de pathologie médicale. Physiopathologie et clinique*, Paris: Masson & Cie, 1947.

Aimé Césaire, *Les Armes miraculeuses*, Paris: Gallimard, 1946.

Paul Césari, *Les Déterminismes et la contingence*, Paris: PUF, 1950.

René Char, *Poèmes et prose choisis*, Paris: Gallimard, 1957.

Paul Chauchard, *Mécanismes cérébraux de la prise de conscience. Neurophysiologie, psychanalyse et psychologie animale*, Paris: Masson & Cie, 1956.

Jean Chesneaux, *Contribution à l'histoire de la nation vietnamienne*, Paris: Éditions sociales, 1955.

Maryse Choisy, *L'Anneau de Polycrate. Essai sur la culpabilité collective et recherche d'une éthique psychanalytique*, Paris: Éditions Psyché, 1948.

[This book on the feeling of guilt, to which Fanon refers in *Peau noire, masques blancs* (p. 134, *Black Skin, White Masks*, p. 70), is marked in several places. The flyleaf bears a note: 'To be consulted: Weulersse, *Noirs et Blancs*, Armand Colin.' Jacques Weulersse's book, *Noirs et Blancs: À travers l'Afrique nouvelle de Dakar au Cap*, Paris: Armand Colin, 1931, is not referenced in Fanon's published works, however. This sentence, notably, is annotated in the margins: 'It is no doubt also possible to conceive at a pinch an ideal, evolved *overman* – perfect, "like a God" – with whom the unconscious has gradually become conscious' (p. 68); an annotation, most likely Fanon's, reads: 'No! That would amount to returning to Valéry: awareness of nothingness on the shores of the "nothing", "power which consumes itself in getting to know itself"' [a recollection of Valéry's 'Cimetière marin']. The following passage is also annotated: 'In his games, the man cub recommences an event, even a disagreeable one, perhaps "so as to be able, through his activity, to master the strong impression he has received of it, instead of confining himself to enduring it by keeping a purely passive attitude" [note: Freud, *Essais de psychanalyse*, p. 47]. This repetition is sometimes a pleasure. In any case, it is a way of making oneself a master of reality. Why will we not have two lives, one of which would serve as a sketch for the other?' (p. 89); annotation: '*Cf.* Lacan (imago)'.]

Édouard Claparède, *L'Éducation fonctionnelle*, Neuchâtel and Paris: Delachaux et Niestlé, 1931.

Henri Claude and Stéphen Chauvet, *Sémiologie réelle des sections totales des nerfs mixtes périphériques. Considérations sur la technique concernant l'étude des troubles des sensibilités, les modifications des réactions vasomotrices et sudorales, les altérations trophiques ostéo-articulaires et cutanées*, Paris: Maloine, 1911.

Paul Claudel, *La Sagesse ou la parabole du festin*, Paris: Gallimard, 1939.

Paul Claudel, *Théâtre (première série). Tête d'or (première et seconde versions)*, Paris: Mercure de France, 1946.

Paul Claudel, *Théâtre*, Paris: Gallimard, ('Bibliothèque de la Pléiade'), 1947.

Raymond Coirault, *Le Syndrome de Guillain-Barré*, Paris: Masson & Cie, Paris, 1958.

Auguste Comte, *Cours de philosophie positive: Discours sur l'esprit positif*, Paris: Garnier frères, 1949.

Constitution de la République Française, 'Statut organique de l'Algérie. Loi portant fixation des circonscriptions électorales pour la désignation des membres de l'Assemblée algérienne, décrets portant règlements d'administration publique pour l'application du statut de l'Algérie', *Journal officiel de la République française et Journal officiel de l'Algérie*, Algiers, November 1950.

Pierre Corneille, *Rodogune*, Paris: Larousse, n.d.

Pierre Corneille, *Cinna. Tragédie*, Paris: Hachette, 1935.

Pierre Corneille, *Le Cid*, Paris: Arthème Fayard, 1946.

Auguste Cornu, *Karl Marx et la révolution de 1848*, Paris: PUF, 1948.

Michel Cournot, *Martinique*, Paris: Gallimard, 1949.

André Cresson, *Les Courants de la pensée philosophique française*, Paris:

Armand Colin, 1946.

[Some annotations in this volume. The first sentence of the introduction ('Human reflection has always oscillated between two poles: the intellectual pole and the moral pole') is notably annotated as follows: 'No, knowledge is not opposed to action. The best knowledge is achieved *through* action.']

André Cresson, *Les Courants de la pensée philosophique française*, vol. 1, Paris: Armand Colin, 1947.

André Cresson, *Les Systèmes philosophiques*, Paris: Armand Colin, 1947.

André Cresson, *Saint Thomas d'Aquin: Sa vie, son œuvre, avec un exposé de sa philosophie*, Paris: PUF, 1947.

Benedetto Croce, *La Poésie: Introduction à la critique et à l'histoire de la poésie et de la littérature*, Paris: PUF, 1951.

Bertrand d'Astorg, *Aspects de la littérature européenne depuis 1945*, Paris: Seuil, 1952.

Henri Damaye, *Psychiatrie et civilisation*, Paris: Félix Alcan, 1934.

Albert Dauzat, *La Philosophie du langage*, Paris: Flammarion, 1912.

Albert Dauzat, *Le Génie de la langue française*, Paris: Payot, 1954.

Jean-Pierre Dehaye, *Contribution à l'étude des états pseudo-démentiels après traumatisme crânien*, Paris, 1955.

Jean Delay, *Colloque international sur la chlorpromazine et les médicaments neuroleptiques en thérapeutique psychiatrique. Paris 20, 21, 22 October 1955, clinique des maladies mentales et de l'encéphale de la Faculté de médecine*, Paris: G. Doin, 1956.

Robert Delavignette, *Les Paysans noirs*, Paris: Stock, 1947.

Victor Delbos, *De Kant aux postkantiens*, Paris: Aubier, 1940.

Jean Delmas and Georges Laux, *Système nerveux sympathique: Étude systématique et macroscopique*, Paris: Masson & Cie, 1952.

Paul Delost and Marthe Bonvallet, *Récents progrès en physiologie*, Paris: PUF, 1956.

Georges Del Vecchio, *La Justice, la vérité: Essais de philosophie juridique et morale*, Paris: Dalloz, 1955.

[In this volume we find a chapter on 'L'obligation juridique de la véracité: Spécialement dans le procès civil'.]

Émile Dermenghem, *Le Culte des saints dans l'islam maghrébin*, Paris: Gallimard, 1954.

[One paragraph is marked with a red cross in the margin; it bears on the Saint of Birmandreis, whose speciality is the 'curing of the mad, neurotics and paralytics' (p. 104).]

René Descartes, *Discours de la méthode pour bien conduire sa raison et chercher la vérité dans les sciences, suivi des Méditations en latin et en français*, Paris: Librairie Delagrave, 1918.

Maurice Despinoy, *Circonstances et signes du début de la schizophrénie*, Lyon: Bosc frères, 1948.

[A dedication from Maurice Despinoy: 'To Doctor Frantz Fanon I offer this dissertation even though it appears to disdain psychology. With best wishes and the hope of soon having the pleasure of being able to work with him again.']

Jean Despois, *L'Afrique blanche française: L'Afrique du Nord*, vol. 1, Paris: PUF, 1949.

Isaac Deutscher, *Staline*, Paris: Gallimard, 1953 (*Stalin: A Political Biography*, Oxford: Oxford University Press, 1949).

Mohammed Dib, *L'Incendie*, Paris: Seuil, 1954.

Denis Diderot, *Textes choisis: Pensées philosophiques, Lettre sur les aveugles, Suite de l'apologie de l'abbé de Prades*, vol. 1, Paris: Éditions sociales, 1952.

Denis Diderot, *Encyclopédie ou dictionnaire raisonné des sciences, des arts et des métiers. Textes choisis, préface et commentaires par Albert Soboul*, vol. 1, Paris: Éditions sociales, 1952.

Denis Diderot, *Textes choisis. De l'interprétation de la nature (Pensées sur l'interprétation de la nature). Articles de l'Encyclopédie (sept premiers tomes)*, vol. 2, Paris: Éditions sociales, 1953.

Denis Diderot, *Les Salons. 1759–1781*, Paris: Éditions sociales, 1955.

Denis Diderot, *Essais sur la peinture. De la manière. Pensées détachées sur la peinture, la sculpture, l'architecture et la poésie. Tableaux de nuit de Skalken*, vol. 5, Paris: Éditions sociales, 1955.

Paul Diel, *Psychologie de la motivation: Théorie et application thérapeutique*, Paris: PUF, 1948.

[Several passages in the introduction to this book are marked, in particular: 'The external world and the internal world are inseparable, they penetrate one another and this interpenetration is called life' (p. 13); 'But psychotherapy perforce exceeds the medical domain. It seeks a meaningful direction of life, a direction toward the meaning of life. A therapy that does not seek to envisage the meaning of life, that seeks to counter the meaning of life, is necessarily meaningless [*insensée*], false. Added to the fundamental difficulty of defining the metaphysical basis is the no less redoubtable difficulty of defining the moral goal' (p. 15); 'With the individual who is unable to valorize his desires in relation to a meaning of life and is only able to satisfy them through the imagination, the separation between the external world and the internal world, the cause of all insufficiency, will become an uncrossable abyss: the suffering will become intolerable' (p. 19).]

John Dos Passos, *Sur toute la terre*, Paris: Gallimard, 1936.
John Dos Passos, *42ᵉ Parallèle*, Paris: Gallimard, 1951.
Fyodor Dostoyevsky, *Mémoires écrits dans un souterrain*, Paris: Gallimard, 1949.
Auguste Dufour, *Paralysies nucléaires des muscles des yeux*, Gand: Impr. Victor van Doosselaere, 1890.
Marc Dufour, *Traité des maladies du nerf optique*, Paris: Doin, 1908.
Mikel Dufrenne and Paul Ricoeur, *Karl Jaspers et la philosophie de l'existence*, Paris: Seuil, 1947.

[Some of the passages in this work are marked. Thus: 'Kierkegaard and Nietzsche knew that the last word of the meditation on existence is neither in the relation of the awareness of being free with objective knowledge, nor even in the relation of existence with itself; the heart of the drama lies in the relation of existence *with some transcendence that it is not but that is nonetheless its reason and its ultimate peace*' (p. 23); 'Well, there is a scandal that can no longer be silenced, in posing the question on being, that is to say the question of the beginning and the end, when the one who questions is neither at the beginning nor at the end, but finds himself caught in a situation between beginning and end, charged with the past, itself mobile, limited by a character, by passions, a birth, a short life, *blinkered information*. The philosopher has to have an awareness of the immensity of his horizon and the precariousness of his perspective: being is only given in profiles, in sketches, which must themselves fail in order to deliver their message' (p. 28).
The whole first page of the chapter on 'La liberté existentielle' (p. 144) is marked in the margin. ('We must therefore see now how it is that freedom is the act of existence, or better how freedom and existence are identified. ... I am the one who choses, and who by his choice decides his own being.')

In this volume, there is a handwritten letter from Pierre Lachièze-Rey (1885–1957), a Kantian philosopher, who had been close to Le Sillon, a left-wing Christian movement, and held now a chair in Lyon. The letter is dated 17 June 1949: 'Dear Monsieur, I regret that circumstances did not allow me yesterday to go further into your

concerns and to reply at greater length to your questions. I repeat that
I remain at your disposal to the extent that you deem I can be of help
to you in your research. I hope that M. Lacroix will equally be able
to be of use to you. I am sending you, as I have promised, an article
that I have written on the method of Maurice Blondel. I recommend
again that you read the first version of this author's *Action*, if you are
able to find it. In this work, you will see what a true transcendence
is. Concerning the problem of values and of destiny, I refer you to an
article that I have published in *Revue de métaphysique et de morale*
in July–October 1947. I implore you to accept my faithful wishes.'
Lachièze-Rey's article (*Revue de métaphysique et de morale*, 52nd
year, nos. 3–4, July–October 1947, pp. 244–58) is titled 'Esquisse
d'une métaphysique de la destinée' ('Sketch of a metaphysics of
destiny'). The book by Maurice Blondel that is recommended
is *L'Action: Essai d'une critique de la vie et d'une science de la
pratique*, Paris: PUF, 1893. Jean Lacroix (1900–1986), a philosopher
from Lyon, himself also on the Christian Left, was close to Emmanuel
Mounier and his journal *Esprit*, which was to publish Fanon's first
texts. André Mandouze (who later became the founder of *Consciences
maghribines* in Algiers, a journal to which Fanon contributed)
attended his clandestine seminars at the end of the war. The question
of the relations between values, action and transcendence obviously
goes to the heart of Fanon's own concerns at the time.]

Georges Dumas, *Le Surnaturel et les dieux d'après les maladies mentales*,
Paris: PUF, 1946.

[There are several markings in the chapters on 'Les psychoses et le
réel' and on 'L'automatisme, les hallucinations'.]

René Dumont, *Terres vivantes*, Paris: Plon, 1961.
Charles Durand, *L'Écho de la pensée*, Paris: G. Doin & Cie, 1941.
Pierre Duranton, *La Schizophrénie infantile*, Paris: Librairie Arnette, 1956.
M.J. Saintes, Léon Ectors and Jacques Achslogh, *Les Compressions de la
    moelle cervicale. Lésions intrinsèques et traumatiques exclues*, Paris:
    1960.
Erasmus, *Éloge de la folie*, Paris: Éditions de Cluny, 1941.
Aeschylus, *Les Perses*, Paris: Hatier, 1933.
Aeschylus, *Tragédies*, trans. Paul Mazon, Paris: Club français du livre, 1955.
Auguste Etcheverry, *Le Conflit actuel des humanismes*, Paris: PUF, 1955.
Étiemble, *Le Mythe de Rimbaud: Structure du mythe*, Paris: Gallimard, 1952.

Henri Ey, *La Psychiatrie devant le surréalisme*, Paris: Centre d'éditions psychiatriques, 1948.

[Most of the pages of this text, a long talk by Henri Ey, are abundantly marked. On Fanon's interest in surrealism, see David Macey, *Frantz Fanon: A Life*, p. 130).]

Henri Ey, *Études psychiatriques: Aspects séméiologiques*, Paris: 1950.
Henri Ey, *Études psychiatriques. Historique, méthodologie, psychopathologie générale*, Paris: Desclée de Brouwer, 1952.
Henri Ey and Julien Rouart, *Essai d'application des principes de Jackson à une conception dynamique de la neuropsychiatrie*, Paris: Doin, 1938.

[The section dealing with 'The third factor of madness. The speed at which dissolution is carried out (speed of the disappearance of control upon persisting evolutionary levels)' is marked with an asterix. In a note to Jackson's text, Ey points out: 'What Jackson says about the importance of the speed of dissolution is of extreme interest and we have never seen it emphasized.' An inscription in the margin of p. 37 indicates: 'On this matter, see Jaspers (Introduction).' On p. 69 of this chapter on 'Les dissolutions de l'activité psychique' ('The dissolutions of psychic activity'), several passages are marked: 'Hallucinatory activity is contingent with respect to the essential structure of such delusions [delusions of paranoid structure]. As a rule, the hallucinatory form expresses the most unconscious affects: hallucinations, when they exist, are manifestly the expression of the paranoid personality.' This passage is marked with two 'yes's' in the margin. 'We were struck, with Lacan, by the extreme importance of the fertile moments in the evolution of such delusions. Everything happens as if the delusional arrangement came together and fed on *states of delusional experience* with an intuitive or *illusional* form.' Only '*illusional*' is underlined by Fanon. This passage is annotated: 'See Lacan dissertation. Case of Aimée.']

Guy Fageot, *Troubles de l'intelligence et du caractère à la suite de brûlures chez l'enfant*, Lyon: Bosc frères, 1953.
Howard Fast, *La Route de la liberté*, Paris: Gallimard, 1948. (*Freedom Road*, New York : Duell, Sloan and Pearce, 1944)
William Faulkner, *Absalon! Absalon!*, Paris: Gallimard, 1953 (*Absalom! Absalom!*, New York, NY: Random House, 1936).
Philippe Fauré-Frémiet, *La Recréation du réel et l'équivoque*, Paris: Alcan/ Presses universitaires de France, 1940.
Jean-Claude Filloux, *Psychologie des animaux*, Paris: PUF, 1950.

Abou'Lkasim Firdousi, *Le Livre de Feridoun et de Minoutchehr, rois de Perse*, Paris: H. Piazza, 1924.

Victor Fleury and Mohammed Soualah, *L'Arabe pratique et commercial. À l'usage des établissements d'instruction et des hommes d'affaires. Lecture, écriture, grammaire, syntaxe, exercices d'application, textes suivis, conversation, lexiques, dictionnaire commercial*, Algiers: La Typo-litho Jules Carbonel, 1950.

Benjamin Fondane, *Baudelaire et l'expérience du gouffre*, Paris: P. Seghers, 1947.

Louis-René des Forêts, *La Chambre des enfants*, Paris: Gallimard, 1960.

Émile Forgue, *Précis de pathologie externe*, Paris: G. Doin & Cie, 1948.

[A note on the inside of the cover indicates: 'Alan Paton, *Pleure ô pays bien aimé*', the French title of Paton's *Cry, the Beloved Country*.]

Michel Foucault, *Histoire de la folie à l'âge classique*, Paris: Plon, 1961.

H. Fraisse and Abdul-Kader Husseini, 'Dégénérescence cancéreuse de la vésicule lithiasique. À propos d'une statistique médico-chirurgicale de 197 cas recueillis dans les services du docteur M. Girard et du professeur Bertrand', *Journal de médecine de Lyon*, vol. 35, 5 February 1954, pp. 121–9.

Simon Frank, *La Connaissance et l'être*, Paris: Fernand Aubier, 1937.

[There are some marks in the translator's introduction. In particular, p. VI: 'In opposition with all the subjectivist doctrines that think they can deify man by turning him, through his knowledge, into the origin of the world in which he lives, but only end up rendering him a stranger to reality by enclosing him in a superficial and fictive representation, [Simon Frank] expresses and defends his unshakeable conviction that we belong intimately to the real.']

Sigmund Freud, *Trois Essais sur la théorie de la sexualité*, Paris: Gallimard, 1923.

[Many marks are contained in the chapters on 'Sexual aberrations' and 'Infantile sexuality'.]

Sigmund Freud, *L'Avenir d'une illusion*, Paris: Denoël et Steele, 1932.

Sigmund Freud, *Introduction à la psychanalyse*, Paris: Payot, 1947. (*General Introduction to Psychoanalysis*, trans. and prefaced by G. Stanley Hall, New York, NY: Boni and Liveright, 1920).

[The chapters on dream are marked in several places. Some of the annotations seem to be by Fanon, in particular those expressing doubts about the symbolism of the sexual organs and the idea of an unconscious knowledge of symbolism. Thus, on p. 137: 'We can only say that the dreamer's knowledge of *symbolism is unconscious, that it is part of his unconscious psychic life* [expression in italics in the original and underlined].' This sentence is accompanied in the margin with 'Stop talking nonsense'. The following sentence, p. 138, is marked with 'Bastard': 'the primitive man made work acceptable at the same time as he used it as an equivalent and substitute for sex-activity'.]

Sigmund Freud, *Essais de psychanalyse. I. Au-delà du principe du plaisir. II. Psychologie collective et analyse du moi. III. Le Moi et le Soi. IV. Considérations actuelles sur la guerre et sur la mort*, Paris: Payot, 1948.

Sigmund Freud, *Psychopathologie de la vie quotidienne*, Paris: Payot, 1948.

Sigmund Freud, *Abrégé de psychanalyse*, Paris: PUF, 1955.

Georges Friedmann, *Problèmes humains du machinisme industriel*, Paris: Gallimard, 1946.

Claude Frioux, *Maïakovski par lui-même*, Paris: Seuil, 1961.

Eugène Fromentin, *Dominique*, Paris: Éditions de Cluny, 1938.

[This book bears the stamp of the Blida-Joinville Psychiatric Hospital.]

Peter Fryer and Patricia McGowan Pinheiro, *Oldest Ally: A Portrait of Salazar's Portugal*, Paris: D. Dolson, 1961.

André Galli and Robert Leluc, *L'Analyse biochimique médicale*, Paris: PUF, 1957.

Jean Garamond, *Images de l'homme immobile*, Paris: Éditions de La Baconnière, 1943.

Alexandre Garde, *Les Complications neurologiques des néoplasmes viscéraux. Rapport de neurologie. Congrès de psychiatrie et de neurologie de langue française*, Paris: Masson & Cie, 1958.

Arthur van Gehuchten, *Les Maladies nerveuses*, Louvain: Librairie universitaire, 1945.

Jean Giraudoux, *Simon le pathétique*, Paris: Grasset, 1926.

Édouard Glissant, *Les Indes. Poème de l'une et l'autre terre*, Paris: Falaize, 1956.

[Copy of one of the deluxe editions, perhaps given to Josie Fanon after Fanon's death. It bears the following dedication: 'This epic of the New World – its sufferings, its humanity – for you, dear Houria, on this first day of the grand Algerian state. Hope! Hope! Éd.']

Kurt Goldstein, *La Structure de l'organisme. Introduction à la biologie à partir de la pathologie humaine* (*Der Aufbau des Organismus*), Paris: Gallimard, 1951.

[Volume marked in several places, without annotation.]

André Gorz, *Le Traître*, Paris: Seuil, 1958.

Marcel Granet, *La Civilisation chinoise*, Paris: Albin Michel, 1929.

Antoine Grégoire, *Le Bégaiement. Conseils indispensables à sa guérison*, Paris: Éditions Lumières, 1948.

Bernard Groethuysen, *Introduction à la pensée philosophique allemande depuis Nietzsche*, Paris: Stock, 1926.

Romano Guardini, *De la mélancolie*, Paris: Seuil, 1952.

Daniel Guérin, *Où va le peuple américain?*, Paris: Julliard, 1951.

Miller Guerra, *Le Syndrome cérébelleux et le syndrome vestibulaire*, Paris: Masson & Cie, 1954.

Georges Gullain and Ivan Bertrand, *Anatomie topographique du système nerveux central*, Paris: Masson & Cie, 1926.

Jean Guillaume, *Les Accidents circulatoires du cerveau*, Paris: PUF, 1957.

Jean Guillaume, *Les Méningiomes: Étude clinique et chirurgicale*, Paris: PUF, 1957.

Jean Guillaume and Jean Sigwald, *Diagnostic neurochirurgical*, Paris: PUF, 1947.

Jean Guillaume, Gabriel Mazars and Stanislas de Sèze, *Chirurgie cérébro-spinale de la douleur*, Paris: PUF, 1949.

Paul Guillaume, *La Psychologie de la forme*, Paris: Flammarion, 1937.

[Volume carrying the stamp of the medical library of the Psychiatric Hospital of Saint-Alban.]

Paul Guillaume, *La Psychologie animale*, Paris: Armand Colin, 1947.

[The section 'L'emploi des symboles' in the chapter on 'Le problème de l'intelligence' is marked in the margin in several places, in particular the passages on the failure of attempts to teach symbolism to monkeys, or its transmission, in contrast to the human child.]

Gérard Guiot, *Adénomes hypophysaires*, Paris: Masson & Cie, 1958.

Georges Gurvitch, *La Sociologie au XXᵉ siècle. Les études sociologiques dans les différents pays*, vol. 2, Paris: PUF, 1947.

[Contains a number of marks.]

Georges Gurvitch, *La Vocation actuelle de la sociologie. Sociologie différentielle*, vol. 1, Paris: PUF, 1957.

[There are some marginal marks in the section bearing on anthropology and cultural ethnology. In particular: 'However, the idea can be seen to establish itself more and more that the social penetrates as far as the psycho-pathological. So, in Muslim societies, sociologists have observed that the insane do not commit suicide so long as they are under the sway of religious prohibitions against suicide, which remain profoundly implanted in the mentality of the patients' (p. 34). Similarly, concerning the symbol in the living collective consciousness, a theme that Fanon often broached: 'Each time that, in a global type of society (in the state of revolution, of war or of transition), or in a particular grouping (group of economic activity, a brotherhood, a mystico-ecstatic grouping, a social class, etc.), what we see predominate are effervescent, innovative, creative collective behaviours, what we can observe is that, on the one hand, activist and volitional communions are at work and that, on the other, the symbols and models that were valid up to then lose their efficacy and their prestige' (p. 84).]

Georges Gurvitch (ed.), *Traité de sociologie*, vol. 1, Paris: PUF, 1958.

[In this collective volume, the pages of section III of the first chapter are cut. This is the article by Roger Bastide, 'Sociologie et psychologie'.]

Georges Gurvitch (ed.), *Traité de sociologie*, vol. 2, Paris: PUF, 1960.

Aron Gurwitsch, *Théorie du champ de la conscience*, Paris: Desclée de Brouwer, 1957.

Georges Gusdorf, *Traité de l'existence morale*, Paris: Armand Colin, 1946.

Georges Gusdorf, *Mémoire et personne. La Mémoire concrète*, vol. 1, Paris: PUF, 1951.

Georges Gusdorf, *Mémoire et personne. Dialectique de la mémoire*, vol. 2, Paris: PUF, 1951.

Georges Gusdorf, *La Parole*, Paris: PUF, 1953.

Daniel Halévy, *La Vie de Proudhon*, Paris: Stock, 1948.

Hervé Harant and Nguyên Duc, *Pathologie exotique*, Paris: Maloine, 1948.

Georges Hardy, *Portrait de Lyautey*, Paris: Existence du monde, 1949.

Georg W. F. Hegel, *Principes de la philosophie du droit*, Paris: Gallimard, 1940.

Georg W. F. Hegel, *Esthétique*, Paris: Aubier, 1944.

Georg W. F. Hegel, *La Phénoménologie de l'esprit*, vols. 1 and 2, Paris: Aubier-Montaigne, 1947. (French translation by Jean Hyppolite of Hegel's *Phänomenologie des Geistes*.)

[Some of the passages of this work are marked in the margins, in particular in the chapter on 'The truth of self-certainty', the section on 'Mastery and Servitude'. For example: '*And it is solely by staking one's life that freedom is preserved* [passage underlined by Fanon. Susbsequent italics are in the original], that the essence of self-consciousness is proven not to be *being*, not the immediate way self-consciousness first emerges, nor its being absorbed within the expanse of life – but rather, through this risk, it is proven that there is nothing present which, in itself, could not be a vanishing moment for it, that is, that self-consciousness is merely pure *being-for-itself*. The individual who has not put his life at stake may admittedly be recognized as a *person*, but he has not achieved the truth of being recognized as an independant self-consciousness (pp. 168–9).
The unessential consciousness is therein for the master the object which constitutes the *truth* of his certainty of himself. However, it is clear that this object does not correspond to its concept. Rather, in the object in which the master has achieved his mastery he finds something entirely different from an independent consciousness [in the margin: "mirror"]. It is not an independent consciousness which exists for him but rather a dependent consciousness' (p. 173).
In the volume edited by André Leroi-Gourhan, *L'Homme, races et mœurs*, the following handwritten note was inserted, perhaps one from a course or lecture on Hegel: 'On Hegel's logic. According to Hegel, only language is sense and sense of sense. There is no effective sense unless through the unity of the in-itself and the for-itself. Via language, there is a passage from the realm of sensation to sense and an inverse passage from thought to its own alienation. How can we go from phenomenology to absolute knowledge? Hegel defines true thought, the concept, as a thinking that gives the Ego [*au Moi*] the consistency of being in-itself, objective value, and to the thing thought the subjective value of the for-itself of consciousness. Kant, in order to go from the realm of sensation to the understanding, spoke of the imagination as a common source. Absolute knowledge with Hegel presumes an active man, since there is no given signification, necessity, but an engendered signification, signification of self: the absolute is subject. With Hegel, speculative logic replaces dogmatic metaphysics. The *logos* as speculative life is *selbst-bewusst-sein* with

its three moments: being as immediate (*sein*), the appearing of being (*bewusst*) and the sense or the self (*selbst*).']

Ernest Hemingway, *L'Adieu aux armes*, Paris: Gallimard, 1948. (*A Farewell to Arms*, New York: Scribner, 1929).

Ernest Hemingway, *Pour qui sonne le glas*, Paris: Gallimard, 1961. (*For Whom the Bell Tolls*, New York: Scribner, 1940).

Angelo Hesnard and René Laforgue, *L'Évolution psychiatrique. Psychanalyse, psychologie clinique*, Paris: Payot, 1927.

[Several passages of the articles making up this historical collection, in which Hesnard did the first history of the psychoanalytic movement in France, are marked:

René Laforgue and Georges Parcheminey, 'Conflits psychiques et troubles organiques': 'Ultimately, psychoanalysis, by broadening the field of consciousness, makes it possible to study in more precise fashion the organo-psychic complexes; as for the intimate explanation of these processes, we can only underline the interest of it here, without claiming to resolve it' (p. 35). 'In the treatment of clinical complexes, with organic involvement, sympathetic and psychic, which have not yielded to the rational treatments used up to now, psychoanalysis appears to us as though it ought to constitue an effective weapon' (p. 44).

Angelo Hesnard, 'Les applications de la psychanalyse à l'étude du mécanisme psychogénétique des psychoses délirantes chroniques': there are several marks here relating to technical points. 'This conception of neurotic symptoms as a morbid solution to the conflict between repressed tendencies and the "conscious ego" which represses is at the basis of the psychoanalytic theory of neuroses' (p. 76, note 1).

Eugène Minkowski, 'De la rêverie morbide au délire d'influence': '*To understand* the content of psychosis hardly seems enough. The point is further to *explain it*, to explain the appearance of mental disorders as well as their particular characters' (p. 157); in the margin there is an accolade linking 'Jaspers' and '*Verstehen-Erklären*'.

Édouard Pichon, 'De l'extension légitime du domaine de la psychanalyse': very negative comments, especially on p. 223 where Pichon seems to advocate a 'noumenal' knowledge of the psyche in opposition to the 'Chinese shadows' that supposedly make up the object of psychoanalysis. Thus: 'A teeny bit of phenomenological reflection would reveal, Pichon, the *pre*-personal field of the empirical consciousness and the *transcendence* of the ego.']

Angelo Hesnard, *L'Univers morbide de la faute*, Paris: PUF, 1949.

Thor Heyerdahl, *L'Expédition du* Kon-Tiki. *Sur un radeau à travers le Pacifique*, Paris: Albin Michel, 1951.

Chester Himes, *La Troisième génération*, Paris: Gallimard, 1954.

Homer, *Iliade*, Paris: Garnier, 1945.

Homer, *Odyssée*, Paris: Armand Colin, 1947.

Victor Hugo, *Les Voix intérieures*, Paris: Garnier frères, 1950.

Johan Huizinga, *Le Déclin du Moyen Âge*, Paris: Payot, 1948.

Edmund Husserl, *Idées directrices pour une phénoménologie*, Paris: Gallimard, 1950.

[Some passages are underlined in the introduction of the translator, Paul Ricœur].

Alex Inkeles, *L'Opinion publique en Russie soviétique. Une étude sur la persuasion des masses*, Paris: Les Îles d'or, 1956.

Anatoli Georgievitch Ivanov-Smolenski, 'Essais sur la physiopathologie de l'activité nerveuse supérieure'. La Raison, *Cahiers de psychopathologie scientifique*, nos. 11–12, 4th trimester 1955.

Max Jacob, *Le Cornet à dés*, Paris: Stock, 1923.

Max Jacob, *Lettres de Max Jacob à Jean Cocteau (1919–1944)*, Paris: Gallimard, 1950.

Cyril Lionel Robert James, *Les Jacobins noirs. Toussaint Louverture et la révolution de Saint-Domingue*, Paris: Gallimard, 1949.

Claude Jamet, *Images mêlées*, Paris: Éditions de l'Élan, 1947.

Pierre Janet, *Les Médications psychologiques*, Paris: Félix Alcan, 1919.

Pierre Janet, *De l'angoisse à l'extase. Études sur les croyances et les sentiments*, vol. 1, Paris: Félix Alcan, 1926.

Pierre Janet, *De l'angoisse à l'extase. Les sentiments fondamentaux*, vol. 2, Paris: Félix Alcan, 1928.

[Several passages are marked in the chapter on 'Les béatitudes', notably pp. 500–32, on the relations between schizophrenia, hysteria, autism and inspired, ecstatic states or states of total inaction.]

Auguste Jardé, *La Grèce antique et la vie grecque. Géographie, histoire, littérature, beaux-arts, vie publique, vie privée*, Paris: Delagrave, 1946.

Alfred Jarry, *Gestes et opinions du docteur Faustroll, pataphysicien*, Paris: Stock, 1923.

Karl Jaspers, *Nietzsche et le christianisme*, Paris: Minuit, 1949. (Nietzsche and Christianity, trans. E.B. Ashton, Henry Regnery Company, [1938] 1961.)

[Some passages are marked in this volume. Thus: 'For it was Christianity which, according to Nietzsche, destroyed all the truth by which man had been living in pre-Christian times – above all, the tragic truth of life as understood by the Greeks before Socrates. To counter this, Christianity put up mere fictions: God, moral world-order, immortality, sin, grace, redemption' (p. 15).]

Andreï Jdanov, *Sur la littérature, la philosophie et la musique*, Paris: Éditions de 'La Nouvelle Critique', 1950.

Francis Jeanson, *La Phénoménologie*, Paris: Téqui, 1951.

[This volume has been very carefully read and contains marks throughout.]

Francis Jeanson, *La Vraie vérité: alibi. Suivi de la récrimination: essai*, Paris: Seuil, 1954.

Francis Jeanson, *Sartre par lui-même*, Paris: Seuil, 1955.

Pierre Jean Jouve, *Ode*, Paris: Minuit, 1950.

Claude Julien, *Le Nouveau Nouveau Monde. L'élite au pouvoir, les syndicats ouvriers*, vol. 1, Paris: Julliard, 1960

Carl Gustav Jung, *L'Homme à la découverte de son âme. Structure et fonctionnement de l'inconscient*, Paris: Éditions du Mont-Blanc, 1940.

[A number of annotations are to be found in this volume, in general negative ones. Thus, all that concerns consciousness from p. 77 on, on the mediately accessible contents of consciousness, is judged 'absurd' or 'simplistic' [*simple*]. Subsequent pages, which localize consciousness in the organic (in opposition to the rest of the psyche) and the passages on 'primitives' are marked with violent comments. Thus: 'Shit, and when I think that there exists a psychoanalysis based on this psychology' in the margin of this paragraph: 'Observe a primitive and you will observe that if he is not breathtaken by some event, nothing happens in him; he remains seated for hours, simply there, in total inertia; if you ask him what he's thinking about, he is offended, because in his eyes thinking is the privilege of madmen! So it cannot be presumed that any thought acts through him; however, his state is also far removed from one of absolute rest: the unconscious exerts in him a vivacious activity, whence sudden and interesting ideas can gush out, the primitive being a master at the "art" of letting his unconscious speak and lending it an attentive ear' (p. 84).

Or else: 'Bastard' in the margin of these phrases: 'At the start of my stay in Africa, I was astonished by the brutality with which the indigenous were treated, whipping being a common practice; first, it seemed superfluous to me, but I had to come to the conclusion that it was necessary; since that moment I constantly bore my rhinoceros-hide whip at my side. I learned to simulate affects that I did not feel, to give out full-throated cries and to stamp my feet with anger. It is necessary to make up in this way for the deficient will of the indigenous' (p. 92).]

Carl Gustav Jung, *Aspects du drame contemporain*, Librairie de l'Université, Paris: George & Cie, 1948.

Franz Kafka, *Journal intime*, Paris: Grasset, 1945.

[Some marks feature in Pierre Klossowski's introduction, such as around this passage, which finds an echo in Fanon's reflections on the relations between illness and religion: 'The patient whose health is refused him can find in illness the path leading beyond health toward saintliness. The man who enjoys health may move to the climes of illness; his own good health has prevented him from living the life of God that he finds at last within the illness of others. In both cases, health appears to obstruct the true path. And it seems that the healthy life proceeds against God' (p. 16).]

Franz Kafka, *L'Amérique*, Paris: Gallimard, 1946.

Franz Kafka, *La Métamorphose*, Paris: Gallimard, 1946.

Franz Kafka, *La Muraille de Chine et autres récits*, Paris: Gallimard, 1950.

Immanuel Kant, *Critique de la raison pure*, Paris: Librairie Joseph Gibert, 1943.

Immanuel Kant, *Fondements de la métaphysique des mœurs*, Paris: Delagrave, 1951.

Søren Kierkegaard, *Ou bien ... ou bien ...*, Paris: Gallimard, 1943.

Søren Kierkegaard, *Vie et règne de l'amour*, Paris: Aubier, 1945.

Søren Kierkegaard, *Crainte et tremblement*, Paris: Aubier, 1946.

Søren Kierkegaard, *Les Miettes philosophiques*, new translation by Paul Petit, Paris: Éditions du Livre français, 1947.

Søren Kierkegaard, *Étapes sur le chemin de la vie*, Paris: Gallimard, 1948. (*Stages on Life's Way*, ed. and trans. with introduction and notes by Howard V. Hong and Edna H. Hong, Princeton, NJ: Princeton University Press, 1988.)

[Some marks in the last section, 'A concluding word'. On pp. 485–6: 'I look at the religious position from all sides, and to that extent I continually have one more side than the sophist, who sees only one side, but what makes me a sophist is that I do not become a religious person. ... Sophists can be grouped in three classes:

1) Those who from the aesthetic reach an immediate relation to the religious. [in the margin: "FF"]. Here, religion becomes poetry, history;

… But the religious consists precisely in being religiously, infinitely concerned about oneself and not about visions [Fr. Tr.: *fantasmagories*], in being infinitely concerned about oneself and not about a positive goal, which is negative and finite because the infinitely negative is the only adequate form for the infinite; in being infinitely concerned about oneself and consequently not deeming oneself finished, which is negative and perdition. This I do know, but I know it with a balance of spirit and therefore am a sophist like the others, for this balance is an offense against the holy passion of the religious.']

Arthur Koestler, *Le Zéro et l'infini*, Paris: Calmann-Lévy, 1938.

Alexandre Kojève, *Introduction à la lecture de Hegel. Leçons sur la phénoménologie de l'esprit*, Paris: Gallimard, 1947.

[Of course, the first section, comprising the famous analysis of chapter 4, section A, of *Phänomenologie des Geistes*, 'Autonomy and dependance of self-consciousness; mastery and servitude', is amply marked in the margins, notably the page on which Kojève comments on the proposition 'Human desire must be directed toward another desire.' The phrase 'human reality can only be social' is underlined. In the last section, in which Kojève returns to the dialectic of recognition, the last sentence of the following paragraph is marked with a line in the margin: 'The man who has engaged in the fight for recognition must remain alive to be able to *live* humanly. But he only lives *humanly* to the extent that he is *recognized* by the other. His adversary must therefore also escape death. The combat must stop short of death, contrary to what Hegel says in his *Lectures* of 1803–1804 (vol. 19, p. 229)' (p. 569).]

Alexandre Koyré, Henri-Charles Puech and André Spaier (eds.), *Recherches philosophiques. 1931–1932*, vol. 1, Paris: Boivin & Cie, 1932.

[There are some annotations on Gaston Bachelard's article on 'Noumène et microphysique'. In particular, this sentence: 'Thus we can no longer see in the description, even painstaking, of an immediate world anything other than a *working phenomenology* in the same sense in which one formerly spoke of a *working hypothesis*' (p. 57).]

Alexandre Koyré, Henri-Charles Puech and André Spaier (eds.), *Recherches philosophiques. 1932–1933*, vol. 2, Paris: Boivin & Cie, 1932.

[Jean Wahl's article on 'Heidegger et Kierkegaard' is marked in several places with added references to Jaspers (pp. 355 and 362) and Husserl (p. 367).]

Alexandre Koyré, Henri-Charles Puech and André Spaier (eds.), *Recherches philosophiques. 1933–1934*, vol. 3, Paris: Boivin & Cie, 1933.

Alexandre Koyré, Henri-Charles Puech and André Spaier (eds.), *Recherches philosophiques. 1934–1935*, vol. 4, Paris: Boivin & Cie, 1935.

[The articles by André Spaier ('Le complexe de l'individualisme') and by Eugène Minkowski ('Esquisses phénoménologiques') are cut and marked in several places.]

Alexandre Koyré, Henri-Charles Puech and André Spaier (eds.), *Recherches philosophiques. 1936–1937*, vol. 6, Paris: Boivin & Cie, 1937.

[Günther Stern (Günther Anders)'s article, 'Pathologie de la liberté: Essai sur la non-identification', is marked in several places. This important volume also contains Sartre's 'La transcendance de l'Ego. Esquisse d'une description phénoménologique' and Jean Wahl's article on 'Le *Nietzsche* de Jaspers'.]

Hugo Krayenbul, *L'Anévrysme de l'artère communicante antérieure*, Paris: Masson & Cie, 1959.

Henri Kréa, *Grand Jour*, Florence: Éditions Spartacus, 1956.

[Dedication dated 20 September 1956: 'To Frantz Fanon, who knows my town of birth and whose intelligence pulverizes the monsters. In fraternity.']

Arthur Kreindler, *La Physiologie et la physiopathologie du cervelet*, Paris: Masson & Cie, 1958.

Roland Kuhn, *Phénoménologie du masque. À travers le test de Rorschach*, Paris: Desclée de Brouwer, 1957.

Henri Laborit and Geneviève Laborit, *Excitabilité neuromusculaire et équilibre ionique. Intérêt pratique en chirurgie et en hibernothérapie*, Paris: Masson & Cie, 1955.

Pierre Lachièze-Rey, *Les Idées morales, sociales et politiques de Platon*, Paris: Boivin & Cie, 1938.

Jean Lacroix, *Le Sens du dialogue*, Neuchâtel: Éditions de La Baconnière, 1944.

[There are some marks in the first section, 'Orgueil et vanité' and 'De la duplicité'.]

Jules Larforgue, *Anthologie poétique. Hamlet*, Paris: Club français du livre, 1952.

André Lalande, *Vocabulaire technique et critique de la philosophie*, Paris: PUF, 1951.

Quentin Lauer, *Phénoménologie de Husserl*, Paris: PUF, 1955.

Louis Lavelle, *De l'acte*, Paris: Montaigne, 1946.

[Some marks. In particular, on the section on 'dialectical action': 'This is enough to show that philosophy and life itself only have a serious character on the conditions that the Absolute is not before me and outside of me as an inaccessible goal, but on the contrary in me and that in it I trace my furrow' (p. 49).]

Guy Lazorthes, *Le Système neurovasculaire*, Paris: Masson & Cie, 1949.

Serge Lebovici and Joyce McDougall, *Un cas de psychose infantile. Étude psychanalytique*, Paris: PUF, 1960.

Auguste Lecoeur, *L'Autocritique attendue*, Paris: Girault, 1955.

Henri Lefebvre, *Le Matérialisme dialectique*, Paris: PUF, 1949.

Henri Lefebvre, *Problèmes actuels du marxisme*, Paris: PUF, 1958.

Michel Leiris, *Contacts de civilisations en Martinique et en Guadeloupe*, Paris: Gallimard/Unesco, 1955.

Michel Leiris, *La Règle du jeu. Biffures*, vol. 1, Paris: Gallimard, 1948.

Michel Leiris, *Race et civilisation*, Paris: Unesco, 1951.

[This volume carries the stamp of Blida-Joinville Psychiatric Hospital.]

Jean Lepoire and Bernard Pertuiset, *Les Kystes épidermoïdes cranio-encéphaliques*, Paris: Masson & Cie, 1957.

René Leriche, *La Chirurgie, discipline de la connaissance*, Paris: La Diane française,1949.

André Leroi-Gourhan, *Ethnologie de l'Union française. Asie, Océanie, Amérique*, Paris: PUF, 1952.

André Leroi-Gourhan (ed.), *L'Homme, races et mœurs*, Paris: Clartés, 1957.

Claude Lévi-Strauss, *Tristes tropiques*, Paris: Plon, 1955.

Emmanuel Levinas, *De l'existence à l'existant*, Paris: Fontaine, 1947. (*Existence and Existents*, trans. Alphonso Lingis, Pittsburgh, PA: Duquesne University Press, 2001.)

[Some marks are contained in the margins pertaining to Levinas' following sentences: 'What was interrupted does not sink into nothingness like a game. This means that the act is inscription in being. And indolence, as a recoil before action, is a hesitation before existence, an indolence about existing' (p. 15); 'Health, the sincere movement of the desiring toward the desirable, that good will that know exactly what it wants, gauges the reality and the concreteness of a human being' (p. 32).]

Georges Lévy, *Formulaire vénérologique du praticien*, Paris: Doin & Cie, 1948.

Jean Lhermitte and Julian de Ajuriaguerra, *Psychopathologie de la vision*, Paris: Masson & Cie, 1942.

[Some marks are contained in the first chapter on hemianopsies (pp. 12–14), including one annotation: 'Nice illustration of *gestalt th*'.]

Maurice Loeper and André Lesure, *Formulaire pratique de thérapeutique et de pharmacologie. Ancien formulaire de Dujardin-Beaumetz-Yvon et Gilbert, Michel*, Paris: G. Doin & Cie, 1948.

Juan José Lopez Ibor, *La Angustia vital. Patología general psicosomática*, Madrid: Paz Montalvo, 1950.

Juan José Lopez Ibor, *El Español y su complejo de inferioridad*, Madrid: Rialp, 'Biblioteca del pensamiento actual', 1954.

Malcolm Lowry, *Au-dessous du volcan*, Paris: Corrêa, 1950.

Georg Lukacs, *Existentialisme ou marxisme?*, Paris: Nagel, 1948.

[Writing on the flyleaf reads: 'Fanon Frantz, 29 rue Tupin' (a street in the centre of Lyon). The pages of the chapters 'Sartre contre Marx' (pp. 141–60) and 'La morale de l'ambiguïté et l'ambiguïté de la morale existentialiste' (pp. 160–211) are cut and bear some marks. For example: 'But this opinion [Sartre's suppressing of the objectivity of nature and history, "since in his eyes, only pure interior subjectivity is worthy of this name"] becomes very difficult to defend, when you have the ambition to defend it against Marxism, qua true philosophy of history' (p. 148); 'No compromise is possible either, between the existentialist conception of freedom and the dialectical and historical unity of freedom and necessity, as established by Marxism' (p. 204). Several pages of the chapter 'Signification dialectique de l'approximation dans la théorie de la connaissance' are cut and marked. Most of the annotations concern the relativism in epistemology defended by Lukacs ('Our knowledge is only ever an approximation of the plenitude of reality and, by the same token, it is always relative' (p. 286)). The commentaries in general express disagreement.]

Georg Lukacs, *La Destruction de la raison. Les débuts de l'irrationalisme moderne de Schelling à Nietzsche*, vol. 1, Paris: L'Arche, 1958.

Nicolas Machiavelli, *Les Pages immortelles de Machiavel*, Paris: Corrêa, 1947.

Gabriel Madinier, *Conscience et amour. Essai sur le « nous »*, Paris: PUF, 1947.

[A loose page of the chapter on 'Espace et durée' from Emmanuel Mounier's *Traité du caractère* (1946, p. 319) is inserted here at p. 66. At issue is a reflection on Bergson. The paragraph that begins as follows was probably of interest to Fanon: 'An overly powerful discovery often blocks reflection into exclusive pathways. By restoring the dignity of lived duration, Bergson has, willy nilly, long prevented our looking with justice at regions where duration approaches space through extension and measured time. As Minkowski remarks, after having erred, in speaking of time, through an excess of statism, since Bergson we err through an excess of dynamism. However, everything today leads us to the idea of a spatiotemporal solidarity that is as close as organo-psychic solidarity.']

Claude-Edmonde Magny, *Les Sandales d'Empédocle. Essai sur les limites de la littérature*, Neuchâtel: Éditions de La Baconnière, 1945.

Claude-Edmonde Magny, *Histoire du roman français depuis 1918*, Paris: Seuil, 1950.

André Malraux, *Les Voix du silence*, Paris: Gallimard, 1951.

André Malraux, *Romans*, Paris: Gallimard, 1951.

Clara Malraux, *Journal psychanalytique d'une petite fille*, Paris: Gallimard, 1928.

Thomas Mann, *Mario et le magicien*, Paris: Stock, 1932.

Octave Mannoni, *Psychologie de la colonisation*, Paris: Seuil, 1950.

[Some marks as far as p. 109. No annotation.]

Gabriel Marcel, *Journal métaphysique*, Paris: Gallimard, 1935.

Jules Marouzeau, *La Linguistique ou science du langage*, Paris: P. Geuthner, 1950.

Luis Martín-Santos, *Dilthey, Jaspers y la comprensión del enfermo mental*, Madrid: Paz Montalvo, 1955.

[There is a handwritten note inserted in this volume that translates the start of chapter 9 of the second part of this book: 'Comprehensive psychology and psychopathology in Jaspers. Psychological understanding consists in applying to individual psychic elements, isolated through a descriptive labour, an ideal schema of motivation, which is situated at the level of the mind. The ideal type is an absolute *a priori* truth that cannot be demonstrated. The relation of motivation, for example between autumn melancholy and the decision to commit suicide, constitutes an absolute truth. This psychological work, which consists in the illustrating of typical motivations, constitutes more an interpretation.']

Jules Masserman, *Principes de psychiatrie dynamique*, Paris: PUF, 1959.
François Mauriac, *L'Agneau*, Paris: Flammarion, 1954.
André Maurois, *Olympio ou la vie de Victor Hugo*, Paris: Hachette, 1954.
Marcel Mauss, *Sociologie et anthropologie*, Paris: PUF, 1950.
Heinrich Meng, *Protection de la santé mentale*, Paris: Payot, 1944.

[A copy of the ward journal of Blida-Joinville Psychiatric Hospital is inserted into this volume (no. 39, 16 September 1954) with this editorial by Jacques Azoulay about the earthquake in Orléansville that occurred on 9 September: 'Thursday morning around 1 am, an earthquake shook the entire hospital. Everyone, surprised in their sleep, felt a displeasing anxiety, which was quickly calmed; when it was time to wake up later on, it was only a topic for discussion, and even for jokes. But during the day, we were informed little by little of the extent of the disaster, which in a few seconds devastated an entire region of our beautiful country. Something that threatened to pass to the status of a scarcely salient event in our memories, was in actual fact to affect us for a longtime, and continues to do so. Something that was likely to quickly become a matter of indifference had all the world talking about it: in London, in Rome, in Paris, everyone spared a thought for our country, for our wounded brothers. And in the hospital, too, we ought to gather ourselves to make room for our comrades of Orléansville who are now homeless. This sad event comes to remind us, as if it were needed, that we must stay in relation with the world, that we must hold onto it, that we must think about it as it must think about us.']

Charles Mentha, *Bases physiologiques de la chirurgie neurovasculaire. Énervations sympathiques, assistance mutuelle des territoires vasculaires*, Paris: Masson & Cie, 1956.

Fernand Mercier (ed.), *Les Médicaments du système nerveux cérébrospinal*, Paris: Masson & Cie, 1959.

Maurice Merleau-Ponty, *La Structure du comportement*, Paris: PUF, 1942 (*The Structure of Behavior*, trans. Alden F. Fisher, Boston, MA: Beacon Press, 1963).

[There are several significant marks, which emphasize in particular the following passages: 'Thus to learn never consists in being made capable of repeating the same gesture, but of providing an adapted response to the situation by different means' (p. 96); 'It [intuition] is one of the possible perspectives upon the structure and immanent meaning of conduct, which constitute the only psychological "reality"' (p. 184); 'The study of reflex has shown us that the nervous system is the place in which an order without anatomical guarantee is realized by means of a continuing organization' (p. 207); 'Higher behaviour retains the subordinated dialectics in the present depths of its existence, from that of the physical system and its topological conditions to that of the organism and its "milieu". They are not recognizable in the whole when it functions correctly, but the disintegration in case of partial lesion attests to their imminence' (pp. 207–8).]

Maurice Merleau-Ponty, *Sens et non-sens*, Paris: Nagel, 1948.
Robert King Merton, *Éléments de méthode sociologique*, Paris: Plon, 1953.
Gaston Milhaud, *Études sur Cournot*, Paris: Librairie philosophique Vrin, 1927.

[In this volume, the pages of chapter 2, 'La définition du hasard de Cournot', are cut. There are some marks in the margins that can be presumed to be Fanon's, since they bear on the idea of a causality that cannot be reduced to a simple determination. Thus, on p. 41: 'Dependency in the largest sense would probably be represented, in Cournot's eyes, by a function or by a set of functions, being expressed only with the aid of constant parameters, containing no variable coefficient, and leading from the precise data in one of the series to precise determinations in the other. Independence, on the contrary – and I hereby arrive at one of the most important and most poorly recognized points of Cournot's thinking – is inseperable from the idea of a multiplicity of possible determinations for one of the series, the other being given.']

Louis Moland, *Théâtre de Marivaux*, Paris: Classiques Garnier, 1951.
Georges Morin, *Physiologie du système nerveux central*, Paris: Masson & Cie, 1948.
Marcel Mouquin, *Manuel de pathologie médicale. Physiopathologie médicale. Cœur-Artères-Veines-Sang*, vol. 1, Paris: Masson & Cie, 1947.
Paul Mousset, *Ce Sahara qui voit le jour*, Paris: Presses de la Cité, 1959.
Henry A. Murray, *Thematic Apperception Test Manual*, Cambridge, MA: Harvard University Press, 1948 (French translation: Centre de psychologie appliquée, 1950).

[This book carries the stamp of Blida-Joinville Psychiatric Hospital.]

Jean Nabert, *Éléments pour une éthique*, Paris: PUF, 1943.
Pierre Naville, *La Psychologie science du comportement. Le behaviorisme de Watson*, Paris: Gallimard, 1942.

[There are some marks in this classic introduction to behaviourism. Some pages are marked along the entire length of the margin. They bear on the articulation of verbal behaviour and physical movement (pp. 182 and 184–5). What may have interested Fanon in this behaviourist theory of language, which was soon to appear obsolete, is the new relation of thought to the world, no longer as representation, but, through language, as a bodily disposition: '[Between words and things an *equivalence of reaction* is established.] It also enables the isolated individual to transport the external world with him, and to manipulate it in solitude. The world, then, is no longer constituted with objects present to the senses, but is stored in the form of a particular bodily organization (including on the front line the throat and the chest with the sensorial organs of the muscles and the nervous system)' (p. 184).]

Friedrich Nietzsche, *Considérations inactuelles, deuxième série*, Paris: Mercure de France, 1922.

[A citation is written in pencil on the title page of the first consideration of this series, 'Schopenhauer as educator': '"Do not let virtue fly away from earthly things and beat against eternal walls with its wings! [...] Like me, guide the virtue that has flown away back to the earth – yes, back to the body and life: so that it may give the earth its meaning, a HUMAN meaning!" F. Nietzsche.' This is an extract from the start of the second section of the sermon 'On the bestowing virtue' at the end of the first part of *Thus Spoke Zarathustra* (The French quote Fanon gives is from Henri Albert's translation of this work: '*Ne laissez pas votre vertu s'envoler des choses terrestre et battre des ailes contre des murs éternels. Ramenez comme moi la vertu égarée sur la terre – afin qu'elle donne un sens à la terre – un sens HUMAIN*' (Paris: Mercure de France, 1903). 'Human' is not in capitals in Nietzsche's text.]

Friedrich Nietzsche, *La Généalogie de la morale*, Paris: Mercure de France, 1943.

[This volume contains some marks. The bulk of the sixth paragraph of the foreword is marked in the margin or underlined. It bears on the critique of moral values and morality as a 'danger *par excellence*'.]

Friedrich Nietzsche, *L'Origine de la tragédie, ou Hellénisme et pessimisme*, Paris: Mercure de France, 1947. (*The Birth of Tragedy*, eds. Ramond Geuss and Ronald Spiers, trans. Ronald Spiers, Cambridge: Cambridge University Press, 1999).

[There are some marks in section 18. For example: 'When Goethe says to Eckermann, speaking of Napoleon, "Yes, my good friend, actions, too, are a form of productivity", he reminds us, with graceful naïveté, that non-theoretical man is something incredible and astonishing to modern man, so that the wisdom of a Goethe is needed to rediscover the fact that even such a surprising form of existence is understandable, indeed forgivable' (p. 85).]

Paul Nizan, *Les Matérialistes de l'Antiquité. Démocrite, Épicure, Lucrèce*, Paris: Éditions sociales internationales, 1936.

Paul Nizan, *Aden Arabie*, Paris: François Maspero, 1960.

Charles-Henry Nodet, *Le Groupe des psychoses hallucinatoires chroniques*, Paris: G. Doin & Cie, 1938.

[There are many marks (up to p. 151) in this volume, which Fanon no doubt read while writing up his dissertation as well as for *Peau noire, masques blancs* (for the chapter 'L'expérience vécue du Noir'). He underlines several passages in the section on Hughlings Jackson's theory of dissolution of functions (applied to psychopathology in Henry Ey's organo-dynamic theory), seeming to accept with a certain reluctance the organic etiology of the psychoses that it implied. In particular, this annotation on p. 105: 'I confess that the problem of psychosomatic interaction found in the neo-Jacksonian organo-dynamism its most elegant compromise.'
After the sentence: 'One can rediscover and reassemble a comprehensible psychological linkage from the concrete event to other situations (objective or subjective) on which it depends', the following phrase is marked with a 'B(ien)' [Good] in the margin: 'But this linkage, reconstituted *après coup*, considered in its historical and lived *outburst*, would appear only to be a realized possibility and not a totally necessary unfolding' (p. 106). 'As close as it holds to the facts, the psychological explanation always comes up against a certain *indetermination*, often reduced, that it will be unable to grasp. … The most disconcerting unknown is not the total explanation of the content of the psychopathological phenomenon, but the reason for its triggering. As understandable as all the psychological springs of a delusion may appear in the last analysis, the problem remains completely intact if the point is to know why this delusion exists. Otherwise said, in

Jacksonian terms, the analysis of the psychopathological structure will never provide the cause of the dissolution. [Italics in the original.]' These sentences are annotated as follows: 'Incommensurability of phenomenology – study of the structures (*necessity*) with psychology – study of the forms (*contingency*)' (p. 107). In the section on 'Les expériences délirantes' (in which one annotation refers to Lacan): 'We understand by this an original disorder of the mind, a fleeting waning of the personality whereby the patient *lives through* a certain morbid episode, more or less conceptualized. This can only be an intuition, a certain state of the soul, a certain delusional humour (*Grundstimmung*). This *Erlebnis* is intensely felt by the patient, who takes a concrete, particular consciousness, a very new one of his Ego, of the outside world, of the relations uniting them. This phenomenological given, fleeting but irresistibly adopted, leaves a deep impression on the patient's personality, in the form of a special signification, of a henceforth more or less diffuse, conceded belief, or of a definitively inscribed attitude in his behaviour' (p. 143).]

Julien Offray de la Mettrie, *Textes choisis*, Paris: Éditions sociales, 1954.

André Ombredane, *L'Exploration de la mentalité des Noirs congolais au moyen d'une épreuve projective, le Congo TAT*, Brussels: Institut royal colonial belge, 1954.

[Bears the stamp of Blida-Joinville Psychiatric Hospital.]

Marcel Pahmer, *Les Méthodes de choc et autres traitements physio-pharmacologiques dans les maladies mentales. Travaux américains de 1940–1946*, Paris: Hippocrate, 1946.

[Some marks refer to points concerning the methodology of these shock treatments and p. 29: 'Overall, *schizophrenia* remains the indication of choice for hypoglycemic treatment, on the condition that we are dealing with *acute cases* of *recent* origin in *young individiuals*, cases that make up the majority of favourable reports, and whose treatment is preceded and followed by all the adjuvant methods in use and in particular psychotherapeutic ones.']

Blaise Pascal, *Pensées. Extraits*, Paris: Hatier, 1921.
Blaise Pascal, *Les Provinciales. Extraits*, Paris: Hatier, 1938.
Jean Paulhan, *Petite Préface à toute critique*, Paris: Minuit, 1951.
Jean Paulhan, *La Preuve par l'étymologie*, Paris: Minuit, 1953.
Charles Péguy, *Clio*, Paris: Gallimard, 1932.
Charles Péguy, *Victor-Marie, comte Hugo*, Paris: Gallimard, 1934.

Charles Péguy, *Cinq prières dans la cathédrale de Chartres*, Paris: Gallimard, 1947.

Roger Peyrefitte, *Les Clés de Saint-Pierre*, Paris: Flammarion, 1955.

Édouard Pichon, *Le Développement psychique de l'enfant et de l'adolescent. Manuel d'étude*, Paris: Masson & Cie, 1936.

Édouard Pichon and Suzanne Borel-Maisonny, *Le Bégaiement. Sa nature et son traitement*, Paris: Masson & Cie, 1937.

Henri Piéron, *Psychologie expérimentale*, Paris: Armand Colin, 1939.

Roger Pinto, *La Liberté d'opinion et d'information*, Paris: Domat, 1955.

Luigi Pirandello, *Quand j'étais fou. « Novelle per un anno »*, vol. 2, Paris: Les Éditions mondiales, 1950.

Thérèse Plainol, *Diagnostic des lésions intracrâniennes par les radio-isotopes (gammaencéphalographie)*, Paris: Masson & Cie, 1959.

Plato, *Œuvres complètes*, vol. 1, Paris: Garnier frères, 1936.

Plato, *Ménon* [*Meno*], trans. Alfred Croiset, Paris: Les Belles Lettres, 1949.

Plato, *La République* [The Republic], Paris: Hatier, 1952.

Plautus, *Amphitryon-Asinaria-Avicularia*, vol. 1, Paris: 1952.

Roger Pluvinage, *Malformations et tumeurs vasculaires du cerveau*, Paris: Masson & Cie, 1954.

Edgar Poe, *Histoires extraordinaires*, Geneva: Au Grand Passage, 1946.

Raymond Polin, *La Création des valeurs. Recherches sur le fondement de l'objectivité axiologique*, Paris: PUF, 1944.

[In this book, the following chapters are marked throughout: ch. 1: 'Le problème d'un fondement des valeurs'; ch. 2: 'Définition du concept d'objectivité'; ch. 3: 'Postulats généraux de toute axiologie objective.' This volume contains a handwritten note on the back of a request form for a police certificate dated 26 September 1947. The request was made by a student from Martinique, Madeleine Lastel, who contributed regularly to *Alizés, revue antillo-guyanaise d'inspiration chrétienne* in the 1950s.[6] The handwritten note

---

[6]On this journal, created by students within the *Aumônerie générale des étudiants d'Outre-Mer*, see the interesting article by Andrew M. Daily, 'Race, citizenship, and Antillean student activism in postwar France, 1946–1968', *French Historical Studies*, vol. 37, no. 2, 2014, pp. 331–57. Daily cites an article by Lastel from October to November 1953, p. 21: 'In an article in *Alizés*, Lastel reports an exchange that she had with a student friend from the Antilles: A young man seriously declared to me, with a tone of reproach in his voice, that I had "Europeanized" myself. "How can you see that?", I asked him. And he replied to me in the same serious tone: "Your short hair!"' Lastel attributes this attitude to the indifference and to the hostility of the Metropole and suggests that some students react to this by donning a rigid and fetichist identity, by becoming critical, or even hostile vis-à-vis those who are perceived as having adapted well to life in the Metropole' (p. 340).

states: 'If it is admitted that God is the creator, it must be further admitted that through his creation God has "committed" himself and that henceforth he finds himself partially engaged in a system of relations.']

Raymond Polin, *La Compréhension des valeurs*, Paris: PUF, 1945.

Georges Politzer, *Le Bergsonisme. Une mystification philosophique*, Paris: Éditions sociales, 1949.

[Several pages are marked here, in particular the pages criticizing the Bergsonian theory of freedom: '*To turn freedom into a purely internal matter, a matter of me with myself,* is as abstract as making it a matter between man and nature: in both cases one conjures away *the concrete life of man*' (p. 77). '*Nothing in the order in which man currently lives is adapted to the unicity of his life* [italics in the original]. He is thrown into a social order whose existence is linked to the fact that the large part of humanity is treated with disregard for the singular life of each of its members, these latter are thus all tossed together in a mass that is no longer human and that one handles like matter; an order that implies at each instant the irreparable devastation and destruction of unique lives, and this stirs no one anymore than the melting of snow. … But these observations are not the most important thing here, but instead the fact that they are inseperable from action. *Since once one really adopts the human point of view, what strikes one are not the things to be said, but the things to be done*' [italics in the original] (p. 91).]

Antoine Porot and Jean Sutter, *Le 'Primitivisme' des indigènes nord-africains. Ses incidences en pathologie mentale*, Marseille: Imprimerie marseillaise, 1939.

[There are no annotations or marks in this article, which Fanon violently attacked in his 'Ethnopsychiatric considerations' in 1955, but p. 3 is torn along the diagonal. Thus missing is the beginning of the section of 'Séméiologie psychiatrique', which notably contains the following paragraph: 'When approaching the practice of psychiatry in the North African milieu, one first gets an *impression of monotony*: all the patients appear to be alike; one gets the impression of a rather uniform greyness in which the rich variety of mental forms that we have come to learn about among Europeans are not distinguished. This diversity nevertheless exists, but it is masked from us by a set of common traits that surprise us because we do not know about them: we must change perspective, we must replace a value scale that no longer has any currency with another scale, one of primitive values, or more exactly, one that participates in the scale of primitive values to the extent that the native mentality proceeds from primitivism.']

Georges Poulet, *Études sur le temps humain. La distance intérieure*, Paris: Plon, 1952.

Ezra Pound, *Cantos et poèmes choisis*, Paris: Pierre-Jean Oswald, 1958.

Maurice Pradines, *Traité de psychologie générale. Le psychisme élémentaire*, vol. 1, Paris: PUF, 1948.

Maurice Pradines, *Traité de psychologie générale. Le génie humain*, vol. 2, Paris: PUF, 1948.

Marcel Proust, *Un amour de Swann*, Paris: Gallimard, 1919.

Raymond Queneau, *Le Chiendent*, Paris: Gallimard, 1933.

Pierre Quercy, *L'Hallucination. Les philosophes: théorie de la perception, de l'image et de l'hallucination chez Spinoza, Leibniz, Bergson. Les mystiques: sainte Thérèse, ses misères, sa perception de Dieu, ses visions*, vol. 1, Paris: Félix Alcan, 1930.

[There are some marks in the introduction. For instance, concerning the visions of saints: 'The most certain thing is the *luminous* certainty of he who is no longer the dreamer and the *dazed* individual of our ordinary wakefulness, but who is finally *awakened* to the divine light.' The last two italicized words are italicized in the original.]

François Rabelais, *Gargantua*, Paris: Les Belles Lettres, 1946.

Jean Racine, *Théâtre complet de Racine. Suivi d'un choix de ses épigrammes concernant son théâtre*, Paris: Garnier frères, 1937.

[Contains some marks, for instance around: *Andromachus* – 'I yield blindly to the transport that carries me away / I love: I come to these places to seek Hermione / to sway her, to snatch her, or to die in her eyes.' *Phaedra* – 'The very light of day is not more pure / Than my heart's core. How could Hippolyte be enthralled by an illicit love ...' (Act IV, Scene II) A handwritten note is inserted into this volume: 'Lyon, 20 August, Certif. special studies in neuropsych'.]

Ramadhan, Algiers: Éditions algériennes Ennahda, 1961.

Charles-Ferdinand Ramuz, *Les Signes parmi nous*, Paris: Grasset, 1931.

Charles-Ferdinand Ramuz, *Besoin de grandeur*, Paris: Grasset, 1938.

John Reed, *Dix jours qui ébranlèrent le monde*, Paris: Éditions sociales, 1958. (*Ten Days that Shook the World*, New York, NY: Boni Liverlight, 1919.)

Martial Rémond, *Djurdjura. Terre de contraste*, Algiers: Baconnière frères, 1940.

Ernest Renan, *Vie de Jésus*, Paris: Calmann-Lévy, 1957.

Joseph Rennard, *Histoire religieuse des Antilles françaises des origines à 1914*, Paris: Société de l'histoire des colonies françaises, 1954.

Retour dans la nuit. Récits par des auteurs chinois contemporains, Beijing: Éditions en langues étrangères, 1957.

Jean Reverzy, *Place des angoisses*, Paris: Julliard, 1956.

Géza Révész, *Origine et préhistoire du langage*, Paris: Payot, 1950.

Louis Revol, *La Thérapeutique par la chlorpromazine en pratique psychiatrique*, Paris: Masson & Cie, 1956.

André Rey, *Étude des insuffisances psychologiques (enfants et adolescents). Méthodes et problèmes*, vol. 1, Neuchâtel and Paris: Delachaux et Niestlé, 1947.

André Rey, *Étude des insuffisances psychologiques (enfants et adolescents). Le Diagnostic psychologique*, vol. 2, Neuchâtel and Paris: Delachaux et Niestlé, 1947.

André de Richaud, *Le Mal de la terre*, Paris: Charlot, 1947.

Walter Riese (with André Réquet), *L'Idée de l'homme dans la neurologie contemporaine*, Paris: Félix Alcan, 1938.

[On the flyleaf, there are two handwritten notes: 'Ba Amadou Hampaté, 51, rue Lauriston, Paris XVIe' (the writing doesn't seem to be Fanon's); '53 *bis*, Quai des Grands-Augustins'. Fanon met Ba at the first International Congress of Black Writers and Artists, held at the Sorbonne between 19 and 22 September 1956.]

Albert Rivaud, *Les Grands Courants de la pensée antique*, Paris: Armand Colin, 1929.

Maxime Rodinson, *Mahomet*, Paris: Seuil, 1961.

Pierre de Ronsard, *Sonnets pour Hélène*, Paris: E. Droz, 1947.

Hermann Rorschach, *Psychodiagnostics. Plates*, New York, NY: Grune and Stratton, 1955.

Hermann Rorschach, *Psychodiagnostic. Méthodes et résultats d'une expérience diagnostique de perception. (Interprétation libre de formes fortuites)*, Paris: PUF, 1947.

[Contains some marks on the technical passages, but no annotations.]

Jacques Roumain, *Gouverneurs de la rosée*, Paris: Les Éditeurs français réunis, 1944.

David Rousset, *Les Jours de notre mort*, Paris: Éditions du Pavois, 1947.

Jean-Jacques Rousseau, *Rêveries du promeneur solitaire*, Geneva: Droz, 1948.

Mario Roustan, *Montesquieu. Morceaux choisis avec une introduction et des notes*, Paris and Toulouse: H. Didier/Éditions Privat, 1921.

Henri Rouvière, *Atlas aide-mémoire d'anatomie*, Paris: Masson & Cie, 1959.

Jean H. Roy, *L'Imagination selon Descartes*, Paris: Gallimard, 1944.

[In this volume, the detached cover of Paul Ricœur's book *Gabriel Marcel et Karl Jaspers* (Paris: Temps présent, 1948) is inserted on p. 112, on which the following sentence is underlined: 'But for Descartes, there is no reasoning of which consciousness is not aware.']

Bertrand Russell, *Histoire de la philosophie occidentale. En relation avec les événements politiques et sociaux de l'Antiquité jusqu'à nos jours*, Paris: Gallimard, 1952. (*A History of Western Philosophy. And its connection with Political and Social Circumstances from the Earliest Times to the Present Day*, London: Allen & Unwin, 1945.)

Raymond Ruyer, *L'Humanité de l'avenir d'après Cournot*, Paris: Félix Alcan, 1930.

Maurice Saillet, *Saint-John Perse. Poète de gloire*, Paris: Mercure de France, 1952.

Antoine de Saint-Exupéry, *Œuvres*, Paris: Gallimard, 1953.

Léonard Sainville, *Dominique. Nègre esclave*, Paris: Fasquelle Éditeurs, 1951.

Henri Salandre and René Cheyssac, *Les Antilles françaises. Histoire et civilisation*, Paris: Fernand Nathan, 1962.

Nathalie Sarraute, *Le Planétarium*, Paris: Gallimard, 1959.

Jean-Paul Sartre, *L'Imaginaire. Psychologie phénoménologique de l'imagination*, Paris: Gallimard, 1940. (*The Imaginary: A phenomenological psychology of the imagination*, revisions and historical introduction by Arlette Elkaim-Sartre, trans. and philosophical introduction by Jonathan Webber, London and New York, NY: Routledge, 2004).

[Most of the pages of this volume contain marks. There are some annotations: 'Roger Stéphane', placed before a quote given by Sartre as follows 'Observation of R. S., student: "I would have liked to convince myself of the idea that every oppressed person or every oppressed group takes from the very oppression they suffer the strength to shake it off"' (p. 119).
The chapter on 'The Imaginary Life' contains a very large number of marks in the margins, such as alongside this passage: 'This is why

the dream world, as with that of reading, is given as entirely magical; we are haunted by the adventures of the dreamed people as by those of the heroes of novels. It is not that the nonthetic consciousness of imagining ceases to grasp itself as spontaneity, but that it grasps itself *as a spellbound spontaneity*' (p. 169; translation modified – SC). The words in italics are underlined and annotated: 'It would be interesting to explain the mechanism of spellbinding.'
'Is not the very first condition of the *cogito* doubt, which is to say the constitution of the real as a world at the same time as its nihilation from this same point of view, and does not the reflective grasp of doubt as doubt coincide with the apodictic intuition of freedom?' (p. 186). 'When the imaginary is not posited as a fact, the surpassing and the nihilation of the existent are stuck in the existent, the surpassing and the freedom *are there* but they are not revealed; the person is squashed in the world, transfixed by the real, and is closest to the thing' (p. 187). Annotation in the margin: 'Hegel'.]

Jean-Paul Sartre, *Situations*, vol. 1, Paris: Gallimard, 1947. (*Sartre: Literary and Philosophical Essays*, trans. Annette Michelson, London: Rider and Company, 1955.)

[This volume is fairly worn out and amply marked and annotated in the margins. Many of these passages have echoes in *Peau noire, masques blancs*. For example: 'That is how things are in his [Giraudoux's] universe: first come truths, first come ideas and meanings that chose their own signs' (p. 43). 'Man's freedom lies less in the contingency of his evolution [*devenir*] than in the exact realization of his essence' (p. 53) [marked with a 'yes' in the margin]. 'Kafka is the novelist of impossible transcendence: the universe is, for him, full of signs that we do not understand; there is something behind the scenery' (pp. 36–7). Annotation by Fanon in the margin of p. 116 [of the French]: 'Camus is right; what Sartre does not see is that we are not foundation [*fondement*] by virtue of our founding of meaning – the absurd is there.'
'They [Kafka, Blanchot] have eliminated the angel's gaze and have plunged the reader into the world with K. and Thomas; but they have left, as it were, a *ghost of transcendence*, floating about within this immanence. *The implements, acts and ends are all familiar to us,* and we are on such intimate terms with them that we hardly notice them. But just when we feel shut up with them in a warm atmosphere of organic sympathy, they are presented to us in a cold, strange light' (p. 72).

This entire paragraph is marked in the margin with a 'TB' (very good) along the last sentence: 'We remember Durkheim's famous precept that we should "treat social facts as things". This is what tempts Mr Bataille in Sociology. If only he could treat social facts and human beings and himself as things, if his inexpiable individuality could only appear to him as a certain given quality, then he would be rid of himself. Unfortunately for our author, Durkheim's sociology is dead: social facts are not things; they are meanings and, as such, they refer back to the being through whom meanings come into the world, to man, who cannot both be scientist and object of science at the same time. You might just as well try to lift the chair you are sitting on by grabbing it by its crossbars. Yet Mr Bataille revels in this vain effort. It is not by chance that the world "impossibility" flows frequently from his pen. He belongs, without a doubt, to that spiritual family whose members are susceptible, above all, to the acid, exhausting charm of impossible endeavours. *The myth of Sisyphus would more aptly symbolize his mysticism than it would Camus' humanism. ...* But we *are* projects, [Sartres' italics], despite what our author says. And we are so not out of cowardice or to flee from an anxiety: *we are projects from the first*' [The English translation of this passage is to be found on pp. 81–2 of *We have only this life left to live: Selected Essays of Jean Paul Sartre, 1939–1975*, eds. Roland Aronson and Adrian Van Den Hoven, New York, NY: New York Review Books, 2013 – translator's note].

'The rest is a matter for psychoanalysis. Yet before anyone protests, I do not have in mind the crude, questionable methods of Freud, Adler or Jung; there are other sorts of psychoanalysis.' Annotation in the margin: 'Can Sartre psychoanalyse Bataille?' (*We have only this life left to live*, p. 82).

'Ponge's movement is opposite: for him it is the thing that exists first, in its inhuman solitude; man is the thing that transforms things into instruments. It is enough, then, to gag in itself this social and practical voice for the thing to be unveiled itself in its *eternal and instantaneous* truth.' Annotation in the margin: 'TB' (Very good) (cf. *Situations 1*, p. 258).

'His end goal, however, is the substitution of a veritable human order for the social order that it undoes. Taking the side of things leads us to the "lesson of things".' Annotation: 'Good'. We find a number of similarly approving remarks in this chapter on Ponge (cf. *Situations 1*, p. 268).

The following citation, by Sartre, of the fourth of Descartes' *Méditations métaphysiques*, an essential text on the will, is marked with a 'capital': 'Since, even as it [the will] is incomparably larger in God than in me, ... *it does not seem larger, however, if I consider it formally and precisely in itself* (cf. *Situations 1*, p. 318).]

Jean-Paul Sartre, *Situations*, vol. 2, Paris: Gallimard, 1948. (*'What is Literature?'And other Essays*, introduction by Steven Ungar, Cambridge, MA: Harvard University Press, 1988.)

[This volume is also marked throughout. Here are some significant marked passages from it. 'Presentation of *Les Temps modernes*': 'Thus, by taking part in the singularity of our era, we ultimately make contact with the eternal, and it is our task as writers to allow the eternal values implicit in such social or political debates to be perceived. ... Far from being relativists, we proclaim that man is an absolute' (p. 254).

'But it is not, we repeat, simply a question of effecting an advance in the domain of pure knowledge: the more distant goal we are aiming at is a *liberation* [word circled in pencil]. Since man is a totality, it is indeed not enough to grant him the right to vote without dealing with the other factors that constitute him. He must free himself totally – that is, make himself *other*, by acting on his biological constitution as well as on his economic condition, on his sexual complexes as well as on the political terms of his situation' (p. 261).

'Without its future, society is no more than an accumulation of raw material, *but its future is nothing other than the self-projection beyond the status quo of the millions of men composing it*' (p. 264).

Long passages on language and literature are underlined in the section 'What is literature?': 'In fact, the poet has withdrawn from language-instrument in a single movement. *Once and for all he has chosen the poetic attitude which considers words as things and not as signs*. For the ambiguity of the sign implies that one can penetrate it at will like a pane of glass and pursue the thing signified, or turn one's gaze towards its *reality* and consider it as an object.' In the margin: 'Lettrism' (p. 29).

'Thus, regarding language: it is our shell and our antennae; it protects us against others and informs us about them; it is a prolongation of our senses, a third eye which is going to look into our neighbour's heart. We are within language as within our body' (p. 35).

'It must be borne in mind that most critics are men who have not had much luck and who just about the time they were growing desperate, found quiet little jobs as cemetery watchmen. God knows how peaceful cemetries are; libraries are the more cheerful of them. The dead are there: the only thing they have done is write. They have long since been washed clean of the sin of living, and besides, their lives are known only through other books which other dead men have written about them' (p. 41).

'And the literary object, though realized *through* language, is never given *in* language. On the contrary, it is by nature a silence and an opponent of the word' (Sartre's italics). In the margin: 'Merleau, indirect language' (p. 52).

'For I call a feeling generous which has its origin and its end in freedom' (p. 58). 'The world is *my* task, that is, the essential and freely accepted function of my freedom is to make that unique and absolute object which is the universe come into being in an unconditioned movement' (p. 65).

'If so, I'd like to be shown a single good novel whose express purpose was to serve oppression, a single good novel which has been written against Jews, Blacks, workers, or colonized peoples. "If there is none," it will be said, "there's no reason why one may not be written some day." But you then admit that you are an abstract theoretician. You, not I. For it is in the name of your abstract conception of art that you assert the possibility of a fact which has never come into being, whereas I limit myself to proposing an explanation for a recognized fact' (note 8, p. 335; translation modified – SC). 'the freedom to which the writer invites us is not a pure abstract consciousness of being free. Strictly speaking, it *is not* [Sartre's italics]; *it wins itself in an historical situation* [underlined in pencil]; each book proposes a concrete liberation on the basis of a particular alienation' (p. 72).

Sartre's pages on *Black Boy* by Richard Wright, whom Fanon admired at the time of *Peau noire, masques blancs*, are underlined in several places (p. 126 *sq.*), above all concerning the nature of the readership that Wright aimed at (Black bourgeoisie and White liberals in America): 'Just as one can catch a glimpse of *eternal freedom at the horizon of the historical and concrete freedom which it pursues, so too is the human race at the horizon of the concrete and historical groups of its readers.* ... But, whatever the good will of the white readers may be, for a black author they represent the *Other*. They have not lived through what he has lived through. *They can understand the negro's condition only by an extreme stretch of the imagination and by relying upon analogies which at any moment may deceive them*'

(p. 79). 'Thus, each of Wright's works contains what Baudelaire would have called a "double simultaneous postulation"; each word refers to two contexts; two forces are applied simultaneously to each phrase and determine the incomparable tension of his tale. Had he spoken to the Whites alone, he might have turned out to be more prolix, more didactic, and more abusive; to the Blacks alone, still more elliptical, more of a partner, and more elegiac. In the first case, his work might have come close to satire; in the second, to prophetic lamentations. Jeremiah spoke only to the Jews. But Wright, writing for a split public, has been able both to maintain and go beyond this split. He has made it the *prextext for a work of art*' (p. 80).

The passages on religion, classicism, enclosure in the past and situatedness also bears several marks (p. 135 *sq.*): 'since the two great earthly powers, the Church and the Monarchy, aspired only to immutability, *the active element of temporality was the past, which is itself a phenomenal degradation of the Eternal*; the present is a perpetual sin which can find an excuse for itself only if it reflects, with the least possible unfaithfulness, the image of a completed era' (p. 86). '*Literature became confused with negativity*, that is, with doubt, refusal, criticism, and opposition. But as a result of this very fact, it led to the setting up, against the ossified spirituality of the Church, of the rights of *a new spirituality, one in movement*, which was no longer identified with any ideology and which manifested itself as the power of continually surpassing the given, whatever it might be' (p. 98).

'*This impassioned sense of the present saved him [the writer] from idealism*; he did not confine himself to contemplating the eternal ideas of Freedom or Equality. For the first time since the Reformation, writers intervened in public life, protested against an unjust decree, asked for the review of a trial, and, in short, decided that the spiritual was in the street, at the fair, in the market place, at the tribunal and that it was by no means a matter of turning away from the temporal, but, on the contrary, that one had to come back to it incessantly and go beyond it in each particular circumstance' (p. 102).

'In a stable society, which is not yet conscious of the dangers threatening it, which possesses a morality, a scale of values, and a system of explanations to integrate its local changes, which is convinced that it is *beyond all historicity* and that nothing important will ever happen any more, in a *bourgeois* France tilled to the last acre, laid out like a chessboard by its secular walls, congealed in its industrial methods, and resting on the glory of its Revolution, no other fiction technique could be conceivable; the new operations that some writers have attempted to introduce were successful only as curiosities or were not followed up. Neither writers, readers, the structure of the collectivity, nor its myths had any need of them' (p. 129; translation slightly modified – SC).

'*Being situated* is an essential and necessary characteristic of freedom. To describe this situation is not to cast aspersions on freedom' (p. 133). 'The spiritual, moreover, always rests upon an ideology, and ideologies are freedom when they make themselves and oppression when they are made' (p. 138). 'In short, literature is, in essence, *the subjectivity of a society in permanent revolution*' (p. 139).

'Thus, it was not a matter [for the surrealists], as has too often been said, of substituting their unconscious subjectivity for consciousness, but rather of showing *the subject as a flimsy illusion at the heart of an objective universe. But the surrealist's second step was to destroy objectivity in turn*' (p. 152).]

Jean-Paul Sartre, *L'Imagination*, Paris: PUF, 1948.

Jean-Paul Sartre, *Les Mains sales*, Paris: Gallimard, 1948.

[On the flyleaf: 'Even if we should soil our hands, freedom will be brought to triumph. Marat. M. J. Dublé [Josie Fanon's maiden name], 29 July 1948.']

Jean-Paul Sartre, *Les Séquestrés d'Altona*, Paris: Gallimard, 1960.

Lucien Sausy, *Grammaire complète*, Paris: Librairie Fernand Lanore, 1947.

Alfred Sauvy, *Théorie générale de la population. Économie et population*, vol. 1, Paris: PUF, 1952.

Paul Savy, *Précis de pratique médicale*, Paris: G. Doin & Cie, 1942.

[On the flyleaf: 'Dr Fanon Frantz, 19, rue Salomon Reinach, Lyon.' There are many marks in the chapter on extrasystolic arrythmia.]

Paul Savy, *Traité de thérapeutique clinique*, vols. 1 and 3, Paris: Masson, 1948.

Paul Sebag, *La Tunisie. Essai de monographie*, Paris: Éditions sociales, 1951.

Gregorio Selser, *Sandino. General de hombres libres*, vol. 1, Havana: Ediciones especiales, 1960.

Seneca, *Dialogues. De la vie heureuse. De la brièveté de la vie*, vol. 2, Paris: Les Belles Lettres, 1949.

William Shakespeare, *Théâtre. Hamlet, prince de Danemark, Othello ou le Maure de Venise, Macbeth*, Paris: Beziat, 1936.

L. William Shirer, *Le Troisième Reich des origines à la chute*, Paris: Stock, 1960. (*The Rise and Fall of the Third Reich: A History of Nazi Germany*, New York, NY: Simon & Schuster, 1960.)

Miguel Sholojov, *Campos roturados*, vol. 1, Moscow: Ediciones en Lenguas Extranjeras, 1960.

René Silvain, *Rimbaud. Le précurseur*, Paris: Boivin, 1945.

Samuel R. Slavson, *Psychothérapie analytique de groupe. Enfants, adolescents, adultes*, Paris: PUF, 1953.

Edgar Snow, *La Chine en marche*, Paris: Stock, 1961.

Leonid Soboliev, *Alma marinera*, Moscow: Ediciones en lenguas extranjeras, 1955.

Albert Spaier, *La Pensée concrète. Essai sur le symbolisme intellectuel*, Paris: Félix Alcan, 1927.

Oswald Spengler, *Le Déclin de l'Occident. Esquisse d'une morphologie de l'histoire universelle*, Paris: Gallimard, 1948.

Baruch Spinoza, *Éthique. Démontrée suivant l'ordre géométrique et divisée en cinq parties*, vol. 1, Paris: Garnier, 1934.

Baruch Spinoza, *Éthique. Démontrée suivant l'ordre géométrique et divisée en cinq parties*, trans. and notes by C. Appuhn, vol. 2, Paris: Garnier, 1953.

Oliver Spurgeon English, *Problèmes émotionnels de l'existence*, Paris: PUF, 1956.

Stendhal, *Le Rouge et le Noir. Chronique du XIXe siècle*, Paris: Les Belles Éditions, n.d.

Stendhal, *La Chartreuse de Parme*, Paris: Éditions du Dauphin, 1948.

Éric Stern, *Le Test d'aperception thématique de Murray (T.A.T.). Description, interprétation, valeur diagnostique*, Neuchâtel and Paris: Delachaux et Niestlé, 1950.

August Strindberg, *Le Fils de la servante. Fermentation. Histoire d'une âme (1867–1872)*, vol. 2, Paris: Stock, 1927.

August Strindberg, *La Sonate des spectres. Pièce en trois actes*, Paris: Stock/Delamain et Boutelleau, 1949.

August Strindberg, *Le Fils de la servante. Dans la chambre rouge. L'Écrivain*, Paris: Stock/Delamain et Boutelleau, 1949.

Raphaël Tardon, *Le Combat de Schœlcher*, Paris: Fasquelle éditeurs, 1948.

[Some passages of this book by the Martinican novelist Raphaël Tardon on the abolitionist Victor Schœlcher are marked with a stroke in the margin: 'So what is a slave in the nineteenth century? It is perforce a negro, often of mixed blood, never a White, in the colonies. What is a negro slave? It is a commodity, a movable (*meuble*) – in the juridical sense of the term – an animal of a livestock, in the end a monkey' (p. 16). Writing in the margin: 'Object of property law'. 'Art. 46 [of the *Code noir*]: "For slave seizures, the formalities of our edicts and the customs for movables seizures" will be applied.' And, lastly, art. 48: 'Prohibits seizing for debt the slaves of a property or the property independently of each other' (p. 17). Writing in the margin: 'The negro is a statutory immovable'.

'No code has regulated the droit du seigneur. The negress is a female. No more' (p. 20).

'Schœlcher speaks: "M. Virey affirms that the dorsal spine of the negro is more hollow in its length and arched at its base than the White's. The negro's occipital hole (this, as is well-known, is the opening situated at the base of the skull, through which passes the spinal cord, the extension of the brain) is as with the brute far closer to the posterior part of the skull, in such a way that an African would be unable to hold his head perpendicular on his shoulders." "The white man, says the doctor, is perfectly straight, the black man leans forward ..." The size of the cervical nerves, with the negroes as with the beasts dictate that physical nature perforce wins out over moral nature. This is why negroes have more developed and active senses than Whites. They are greedy, drunkards; they have a piercing sight and a sense of smell keen enough "to scent the snakes and follow the tracks of the animals that they hunt". The negro's blood, bilious humours, viscera, bladder, etc., are impregnated with a blackish tint. (Merckel, a Prussian doctor, copying Herodotus and Aristotle, had already written in 1757 that the negroes "are a separate race of men, because their brain and their blood are black"' (p. 40).)]

Lê Thank Khôi, *Histoire de l'Asie du Sud-Est*, Paris: PUF, 1959.

Gérard Thiriet, *Contribution à l'étude des kystes vrais et des pseudo-kystes nécrotiques du pancréas*, Lyon: Bosc frères, 1949.

André Tilquin, *Le Behaviorisme, origine et développement de la psychologie de réaction en Amérique*, Paris: J. Vrin, 1942.

Leo Tolstoy, *Anna Karenine*, Moscow: Imprimeries réunies de Chambéry, 1956.

Palmiro Togliatti, *Le Parti communiste italien*, Paris: François Maspero, 1961.

Joseph de Tonquedec, *Une philosophie existentielle. L'existence d'après Karl Jaspers*, Paris: Beauchesne et ses fils, 1945.

[Several passages are underlined, bearing on the essential relations between freedom and existence in Jaspers. Thus: 'In action and decision, I am the origin (*Ursprung*) of my action and of my being at one and the same time' (p. 23). '*This choice is the decision to be myself in* Dasein ["decision" in italics in the original]. ... [He implies] that by wanting, I can be, properly speaking. ... *Decision as such is above all a leap* (or only consists in a leap: *ist erst im Sprunge*)' (p. 27). Facing the next passage, 'Engagement' is written in the margin: 'But the great source of clarity, which illuminates above all the theatre, in which freedom has to be produced, is what Jaspers calls *Weltorientierung*, orientation in the world. Man explores the universe without letting up, in order to uncover its mystery, to find himself within it and to act within it. He discovers in it, as far as the eye can see, the conditions and possibilities for action; he becomes aware of the motives that can solicit him in diverse senses' (p. 29). The title of the section 'Liberté et nécessité', in the chapter on liberty, is underlined. In this section we find familiar themes from *Peau noire, masques blancs*, in particular concerning the constitutive historicity of all human existence (p. 37).]

Sékou Touré, *L'Action politique du Parti démocratique de Guinée pour l'émancipation africaine*, Conakry: Imprimerie nationale, 1958.

Rodolphe Tourneur and François Contamin, *Dossier de pathologie médicale pour l'internat des hôpitaux de Paris*, Toulouse: Jean Bertrand, 1951.

Arnold J. Toynbee, *La Civilisation à l'épreuve*, Paris: Gallimard, 1951.

Arnold J. Toynbee, *L'Histoire. Un essai d'interprétation*, Paris: Gallimard, 1951.

Tsouen Tsing, *Le Vieux Messager*, Beijing: Éditions en langues étrangères, 1956.

Union of the populations of Angola, *Populations de l'Angola. La lutte pour l'indépendance de l'Angola. Déclaration du comité directeur de l'Union des populations de l'Angola*, 1960.

Paul Valéry, *Poésies*, Paris: Gallimard, 1942.

Paul Valéry, *Souvenirs poétiques*, Paris: Guy Le Prat, 1947.

Paul Valéry, *Traduction en vers des Bucoliques de Virgile*, Paris: Gallimard, 1956.

Gisèle Vallerey, *Contes et légendes de l'Afrique noire*, Paris: Fernand Nathan, 1955.

Joseph Vendryes, *Le Langage. Introduction linguistique à l'histoire*, Paris: Albin Michel, 1950.

Paul Verlaine, *Nos Ardennes. Huit dessins de Paul Verlaine, Ernest Delahaye, Germain Nouveau*, Geneva: P. Cailler, 1948.

Louis Vidal, *Dictionnaire de spécialités pharmaceutiques*, Paris: Office de vulgarisation pharmaceutique, n.d.

Alfred de Vigny, *Poésies complètes*, Paris: Éditions de Cluny, 1937.

Voltaire, *Zadig et autres contes*, Paris: Éditions de Cluny, 1950.

Voltaire, *L'Ingénu. Anecdotes sur Bélisaire*, Paris: Éditions sociales, 1955.

Jean Wahl, *Le Choix, le Monde, l'Existence*, Grenoble: Arthaud, 1947.

Simone Weil, *Intuitions préchrétiennes*, Paris: La Colombe, 1951.

[Pages 92 to 107 are cut. They bear on Aeschylus' *Prometheus* and its Christian posterity.]

Jean Weill and Justine Bernfeld, *Le Syndrome hypothalamique. Synthèse endocrinienne, métabolique, végétative et psychique*, Paris: Masson & Cie, 1954.

Edward Weiss and Olivier Spurgeon English, *Médecine psychosomatique. L'application de la psychopathologie aux problèmes cliniques de la médecine générale*, Neuchâtel and Paris: Delachaux et Niestlé, 1952.

Pierre Wertheimer and René Leriche, *Neurochirurgie fonctionnelle*, Paris: Masson & Cie, 1956.

Walt Whitman, *Feuilles d'herbe*, Paris: Mercure de France, 1955.

Oscar Wilde, *Le Portrait de Dorian Gray*, Paris: Stock, 1947.

[Written on the flyleaf: '26 May 1952. Errance and aberrance'.]

Thomas Wolfe, *Aux sources du fleuve*, Paris: Stock, 1929.

Richard Wright, *Les Enfants de l'oncle Tom*, Paris: Albin Michel, 1946.

Richard Wright, *Black Boy*, Paris: Gallimard, 1947. (*Black Boy (American Hunger)*, New York, NY: Harper Brothers, 1945.)

[Some passages are marked in the margins, in particular: 'Though I had long known that there were people called "white" people, it had never meant anything to me emotionally. I had seen white men and women upon the street a thousand times, but they had never looked particularly "white". To me they were merely people like other people, yet somehow strangely different because I had never come in close touch with any of them; they simply existed somewhere in the background of the city as a whole' (p. 23). 'He asked me questions in a quiet, confidential tone, and quite before I knew it he was not "white" any more' (pp. 31–2).

'And when I brooded upon the cultural barrenness of black life, I wondered if clean, positive tenderness, love, honor, joy, loyalty, and the capacity to remember were native with man. I asked myself if these human qualities were not fostered, won, struggled and suffered for, preserved in ritual form from one generation to another' (p. 37).

'I would stand for hours on the doorsteps of neighbors' houses listening to their talk, learning how a white woman had slapped a black woman, how a white man had killed a black man. It filled me with awe, wonder and fear, and I asked ceaseless questions' (p. 73).

'Like "K" of Kafka's novel, *The Castle*, he tried desperately to persuade the authorities of his true identity right up to the day of his death, and failed' (p. 140).

The first two sentences of this paragraph are marked with a line in the margin: 'Inside of me my world crashed and my body felt heavy. I stood looking down the quiet, sun-filled street. Bob had been caught by the white death, the threat of which hung over every male black in the South. I had heard whispered tales of black boys having sex relations with white prostitutes in the hotels in town, but I had never paid any close attention to them; now those tales came home to me in the form of the death of a man I knew' (p. 172).

'In my dealing with whites I was conscious of the entirety of my relations with them, and they were conscious only of what was happening at a given moment. I had to keep remembering what others took for granted; I had to think out what others felt' (p. 196).

'Here, in this underworld pocket of the building, we munched our lunches and discussed the ways of white folks toward Negroes. When two or more of us were talking, it was impossible for this subject not to come up. Each of us hated and feared the whites, yet had a white man put in a sudden appearance we would have assumed silent, obedient smiles' (p. 229).

'(There are some elusive, profound, recondite things that men find hard to say to other men; but with the Negro it is the little things of life that become hard to say, for these tiny items shape his destiny. A man will seek to express his relation to the stars; but when a man's consciousness has been riveted upon obtaining a loaf of bread, that loaf of bread is as important as the stars.)' (pp. 232–3).]

Joseph Zobel, *La Rue Cases-nègres*, Paris: Jean Froissart, 1950.

Émile Zola, *Les Rougon-Macquart. Histoire naturelle et sociale d'une famille sous le Second Empire*, Paris: Fasquelle éditeurs, 1960.

Marxism and political brochures

Chassons les impérialistes Américains de l'Asie!, Beijing: Éditions en langues étrangères, 1960.

Constitution de la République populaire de Chine. Adoptée le 20 septembre 1954 à la première session de la première Assemblée populaire nationale de la République populaire de Chine, Paris: Éditions en langues étrangères, 1960.

Constitution de la République socialiste tchécoslovaque, Prague: Orbis, 1960.

Ivo Babic, Marijan Filipovic and Mihailo Milosevic, *Les Institutions scientifiques de Yougoslavie*, Belgrade: 1958.

Commission médicale du centre culturel et économique France-USSR, *Orientation des théories médicales en URSS*, Paris: Centre culturel et économique France-URSS, 1951.

Friedrich Engels, *Études sur* Le Capital. *Suivies de deux études de Franz Mehring et de Rosa Luxemburg sur* Le Capital, Paris: Éditions sociales, 1949.

Friedrich Engels, *Anti-Dühring*, Paris: Éditions sociales, 1950.

[Alice Cherki reports that in Tunis 'Rédha Malek, who undertook studies in philosophy before 1955, gave Fanon Engel's *The Role of Force in History* and *Anti-Dühring* to read. Fanon was reserved. He found these texts too removed from the qualitative experience that an individual has of violence' (*Frantz Fanon: A Portrait*, p. 108). Most of the opening of the first chapter *Anti-Dühring* is marked with long lines in the margins. 'We know today that the *reign of reason* was nothing other than the *idealized reign of the bourgeoisie*; that eternal justice found its realization in bourgeois justice; that equality amounted to bourgeois equality before the law; that to be proclaimed as one of the essential rights of man was ... bourgeois property' (p. 50). In French translations the traditional title of Engels' essay is *Le Rôle de la violence dans l'histoire*.]

Friedrich Engels, *L'Origine de la famille. De la propriété privée et de l'État. Sur l'histoire des anciens Germains. L'époque franque. La Marche*, Paris: Éditions sociales, 1954.

Ho Chi Minh, *Œuvres choisies. Le procès de la colonisation française*, Hanoi: Éditions en langues étrangères, 1960.

[This volume carries a dedication: 'As a testament to our fraternity in struggle. Boualem and Ali. W[ilaya]4.']

Vladimir Ilitch Lenin, *L'État et la Révolution. La doctrine du marxisme sur l'État et les tâches du prolétariat dans la révolution*, Moscow: Éditions en langues étrangères, 1918.

Vladimir Ilitch Lenin, *La Maladie infantile du communisme (le communisme de gauche), essai de vulgarisation de la stratégie et de la tactique marxistes*, Paris: Éditions sociales internationales, 1930.

Vladimir Ilitch Lenin, *L'Impérialisme, stade suprême du capitalisme*, Paris: Éditions sociales, 1945.

Vladimir Ilitch Lenin, *Deux tactiques de la social-démocratie dans la révolution démocratique*, Moscow: Éditions en langues étrangères, 1949.

Vladimir Ilitch Lenin, *Notes critiques sur la question nationale. Du droit des peuples à disposer d'eux-mêmes*, Paris: Éditions sociales, 1952.

[This volume is marked in several places.]

Vladimir Ilitch Lenin, *L'Alliance de la classe ouvrière et de la paysannerie*, Moscow: Éditions en langues étrangères, 1954.

Vladimir Ilitch Lenin, *La Faillite de la IIe internationale*, Moscow: Éditions en langues étrangères, 1954.

[This volume is marked in several places.]

Vladimir Ilitch Lenin, *Que faire?*, Moscow: Éditions en langues étrangères, 1958.

Vladimir Ilitch Lenin, *Sur le parti révolutionnaire du prolétariat de type nouveau*, Beijing: Éditions en langues étrangères, 1960.

Vladimir Ilitch Lenin, *L'État et la Révolution. La doctrine du marxisme sur l'état et les tâches du prolétariat dans la révolution*, Moscow: Éditions en langues étrangères, n.d.

Vladimir Ilitch Lenin, *L'Impérialisme, stade suprême du capitalisme. Essai de vulgarisation*, Moscow: Éditions en langues étrangères, n.d.

Liu Shaoqi, *Rapport sur le projet de constitution de la République populaire de Chine. Constitution de la République populaire de Chine*, Beijing: Éditions en langues étrangères, 1954.

Liu Shaoqi, *Le Triomphe du marxisme-léninisme en Chine. Écrit pour la Nouvelle Revue internationale. Problèmes de la paix et du socialisme à l'occasion du Xe anniversaire de la République populaire de Chine, 14 septembre 1959*, Beijing: Éditions en langues étrangères, 1959.

Mao Zedong, *La Guerre révolutionnaire*, Paris: Union générale d'éditions, 1955.

Mao Zedong, *De la juste solution des contradictions au sein du peuple. Discours prononcé le 27 février 1957 à la onzième session élargie de la Conférence suprême de l'État*, Beijing: Éditions en langues étrangères, 1958.

Mao Zedong, *Analyse des classes de la société chinoise*, Beijing: Éditions en langues étrangères, 1960.

Mao Zedong, *À propos de la pratique*, Beijing: Éditions en langues étrangères, 1960.

Mao Zedong, *Contre le libéralisme*, Beijing: Éditions en langues étrangères, 1960.

Mao Zedong, *De la guerre prolongée*, Beijing: Éditions en langues étrangères, 1960.

Mao Zedong, *Discours prononcé à l'assemblée de la région frontière Chensi-Kansou-Ninghsia*, Beijing: Éditions en langues étrangères, 1960.

Mao Zedong, *Discours prononcé à une conférence des cadres de la région libérée du Chansi-Souei-Yuan*, Beijing: Éditions en langues étrangères, 1960.

Mao Zedong, *Entretien avec la journaliste américaine Anna Louise Strong*, Beijing: Éditions en langues étrangères, 1961.

Mao Zedong, *La Démocratie nouvelle*, Beijing: Éditions en langues étrangères, 1960.

Mao Zedong, *La Dictature démocratique populaire. En commémoration du 28ᵉ anniversaire du Parti communiste chinois*, Beijing: Éditions en langues étrangères, 1960.

Mao Zedong, *La Ligne politique, les mesures et les perspectives de la lutte contre l'offensive japonaise*, Beijing: Éditions en langues étrangères, 1960.

Mao Zedong, *La Révolution chinoise et le Parti communiste chinois*, Beijing: Éditions en langues étrangères, 1960.

Mao Zedong, *La Tactique de la lutte contre l'impérialisme japonais*, Beijing: Éditions en langues étrangères, 1960.

Mao Zedong, *Le Camarade Mao Tsé-toung sur* L'Impérialisme et tous les réactionnaires sont des tigres en papier. *Département de la rédaction du* Renmin Ribao (*27 October 1958*), Beijing: Éditions en langues étrangères, 1960.

Mao Zedong, *L'Impérialisme et tous les réactionnaires sont des tigres en papier*, Beijing: Éditions en langues étrangères, 1960.

Mao Zedong, *Le Rôle du Parti communiste chinois dans la guerre nationale*, Beijing: Éditions en langues étrangères, 1960.

Mao Zedong, *L'Orientation du mouvement de la jeunesse*, Beijing: Éditions en langues étrangères, 1960.

Mao Zedong, *Les Problèmes stratégiques de la guerre révolutionnaire en Chine*, Beijing: Éditions en langues étrangères, 1960.

Mao Zedong, *Les Questions de stratégie dans la guerre de partisans antijaponaise*, Beijing: Éditions en langues étrangères, 1960.

Mao Zedong, *Les Tâches du Parti communiste chinois dans la période de la résistance aux envahisseurs japonais*, Beijing: Éditions en langues étrangères, 1960.

Mao Zedong, *L'Indépendance et l'autonomie au sein du front uni*, Beijing: Éditions en langues étrangères, 1960.

Mao Zedong, *Luttons pour entraîner les masses dans le front national antijaponais uni*, Beijing: Éditions en langues étrangères, 1960.

Mao Zedong, *Luttons pour la mobilisation de toutes les forces pour remporter la victoire dans la guerre antijaponaise*, Beijing: Éditions en langues étrangères, 1960.

Mao Zedong, *Mener la révolution jusqu'au bout*, Beijing: Éditions en langues étrangères, 1960.

Mao Zedong, *Pour la parution de* Le Communiste, Beijing: Éditions en langues étrangères, 1960.

Mao Zedong, *Pourquoi le pouvoir rouge peut-il exister en Chine*, Beijing: Éditions en langues étrangères, 1960.

Mao Zedong, *Pour un gouvernement constitutionnel de démocratie nouvelle*, Beijing: Éditions en langues étrangères, 1960.

Mao Zedong, *Problèmes de la guerre et de la stratégie*, Beijing: Éditions en langues étrangères, 1960.

Mao Zedong *Rapport sur l'enquête menée dans le Hunnan à propos du mouvement paysan*, Beijing: Éditions en langues étrangères, 1960.

Mao Zedong, *Réformons notre étude*, Beijing: Éditions en langues étrangères, 1960.

Mao Zedong, *Soucions-nous davantage des conditions de vie des masses et portons plus d'attention à nos méthodes de travail*, Beijing: Éditions en langues étrangères, 1960.

Mao Zedong, *Sur les dix grands rapports*, Beijing: Éditions en langues étrangères, 1960.

Mao Zedong, *Sur quelques questions importantes de la politique actuelle du Parti*, Beijing: Éditions en langues étrangères, 1960.

Mao Zedong, *Une étincelle peut mettre le feu à toute la plaine*, Beijing: Éditions en langues étrangères, 1960.

Mao Zedong, *À propos des méthodes de direction*, Beijing: Éditions en langues étrangères, 1961.

Mao Zedong, *La Situation et notre politique après la victoire dans la guerre de résistance contre le Japon*, Beijing: Éditions en langues étrangères, 1961.

Mao Zedong, *La Situation actuelle et nos tâches*, Beijing: Éditions en langues étrangères, 1961.

Mao Zedong, *L'Élimination des conceptions erronées dans le Parti*, Beijing: Éditions en langues étrangères, 1961.

Mao Zedong, *L'Enquête à la campagne*, Beijing: Éditions en langues étrangères, 1961.

Mao Zedong, *Poèmes*, Beijing: Éditions en langues étrangères, 1961.

Mao Zedong, *Préface et postface à* L'Enquête à la campagne, Beijing: Éditions en langues étrangères, 1961.

Mao Zedong, *Raffermir le système du comité du Parti*, Beijing: Éditions en langues étrangères, 1961.

Mao Zedong, *Rapport à la deuxième session plénière du Comité central issu du VIIe congrès du Parti communiste chinois*, Beijing: Éditions en langues étrangères, 1961.

Mao Zedong, *Sur le Livre blanc américain*, Beijing: Éditions en langues étrangères, 1961.

Mao Zedong, *Sur le problème de la coopération agricole. Rapport présenté le 31 juillet 1955 à une réunion des secrétaires des comités des provinces, municipalité et régions autonomes du Parti communiste chinois*, Beijing: Éditions en langues étrangères, 1961.

Mao Zedong, *Sur les négociations de Tchongking*, Beijing: Éditions en langues étrangères, 1961.

Mao Zedong, *Sur notre politique*, Beijing: Éditions en langues étrangères, 1961.

Mao Zedong, *Sur quelques questions importantes de la politique actuelle du Parti*, Beijing: Éditions en langues étrangères, 1961.

Karl Marx, *Les Luttes de classes en France (1848–1850). Le 18-Brumaire de Louis Bonaparte*, Paris: Éditions sociales, 1948.

Karl Marx, *La Guerre civile en France, 1871*, Paris: Éditions sociales, 1953.

Karl Marx, *Salaire, prix et profit*, Paris: Éditions sociales, 1955.

Karl Marx, *Le 18-Brumaire de Louis Bonaparte*, Paris: Éditions sociales, 1956.

Karl Marx, *Contribution à la critique de l'économie politique*, Paris: Éditions sociales, 1957.

[There are some markings in the first chapter on the commodity, as well as at the start of the famous passage on the relations of Greek art and Shakespeare's art with our time (p. 174).]

Karl Marx, *Manifeste du Parti communiste*, Paris: Éditions sociales, 1960.

Karl Marx and Friedrich Engels, *Études philosophiques*, Paris: Éditions sociales, 1951.

[There are several markings on the pages on Hegel in the essay on Ludwig Feuerbach. A cut-out of newspapers from 1964 rejecting the idea that torture is still used against the counter-revolutionaries in Algeria is inserted in this volume, a sign that it was perhaps annotated by another reader.]

Georges Plekhanov, *Les Questions fondamentales du marxisme*, Paris: Éditions sociales, 1947.

[The chapters on 'La philosophie de Hegel' (up until p. 123) and 'Dialectique et logique' are marked throughout.]

Georges Plekhanov, *L'Art et la vie sociale*, Paris: Éditions sociales, 1953.

Union international des étudiants, *Réalités économiques martiniquaises*, Prague: 1960.

Récits de l'Armée rouge chinoise, Beijing: Éditions en langues étrangères, 1961.

Ts'ien Siao, *Leur Terre, ils l'ont gagnée*, Paris: Les Éditeurs français réunis, 1954.

Conference proceedings, article offprints, medical brochures

Congrès des médecins aliénistes et neurologues de France et des pays de langue française, 54ᵉ session, Bordeaux, August 30-September 4 1956. Rapport d'assistance, Paris, 1956.

Congrès des médecins aliénistes et neurologistes de France et des pays de langue française, 55ᵉ session, Lyon. Rapport de neurologie (Paul Castaigne and Jean Gambier), *Valeur des examens paracliniques au cours des accidents vasculaires cérébraux*, Paris: Masson & Cie, 1957.

Les Collagénoses. Rapports présentés au XXXIᵉ congrès français de médecine, Paris, 1957, Paris: Masson & Cie, 1957.

Jean Bancaud, Vincent Bloch and Jacques Paillard, 'Contribution EEG à l'étude des potentiels évoqués chez l'homme au niveau du vortex', *Revue neurologique*, vol. 89, no. 5, 1953.

E. Berard and Gabrielle C. Lairy-Bounes, 'Quelques remarques sur l'électro-encéphalogramme au cours de l'hibernation artificielle',

Electroencephalography and Clinical Neurophysiology, vol. 7, no. 4, November 1955.

Henry Christy, 'Encéphalite psychosique suivie d'un syndrome de démence précoce. Pyrétothérapie. Apparition d'un érythème noueux. Rémission actuelle', *Comptes rendus du congrès des médecins aliénistes et neurologistes*, Brussels, 22–28 July 1935.

Henry Christy, 'Phénomènes de balancement psychosomatique. Expression particulière d'une loi générale dans les localisations viscérales tuberculeuses. Rôle du terrain', *Comptes rendus du congrès des médecins aliénistes et neurologistes*, Nancy, 30 June–3 July 1937.

Henry Christy, 'Discussion du rapport de M. Hans W. Maier sur la thérapeutique des psychoses dites fonctionnelles', *Comptes rendus du congrès des médecins aliénistes et neurologistes*, Bâle-Zurich-Berne-Neuchâtel, 20–25 July 1936.

Georges Daumézon, Yves-Henri Champion and Jacqueline-Louise Champion-Basset, 'Étude démographique et statistique des entrées masculines nord-africaines à l'hôpital psychiatrique Sainte-Anne de 1945 à 1952', *L'Hygiène mentale*, no. 43, 1954, pp. 1–20 and 85–107.

Michelle B. Dell, Colette Dreyfus-Brisac and Gabrielle C. Lairy-Bounes, 'Le problème des complexes pointe-onde dans l'épilepsie', *L'Encéphale*, no. 4, 1953, pp. 353–76.

Michelle B. Dell, 'L'électroencéphalographie dans l'épilepsie', *Encyclopédie médicochirurgicale, Psychiatrie, Méthodes de diagnostic*, 1955.

James Gray, 'Le mécanisme du mouvement ciliaire' [translation of 'The mechanisms of ciliary movement. Photographic and stroboscopic analysis of ciliary movement', *Proceedings of the Royal Society of Biology*, no. 107, 1930, pp. 313–18].

Paul Hazoumé, 'La révolte des prêtres', *Présence africaine*, nos. 8-9-10, June–November 1956, pp. 29–42. Actes du 1ᵉʳ Congrès international des écrivains et artistes noirs, held at the Sorbonne from 19 to 22 September 1956.

[It is hardly surprising that Paul Hazoumé's remarkable article attracted Fanon's attention, since it joins his interests on the relation between religion and madness, popular spirituality and the disalienation of the colonized. The set of events and ceremonies which Hazoumé describes and which amounts to a revolt by the caste of priests in Dahomey upon an individual expressing a sacrilegeous opinion (for example, by stubbornly calling a priest by his previous layperson's name), consist in organizing an outbreak of social 'madness', to the point of blocking all economic activity, and reasserting this caste's power over the political authorities. Hazoumé concludes his articles with a comparison with the profanations demanded by atheist as well as falsely religious colonialists and suggests the possibility of future outbursts against the colonial power, henceforth denuded of all spiritual authority. See also the discussion between Hazoumé and Achille (a friend of Fanon's) on the relations between 'animist beliefs and the inevitable spread of the scientific spirit' (p. 79).]

Laboratoires Laroche-Navarron, *Actualités sur le diabète. 5ᵉ partie, 'Le coma diabétique'*, scientific documentation, record no. 25, January 1954.

Laboratoires Laroche-Navarron, 'Le virilisme pilaire de la femme: définition', scientific documentation, record no. 26, January 1955.

Laboratoires Laroche-Navarron, 'Données récentes sur la cortine naturelle Laroche-Navarron', scientific documentation, record no. 40, January 1956.

Gabrielle C. Lairy-Bounes and Joseph Benbanaste, 'Quelques aspects électroencéphalographiques particuliers des syndromes post-traumatiques tardifs', *Annales de médecine légale*, vol. 34, no. 1, 1954.

Jacques Rabemananjara, 'L'Europe et nous', *Présence africaine*, nos. 8-9-10, June–November 1956, pp. 20–8. Proceedings of the 1ᵉʳ Congrès international des écrivains et artistes noirs, held at the Sorbonne from 19 to 22 September, 1956.

[Rabemananjara's famous address expresses a distance to the idea of négritude (nevertheless associated with an admiration for Césaire) that is similar to Fanon's position in many points.]

Léopold Sédar Senghor, 'L'esprit de la civilisation ou les lois de la culture négro-africaine', *Présence africaine*, nos. 8-9-10, June–November 1956, pp. 20–8. Proceedings of the 1ᵉʳ Congrès international des écrivains et artistes noirs, held at the Sorbonne from 19 to 22 September 1956.

Georges Verdeaux and Jacqueline Verdeaux, 'Étude électro-encéphalographique d'un groupe important de délinquants primaires ou récidivistes au cours de leur détention', *Annales médicopsychologiques*, 113th year, vol. 2, November 1955, pp. 644–58.

Georges Verdeaux and Gabrielle C. Lairy-Bounes, 'Valeur et limites actuelles de l'électroencéphalographie en criminologie'.

Georges Verdeaux, 'Utilisation de l'électroencéphalographie dans l'expertise médico-légale', *L'Encéphale*, vol. 47, no. 1, February 1958, pp. 1–30.

World Health Organization, 'L'hôpital psychiatrique public', *Troisième rapport du Comité d'experts de la santé mentale, Série de rapports techniques*, no. 73, November 1953.

Periodicals

Bulletin de l'ordre des médecins, 1953: 4; 1956: 2.
Cahiers du communisme, 1950: 12; 1954: 6–7.
Cahiers du Sud, 1948: 291; 1953: 320.
Cahiers internationaux de sociologie, 1952: vol. 12; 1965: vol. 39.
Esprit, 1948: 10; 1952: 5–6; 1953: 2, 4, 5, 8, 9; 1954, 5; 1955: 6, 7, 12; 1956: 6, 9.
L'Évolution psychiatrique. Cahiers de psychologie clinique et de psychopathologie générale, 1929: 1; 1931: 2; 1947: 1–4; 1948: 1, 2; 1949: 2–4; 1950: 1; 1953: 2.

[Some of the texts published in this important journal are not easily accessible. Since they provide the background of the evolution of his psychiatric thought, I give extensive quotes from issues Fanon anotated.

In issue 2 of 1947, the article by Jan Hendrik van Den Berg, 'Bref exposé de la position phénoménologique en psychiatrie', has been attentively read, in particular concerning the distinction, which phenomenology suspends, between the subjective and the objective. Most of the annotations seem to indicate a certain distance. The following phrase is marked and annotated: 'The demand of *the pre-reflexive attitude* (die Vorwissenschaftlichkeit) *is to let speak all that exists in order to give it the possibility to show what it is in reality, that is to say, its essence, its sense.*' Annotation: 'this is only *one* aspect of the phenomenological approach' (p. 30).

In volume 4 of 1947, Sacha Nacht's article, 'Le rôle du moi dans la structure du caractère et du comportement', contains several marks. The passages on the psychoanalysis of masochism, of fear and of failure neurosis are especially underlined (with a reference in the margin to Lacan concerning the primary identification at the oral stage, p. 62).

In issue 2 of 1948, titled 'Neuropsychiatrie', Henri Hécaen's article on 'La notion de schéma corporel et ses applications en psychiatrie' is abundantly underlined and favourably commented. We know that the notion of the body schema, inherited from Lhermitte and from Merleau-Ponty, is crucial in *Peau noire, masques blancs* and *L'An V de la révolution algérienne*, since what the racist gaze produces is conceived in it as a pathology of the body schema.[7] Fanon marks with

---

[7] See Jean Khalfa, 'Fanon, *corps perdu*', *Les Temps modernes*, nos. 635–6, November–December 2005/January 2006).

a '*Bien*' ('Good') and a '*Oui*' ('Yes') the following paragraphs: 'What we said above about the development of the ego images enables us to conceive that the affective disorders are liable to modify the knowledge of our body. It does not appear impossible to admit that the incessant alternate process of construction and of destruction, which gives us our model of posture, no longer works, or at least is abnormally realized, when the *energy* that maintains and directs it, that is to say the emotional processes, is perturbed. [Added: "*Cf.* Janet."]. It will easily be grasped that, in anxious melancholias in which the subject's aggressiveness gets intensely expressed against his own ego, identified, according to the psychoanalysts, with the lost object, knowledge of the physical ego, henceforth deprived of its propulsive element, fades until its disappears from consciousness or is only manifested there in a strange fashion' (p. 97).

In the margin of a reflection on heautoscopy (the perception of one's body as split into two) in its link with introspective habits: '*Cf.* J.P. Sartre's self-observation, related by M. MP in his "phéno de perception"' (p. 110).

The following phrase is marked with a 'most certainly': 'The feeling of the physical ego cannot be separated from that of the moral ego, both being profoundly integrated together by our affective life, which assures their unity; all that tends to dissociate one is reflected in the other. No distinction can be formally made between depersonalization and hemiasomatognosia [affection where the patient does not recognize the paralysed part of his body as his own]' (p. 112).

Significant disagreement is also expressed. Hence, on p. 114, Hécaen designates as a schizophrenic one of his patients 'all of whose activities are now only centered on the search for the ideal ego that he possessed in his younger years' and whose bodily perception is totally deformed.' This observation is annotated in the margin with a: 'No! This is a *psychasthenic* patient.' Psychasthenia, a concept forged by Janet to designate a pathology involving a fundamental inadaptation to social life, was an essential parameter for Fanon.

In issue 1 of 1949, Hubert Mignot's article, 'Étude critique de l'exploration du psychisme sous état hypnagogique provoqué par les barbituriques', was read and marked with care. The point of it was to examine 'narco-analysis'.

Issue 3 of 1949 is important owing to Henri Ey's article on the 'Efficacy of Psychotherapy'. Fanon's annotations reveal his preoccupations at the time, such as the one bearing on these sentences: 'For us, only a dynamist conception of the relations between the physical and the moral, which presumes that the latter is a form of integration of the former, can enable us to overcome these difficulties. By virtue of this hypothesis, which seems to us to conform to the nature of things, mental illness is defined as a *regression of psychic life conditioned by a disorder of its organic infrastructure.*' Concerning this summary of organo-dynamism, which emphasizes the organic aspect, Fanon wrote: 'Beware! [*Alerte!*]' (p. 291).

Similarly, on p. 292, the first part of the following paragraph is marked with a 'yes', whereas the second is marked with a 'Beware!': 'This way of looking at things situates at the centre of every "mental illness" the individual sufferers' psychic life (that is, the totality of relational life), such that this mental illness appears phenomenologically as a way of being inferior as regards adaptation to reality, to society, to events, but all the same as a way of "being-in-the-world", a disturbed *"Dasein"*, the object of a structural analysis or of a necessary *"Daseinanalysis."* But it supposes that this abnormal organization of psychic life *depends* on an inherited or acquired disorder of the *organic* infrastructure, the essential object of a physiopathology. It is evident, as a result, that it posulates both the necessity and the limit of psychotherapy.'

On p. 297: the following paragraph is marked with a line in the margins and a cross: 'What we call "psychosis" is hardly an immobile and static structure with rigid nosographical characteristics, but a certain more or less typical form of evolution, which passes via a series of levels of dissolution and secondary organization of the personality – and, during this psychopathological "work", *some phases* are favorable to psychotherapy. The entire *practical* problem consists in accurately evaluating evolutive work and not losing sight of the opportunities for the psychotherapeutic act, which may be decisive.'

We then find some marks on Eugène Minkowski's article on 'Les voies d'accès à l'inconscient', displaying some skepticism concerning the diverse distinctions examined pertaining to the unconscious and consciousness, such as the possibility of explaining the unconscious as a conservation 'in the form of traces of a physiological order' (annotation: 'Slippery terrain!'), and towards all static conceptions. On the other hand, Minkowski's presentation of Janet's conception of things is marked with a line and a cross: 'Here, the unconscious trace, if trace there is, hardly serves in being evoked from time to time, but it is what at a given moment will determine my conduct;

far from serving for the simple reproduction of the past, it will bear within it a sort of propulsion toward the future, which at the desired time will enter into action. I recall here the role that Pierre Janet attributed to the *deferred act* in the constitution of the notion of time: he considers it to be the first element' (p. 390). Janet's dynamic ontology indeed has important echoes in Fanon's dissertation.

The following sentences, which might appear Wittgenstinian, define consciousness in the pragmatic terms of 'lived experience'. They are marked with a line in the margin: ['Remorse, hope, prayer, belief] exceed the "field of consciousness", not in the sense that they are situated outside this field, but in the sense that they are associated with an entirely different way of being, which, much larger, overflows the one determined by the couple conscious/subconscious. They pertain to *lived experience (le vécu)*; and consciousness, together with its field, now seems to detach from this lived experience, in part by impoverishing it, and to be only one of its forms, and certainly not the most alive one' (p. 393). Such a conception corresponds to the descriptions that Fanon gives both of the experience of racism (lived experience structuring the alienated consciousness) and of the colonial reification of cultures, transformed into 'forms' of consciousness and into objects of knowledge.

The conception of the unconscious as *depth* of consciousness, underlined in the following sentences, is indeed necessary to an analysis of ideology: 'Besides the conscious, there is the *lived* (vécu), with the features that are proper to it. The latter, which is much larger, embraces the former' (p. 394). 'All that is connected to research, creation, discovery, is in part elaborated outside of the operations of conscious thought to *arise*, or better still *burst out* [*jaillir*], at a given moment, certainly not in the details, but in a condensed view of the whole, in the manner of a ray of light, within consciousness' (p. 395). 'This unconscious is situated in relation to the conscious not under the sign of the "alongside", as is the subconscious in the field of the conscious, but under the sign of *depth*. It constitutes the ground [*fond*] of our life, from which spring the very personal, diverse experiences of this life' (p. 397).

This paragraph on time is marked with a 'Yes': 'Past, present, future are hardly for us simply "cardinal points", slices of time, but instead present, each for itself, as I have attempted to show in previous works, a particular mode of living of time. These differences have also been found here in relation to the unconscious' (p. 399).

Concerning a paragraph in which it is stated that, 'the unconscious is not exclusively a deposit of repressed complexes', Fanon notes: 'Good God! Is it so difficult – especially for a philosopher – to "signify" the libido by recognizing it as an *indeterminate* power of "fixation" and of "investment"?' (p. 401). In a page on the need to preserve the relation of consciousness to liberation and therefore to revise the role attributed to the unconscious, Minkowski writes: '*It is consciousness which liberates.*' Fanon underlines the word 'alone' here: 'On the psychological and philosophical level it is thus affirmed – and this seems to me important above all else – that this faculty to liberate and to liquidate is a fundamental trait of consciousness alone' (p. 403). The following paragraph is marked with a 'Yes' ('Oui'): 'Every doctrine relative to the human being must respect the fundamental features that confer on this being the human aspect and that thereby comprise its essence. There thus exists for doctrines of this sort a specific *criterion of the human*. They take a fatally wrong path inasmuch as they move away from it through an *excessive* concern for what it is customary to call a scientific explanation, based on the principles of evolution, causality, determinism and universal ends' (pp. 403–4).

Lastly, p. 404, which raises an important question about the nature of the unconscious and the complex, is amply annotated: 'The opposition between latent and manifest dream content, and, thereafter, between the latent and manifest content of psychosis, leads us to a crossroads. At this point the paths diverge: does the latent content condition the dream state or solely determine its content? [Fanon's annotation: "Why *abstract* the signification from the content?"]. It certainly seems that the answer ought to concur with the second sense. Similarly, for psychosis. But thereupon the generative role of the complex comes to be limited; it only appears to be called to secondarily fill with a precise content the particular form of life, itself determined by other mechanisms. It may well be that the psychogenesis to which psychoanalysis lays claim is in actual fact neither genesis nor "psycho".' The annotation in the margin of these last two sentences reads: 'In other terms: *reductibility* of the complex to primary forms of signification, i.e. seek in the complex – as archaic as it may be – the announcement and the first sketch of the human *drama*.'

Issue 3 (1950) carries the stamp of the medical library of the psychiatric hospital of Saint-Ylie (where Fanon had his first position). It is a special issue paying 'Homage to Pierre Janet'. There is no annotation, but it is indicative of Janet's importance for Fanon that he held onto this issue.

In the table of contents of issue 4 (1950), many articles are marked with a cross, which Fanon did to indicate the important sections of a book or of a journal. Alexandre Vexliard's remarkable article on 'Le clochard, les phases de la désocialisation' [The tramp, phases of de-socialization] is marked throughout.[8] Thus in the analysis of the third phase of regressive adaptation of the homeless person to the situation of social destitution, Fanon marks the following paragraph with several lines: 'Consciousness, whose usual role is to be a guide for action, is barely able to keep up with the events that devalorise the ego. However, if the individual effectively had an awareness of his situation, he would have been able to adopt in advance dispositions that would (perhaps) have allowed him to adapt better to the new situation instead of seeking to re-establish the past' (p. 633). The article's conclusion is underlined with a thick line: 'The social contact [*contact social*] is broken, because the needs, the motivations, the values and the mechanisms of behaviour, which enable a normal social life, have almost completely disappeared, under the invading upsurge of an existence in which the old values have lost all signification, all power to inspire' (p. 639).

The second article marked in this issue is Hubert Mignot's analysis of Henri Ey's thought in his *Études psychiatriques*. In it, Fanon underlines everything that concerns the relation to time and memory. Thus, among the numerous passages pointed to, we find this paragraph, which corresponds clearly to Fanon's analysis of the relation to memory in colonial alienation, in which the past has no longer any relation with possible existence: 'And to conclude, H. Ey emphasizes that "memory disorders can be considered as the phenomenological substance of all the symptoms of the neuroses and the psychoses, insofar as they are more or less direct effects of the *dissolution of consciousness*, i.e., of the alteration of the links that unite in time the form of existence currently lived to buried existence and to possible existence"' (p. 647). Notable also are some marks on the relations between the spatial order of cerebral localisations and the temporal order of evolution in psychiatry in the article that Ey devotes to Guiraud's *Psychiatrie*

---

[8]On Vexliard, pioneer of the psychosociological analysis of social destitution, see Laurent Mucchielli, 'Clochards et sans-abri: actualité de l'œuvre d'Alexandre Vexliard', *Revue française de sociologie*, vol. 39, no. 1, 1998, pp. 105–38.

générale (to which Fanon's dissertation refers), in particular p. 653. Elsewhere in this issue, some marks are to be found that underline in particular Fanon's interest in the developments of psychosomatic medicine in the United States, but no annotation is made on the edifying review that Henri Aubin wrote about Sartre's *Orphée noir*. Aubin, one of Porot's former students and a contributor to the sections of colonial ethnography in the *Manuel alphabétique de psychiatrie* (Paris: PUF, 1952), sees Sartre's article as an attempt at a 'sincere comprehension of the black soul'. He notes, however, that 'recent physiological research reveals in the Black of tropical Africa certain electro-encephalographic characteristics that attest to an "incontestable neuronal immaturity" of the cortex'. If Fanon read this article (marked with a cross in the table of contents), perhaps he found in it an opportunity to reflect in parallel on negritude and on contemporary ethnopsychiatry. There is no mark in issue 1 from 1951, but it contains the second part of Vexliard's article as well as an article, cut, by E.L.K. Zeldenrust, on 'L'art et la folie: étude ontologique et anthropologique' [Art and madness, ontological and anthropological study], which revisits (p. 84) Ey's reflections on art and madness in the study on psychiatry and surrealism, which Fanon cited in his dissertation.]

L'Information psychiatrique. Livraisons mensuelles publiées par le Syndicat des médecins des hôpitaux psychiatriques, 1954: 1–10 (3 is missing); 1955: 1–10; 1956: 1–10 (4 is missing).

[No. 1 of 1955 is dedicated to psychiatry in the colonies. This is the issue in which Fanon and his collaborators published 'Current aspects of mental care in Algeria'. The article of Doctor Le Mappian on 'La psychiatrie à l'île de la Réunion' depicts the difficulties of conducting psychotherapies in the local milieu there (see p. 43 in particular).]

La Nouvelle Critique, 1953: 45; 1954: 51, 53; 1955: 66, 67.

[No. 66, from June 1955, is a special issue on the theme of 'Racism, colonialism and civilization'. It contains a famous article by Maxime Rodinson, 'Racisme et civilisation', which targets the 'agnosticism of bourgeois ethnography', which is ignorant of Marxism; the underlined passage in the following sentence is also marked with two lines made with a pen in the margin: 'But it is necessary to see clearly that the attitude that I have just described [the relativism that consists in putting all "cultures" on the same level] serves many ethnologists

(I do not say all), whether consciously or not, to support a policy that *locks the "native" within his tribal, archaic life, within his traditional activities* (since all civilizations are equivalent and since "progress does not produce happiness"), whereas the Whites continue to bear their burden, as Kipling cynically said: the government of these sympathetic peoples' (pp. 131–2).]

La Nouvelle Revue française, 1948: 10; 1953: 6; 1954: 16–17; 1955: 25.
La Nouvelle Revue internationale, 1959: 14, 16. *Les Lettres et les Arts*, 1956: 1.

[This issue, edited by Michel Beaugency and Henri Kréa (see the dedication to Fanon in his book *supra*), contains a section titled 'Trois poètes noirs: Charles Calixte, Édouard Glissant, Léopold Sédar Senghor'.]

Les Temps modernes, 1948: 29, 31, 32; 1949: 48, 49, 50, 52; 1951: 63, 68, 70, 73, 74; 1952: 75, 76, 78, 79, 81, 82, 83; 1953: 92, 93–4; 1954: 102, 108; 1955: 109, 110, 111, 114, 115; 1956: 121, 122, 126.

[In no. 29 from 1948, the second part of Francis Jeanson's article 'La récrimination' (published in three parts in nos. 28, 29 and 30) is marked right throughout. For example: 'Thus may I recriminate against the evil of living in a world in which my life is stolen from me just as I may against one in which I *wanted my life to be mine fully* [note in the margin: "Fanciful self-possession"] and where I come up against the impossibility to assert myself once and for all. These two forms of recrimination I will now bring to light by addressing, by turns, the diverse aspects of the situation in the sense I have already made clear, that is to say in what in it seems to be *objective and fatal – for a consciousness, all of whose effort consists precisely in admitting that everything already has a meaning, and that this meaning does not depend upon it*' (p. 1420). Annotation in the margin: '*Cf. Robert Browning* (life has a meaning and it is vital for the ego to discover it)'. '"When my meaning is not at stake" I identify myself with my body – and this is why I hold to it so much. However, because in that the "I" will be able to escape itself into an irresponsible gaze, this "me" will become frozen as an "object", as a bundle of characteristics, as a "character," a temperament, a nature; correlatively, my body will receive from this a sort of objectivated, solidified signification. But when a difficulty arises, when I suddenly find myself in immediate peril, then I frankly break with this body and this "me"; *having turned them into objects*, I can become disinterested with them, I can leave them behind to constitute myself as a pure subject – and this is close to what André Breton said, in the wake of Freud: *that in case of a serious scare, the psychic accent is withdrawn from the ego and transferred to the "superego"'* (p. 1422). In *Peau noire, masques blancs*, Fanon notes that such a break is not possible for anyone who is the object of the racist gaze.

Next to a passage on death, we find this annotation in the margin: 'Read the formidable chapter of *L'Être et le Néant*, "My Death"'[9] (p. 1429). 'If the thought of death can spoil my life and prevent me from really living it, then this occurs to the extent to which I persist *childishly* [underlined with a double line] *to think of death* as being for me the supreme peril and the most definitive of catastrophes. [Annotation: "This is indeed a fundamental ineptitude". And we cite merely for our recollection the Spinozist thought according to which *"a free man thinks of death least of all things, and his wisdom is a meditation not of death but of life* [this last word is underlined with a double line]", a thought that ought obviously to be constrasted with the opposite tradition, which leads to Heidegger' [Annotation: 'And his "being-toward death"'] (p. 1430).

'As we see, all these behaviours are understood in reference to some *absolute self-possession*. Whether I abandon myself to the anonymity of a collective destiny or I rise up without respite against any despoliation, wherever it comes from, it is always for having *posited* [underlined with a double line] in principle that *the ideal form of existence and the perfect type of happiness resided in the total satisfaction of my right of propriety over myself.*' Annotation facing '*absolute self-possession*': 'That is, coincidence of self with self–abolition of that distance to the self whose permanence conditions all authentic "lack of being"'[10] (p. 1432).

---

[9]See Jean-Paul Sartre, *Being and Nothingness*, trans. Hazel E. Barnes, London: Methuen 1957, pp. 531–53. It is evident that Fanon also found the previous section interesting, 'My Fellowman', pp. 509–31, in particular pp. 525–31 on the 'total alienation of the person' produced by the racist gaze in the case of anti-Semitism, a theory developed in *Réflexions sur la question juive*, which Fanon mentions several times in *Peau noire, masques blancs*.

[10]On the 'lack of being', see Sartre, *Being and Nothingness*, p. 129 *sq*. It is well-known just how Fanon was able to commit himself absolutely while always putting into question what had seemed to be of the order of certainties, as his analysis of neo-colonialism also shows. The ending of *Peau noire, masques blancs* is a celebration of the very posture of questioning as an ultimate end.

Facing the following description of an attitude refusing engagement, 'BIEN' ('GOOD') and 'that is the node of the *inauthentic*': 'At issue – in the narrow frame of my life or in its compact vacuity, made of perpetual refusals – not *to give way to the* upheaval of the instant, *to the catastrophic upsurge of an interrogation that would no longer be part of the system, but would put the entire system in question*' (p. 1435). 'All efforts at moralization imply a *practice of the social as a human milieu, a place of ineluctable co-existence* [this last term is underlined twice] for beings *each one of whom possesses inwardly the same power of liberation*, but whose situations differ on the exterior and *none of whom could manage to liberate themselves all alone*' (p. 1445).

In no. 31 (1948), Harold Rosenberg's article, 'The Stages: Geography of Action', translated as 'Du jeu au je. Esquisse d'une géographie de l'action', an article on the theatre, in particular Shakespeare, is marked in several places, above all at the points concerning the free act, human will, spontaneity and madness (pp. 1740 *sq.*). There are also some marks in the text of Sartre's *Mains sales* (pp. 1773 and 1800).

In no. 50 (1949), Francis Pasche's article, 'Le psychanalyste sans magie', contains several marks. The article aims to reply to Lévi-Strauss' critique, which compares psychoanalysis to chamanism, whose therapeutic successes can be reduced to 'a simple reintegration into the irrational system of beliefs of the group' (p. 961). The following paragraph is marked with an 'Of course!': 'What is left is to examine the most serious accusation that can be made against psychoanalysis: "Perhaps you abolish domestic cults, but to the benefit of a state religion, since by interpreting as a disorder of familial origin that which may result from a conflict of classes, you deliver the patient to the collective myths that alienate him. You cure him by *adapting* him, whatever the cost, to the society of which you are both part, even if it is untenable in reality, which comes down to absolving the objectively privileged oppressor and to getting the oppressed to accept his yolk"' (p. 971). Annotations in the margin: 'Official psychoanalysis can have no other ambition'. Further below, opposite the last sentence: 'Absolute regression in relation to the "previous conflict situation".' 'Our ambition will there be, to adopt Lévi-Strauss' terminology, to disadapt them [the exploited]: the awakening of their social consciousness and not euthanasia.' In the margin: 'I doubt so' (p. 972).

No. 57 (1950) contains Francis Jeanson's review of Octave Mannoni's book *Psychologie de la colonisation*. It contains no mark or annotation.

This subtle and dense analysis ought probably to be related to Fanon's ambivalence toward Mannoni in *Peau noire, masques blancs*.

No. 60 (1950) contains Else Frenkel Brunswik and R. Nevitt Sanford's article 'La personnalité antisémite. Essai sur quelques conditions psychologiques de l'antisémitisme.' The several marks in this text, which undertakes an analysis of the anti-Semitic personality, show that Fanon may have been interested in it not only on account of the topic (in *Peau noire, masques blancs*, he states that Sartre's 1946 book *Réflexions sur la question juive* is essential to his own thought), but also for its use of psychological tests based on the interpretation of images.

On the back of no. 81 (July 1952), which contains the first part of Sartre's article 'Les communistes et la paix', there is the following handwritten note: 'Vocabulary of psychiatry, of psychology. Husserl's *Ideas* by Ricœur. Coll. TM'.]

Présence africaine, 1947: 1, 1948: 4, 5; 1949: 7; 1950: 8/9; 1951: 10/11, 12

[In no. 4 of 1948, Horace R. Cayton's article, 'A psychological approach to race relations', is marked right throughout and its title is circled and marked with a cross in the table of contents. Similarly, there are some marks on Paul Niger's long poem, which follows it, 'Je n'aime pas l'Afrique' ['I do not like Africa'].

In no. 7 from 1949, Francis Jeanson's important article on 'Sartre et le monde noir' ['Sartre and the black world'] is heavily marked. The following passage is annotated in the margin with 'yes'. *Oncle Rémus*' (Fanon discusses the tales of Uncle Remus and the film that Disney made of it in 1946 in *Peau noire, masques blancs*): 'The master expects from the slave something in addition to his work: he expects him to perform without any reticience at all, and to present his perfect resignation through a perfectly carefree attitude' (p. 209). A good part of p. 214 is marked, in particular: 'Moreover, the entire question is to know to what extent incomprehension, hostility and bad faith will play here against the black revolutionaries and reject them either on the side of a forgetting of the universal meaning that their project bears, or else on the side of its hijacking for the benefit of some theoretical certainty, some vain arrogance as regards history.'

No. 12 from 1951 is an important issue, edited by Alfred Métraux, and devoted to 'Haïti: poètes noirs'.]

Présences. Revue trimestrielle du 'monde des malades', 1956: 54, 'Le malade mental. *Qu'en avons-nous fait?*'

[There are no marks, but this issue does include several articles by psychiatrists that Fanon knew, for example Philippe Paumelle ('Folie et conscience de la maladie'), Paul Balvet and Nicole Guillet ('Le malade mental, un malade comme les autres'), Louis Le Guillant and Paul Béquart ('Relations avec les familles et le milieu extérieur'), Paul Sivadon ('La sortie de l'hôpital psychiatrique') and Jean Oury ('Désaliénation en clinique psychiatrique').]

Psyché. Revue internationale des sciences de l'homme et de psychanalyse, 1948: 15; 1949: 27–8.

[No. 15 contains the first part of Octave Mannoni's article, 'Ébauche d'une psychologie coloniale. Le complexe de dépendance et la structure de la personnalité.' It is unmarked.

Nos. 27–8 contain Maryse Choisy's 'Quelques réflexions sur la guerre de la paix', Angelo Hesnard's 'Le drame de l'aveu' and René Laforgue's 'Au-delà du scientisme. Freud et le monothéisme. Psychologie du mérite.' Fanon has amply annotated Choisy's article, whose work on collective guilt *L'Anneau de Polycrate* he cites in *Peau noire, masques blancs*. Some passages are marked, in particular on creation, genius and boredom. Also, we find this citation of Nicolas Berdiaeff: 'If communism threatens the mind with its totalitarianism, socialism threatens it *with its boredom and its mondanity*. The problem of boredom is a serious problem. The virus of boredom exists in all Christian parishes of all confessions as well as in traditional Christian literature, which in this regard is able to compete with the socialist press. The antidote to boredom is creative power or the power of hatred' (p. 71).

On p. 78, there is a half-sheet of paper that serves as a bookmark and has typed and handwritten text on it: '*Éléments pour une éthique* de Nabert', p. 110: 'Well, as humble, as fleeting as it may be, at the first, the feeling of contrast between the *depth of inclination* and the *satisfaction received* after the tendency had in some sense been thrown outside of itself *on the search for the object*, it is the condition of possibility, as much as the indice, of a consciousness in which a desire is born that is no longer to be confounded with object-oriented desire, that is, the desire that depends on the object and only knows itself as such through the interval that separates it out from it, through the resistances it encounters and through the internal tensions accompanying them. This desire that awakens in the depths of desire attests that consciousness, which was only the experience of a certain opposition that simultanesously had to be endured and overcome, does not move back into the night. Since, in order to shed light on the tendency, it makes use of the light it owes to the contraried expansion of the inclination.' The piece of paper is torn here. On the back: 'Since the subjectivity that is produced to appease this opposition can do so only by an appropriation of the inclination for a goal that it is called to serve, although it passes over it. Whereby is discovered that paradox of ethics according to which the roots of the liking ought never be cut, to which the sap of the liking must circulate through the most distant ends of the primary function of the tendency.' This dialectic (which is a religious one in Nabert's work) of a desire that, by reflecting on its very exercise, unties itself progressively from the object, may well have found Hegelian echoes in Fanon. It was to be transformed in one of his contemporaries, Deleuze, into a theory of desire no longer as a lack of object but as creativity.

A handwritten note on another piece of paper is inserted in this issue: 'Grace and merit. Health, said Laforgue (*Psyché*, 27–8, p. 41), is a balance between several illnesses. Eliminate one of them and illness explodes. Laforgue does not conceive of the good without the bad. The moral ghetto.'

Two other articles are marked: Marie-Madeleine Davy, 'Des limites de la psychanalyse à la forme de la mystique', the marked passage is as follows: 'Delusion is characterized by a false interpretation of everyday events, whereas the *mystical sentiment allows common sense to subsist entirely*' (p. 110); François Piazza, 'Sur le *Chien andalou* de Luis Buñuel et Salvador Dalí'. This is a 'psychoanalytic examination of the essential themes of the screenplay'. The parts of the article devoted to the symbolism of the film sequences (pp. 148–54) are underlined in multiple places.]

Revue de la nouvelle médecine, 1953: 1, 2; 1954: 3.

[This was a journal put together by communist doctors and edited by Yves Cachin. There are several articles linked to Pavlov or bearing on medicine in the USSR or in Romania. No. 3 is devoted to painless childbirth.]

Revue française de psychanalyse, 1948; 3, 4; 1949: 2.

[In no. 3 of 1948, there are some marks in the article by Nacht on 'Les manifestations cliniques de l'agressivité et leur rôle dans le traitement psychanalytique'. Lacan's article on 'L'agressivité en psychanalyse' is not marked.

In no. 4 of 1948, Marie Bonaparte's article 'De l'angoisse devant la sexualité (notes du 23 juillet 1935)' is copiously marked. Mostapha Ziwar's article, 'Psychanalyse des principaux syndromes psychosomatiques', which undertakes a systematic analysis of cases of physical disorders (asthma, ulcers, hypertension, etc.) to relate them to neuroses, was carefully read and marked in several places. Many of the bibliographical references are underlined. Fanon took an early interest in psychosomatic medicine, which would later come to play a major role in his understanding of the 'lived experience' of alienation. See *The Psychiatric Writings from Alienation and Freedom*, pp. 9 and 107.

This paragraph, which sheds light on certain psychogenic vision disorders, is marked with two lines in the margin: 'Freud thus distinguishes two categories of functional disorders; one of a physical nature and that essentially consists in physiological alterations brought about by the untimely use of a given function; and another that includes functional disorders with a precise unconscious meaning, disorders that are the expression of fantasies in a bodily language and are directly accessible to psychoanalysis in the same way as dreams. These disorders are evidently "conversions". The former are currently referred to as psychosomatic' (pp. 507–8).

The article's conclusion (p. 539) is marked with a cross: 'However, it is necessary to consider these psychological characteristics as etiological factors. The specificity of the psychic picture does not imply psychogenesis, no more, moreover, than the therapeutic successes obtained by psychoanalysis. As Bonger and his collaborators point out, in the current state of our knowledge, we can only consider psychic disorders and somatic disturbances to be two expressions of the fundamental failure of adaptation.'

Fernand Lechat's article, 'De la sublimation', is underlined in several areas. The passages on the difference between sublimation and schizophrenia in relation to mysticism may have found an echo in Fanon's dissertation. Hence, on pp. 580–1, the following paragraph is marked several times in the margins: 'It must be emphasized here, to ward off all confusion, that there is an essential difference between sublimation and the schizophrenic attitude: the exalted individual [*le sublime*] and the schizophrenic [*le schizophrène*] have the same taste for abstraction and tend to place their main interests outside the field of human relations, but that is the only common feature they share. One important factor eliminates any resemblance between their structures,

which is social contact. ... And that leads me to oppose true sublimation to mysticism, no matter the ideology on which the latter depends. To my mind, mysticism, as I conceive it, is a pathological fact belonging to a schizophrenic constitution: it is an autism externalized in acts and the acts it inspires are marked with the psychotic seal, as is attested by the permanent delusions of the mystics and psychopathological manifestations, from the hallucinations of some to the insane acts of others.'
To be noted here is a question mark in the margin of p. 577 referring to Lechat's mention of the 'Groupe lyonnais d'études médicales, philosophiques et biologiques (1947)'. This group, led by Gustave Thibon, was therefore not known to Fanon.]

Revue pratique de psychologie de la vie sociale et d'hygiène mentale, 1954: 3, 4; 1955: 1, 2; 1956: 1, 2.

Key Dates of Fanon's Life
Chronology prepared by Robert J.C. Young

1925   20 July: Frantz Marguerite Victor Fanon is born in Fort-de-France, Martinique. Fanon lives in the family home at 33, rue de la République, Fort-de-France. He goes to school at École de la rue Pérrinon, then at the Lycée Schœlcher.

1939   Start of the Second World War. The schools in Fort-de-France are closed. September: the admiral Georges Robert arrives in Martinique. The period of '*Tan Robè*' begins on the island.

1940   June: Armistice between France and Germany. Robert announces his support for Pétain and for the Vichy government. November: Frantz and Joby are sent to Le François to stay with Uncle Édouard. The lycée there is still open.

1941   Schools reopen and the boys return to Fort-de-France. Fanon meets Aimé Césaire, then a twenty-six-year-old teacher at the Lycée Schœlcher.

1943   January: on the day of his brother Félix's marriage, Fanon, seventeen years old, makes a clandestine crossing to Dominica to join the Free French Forces.
June: Admiral Robert is toppled by the Gaullist Henri Tourtet. Fanon, repatriated from Dominica, goes back to the lycée.

1944   Fanon, enlisted in the Free French Forces, is assigned to the 5th Bataillon de marche antillais (BMA5).
March: the battalion disembarks at Casablanca, from where it is transported to Guercif and then to El Hajeb camp close to Meknès, Morocco.
May: transfer to Bougie (Béjaïa), in Algeria.
August: beginning of operation Anvil, launched by the US First Airborne Task Force, in the south of France; liberation of Paris.
August: Fanon crosses the Mediterranean and alights close to Saint-Tropez. Fanon is reassigned to the 6th regiment of *tirailleurs sénégalais*. They advance toward the north as far as the Rhone Valley.
September: Lyon is liberated.
November: The French advance in Alsace begins.
15 November: while fighting close to Montbéliard in the Doubs, Fanon is wounded in the chest by shrapnel. He is hospitalized in Nantua and then awarded the Croix de guerre with a bronze star. Recovered, he goes to Paris.

1945   January: he rejoins his regiment on the shores of the Rhine.
May: Germany capitulates.
September: Fanon is sent to Rouen and stationed in the Château
du Chapitre.
September: he takes the *San Mateo*, a cargo ship, to Martinique.
Fanon returns to the Lycée Schœlcher to finish his baccalauréat.

1946   Autumn: Fanon departs for Le Havre, from where he takes the
train to Paris, with the intention of studying dentistry. After
some weeks, he leaves Paris to study medicine in Lyon. He takes
courses in biology, physics and chemistry.

1947   January: Félix Casimir Fanon, Fanon's father, dies at the age of
fifty-six.
Fanon is clubbed by the police at a demonstration for the liberation
of Paul Vergès, the head of the Communist Party of Réunion.

1948   February: Fanon publishes a small student magazine, *Tam-Tam*.
He begins a relationship with Michelle B.; birth of his daughter
Mireille.

1949   Fanon meets Marie-Josèphe Dublé (Josie) at Célestins, a theatre in
Lyon. He writes two plays, *L'Oeil se noie* and *Les Mains parallels*.

1949-   He begins his specialization in psychiatry. He follows a
1951   course at the psychiatric hospital of Vinatier, then he decides
to study at the Faculty of Medicine at Lyon University under
the supervision of Professor Jean Dechaume. He meets Nicole
Guillet, who will introduce him to the psychiatrist François
Tosquelles (probably in 1952).

1950   December: Fanon is required to give up a temporary, irregular
position as an intern at the hospital of Saint-Ylie in Dole (Jura).

1951   April: Fanon's proposal, originally made in November 1950,
to submit an early version of what would become *Peau noire,
masques blancs* as his dissertation, entitled 'Contribution to
the study of the psychological mechanisms likely to hinder a
healthy understanding between different members of the French
Community', is rejected.
November: viva voce for his dissertation *Altérations mentales,
modifications caractérielles, troubles psychiques et déficit
intellectuel dans l'hérédo-dégénération spino-cérébelleuse.*

1952   February: he publishes his first article, 'The North African
Syndrome', in *Esprit*.
February-March: a stay in Martinique.
Returning to France, he visits the psychiatric hospital of Saint-
Alban-de-Limagnole (Lozère), where he works as an intern with
François Tosquelles.

April: publication of *Peau noire, masques blancs* by Éditions du Seuil.

October: Fanon and Josie are married.

1953   June: Fanon passes the medical examinations for psychiatric hospitals, which enables him to take up a position as *médicin-chef*. He applies for a position in Guadeloupe.

September: he takes up a position as a temporary replacement at Pontorson, La Manche.

November: Fanon is appointed to a position at Blida-Joinville psychiatric hospital in Algeria. There he begins to reform current practice and establishes an institutional psychotherapy on the model of Saint-Alban. His interns include Jacques Azoulay and, from 1956, Charles Geronimi.

1954   1 November: start of the war in Algeria.

1955   Fanon makes first contact with the FLN. Birth of his son, Olivier. February: death of his sister Gabrielle, aged thirty-three.

April: a state of emergency is declared in Algeria. During the summer, Fanon publishes an unsigned article criticizing the psychiatry of the Algiers School in *Consciences maghribines*.

1956   July:[1] Fanon sends letter of resignation to the Resident Minister in Algiers.

September: talk at the first World Congress of Black Writers and Artists in Paris, on 'Racism and culture'.

1957   January: expelled from Algeria. Fanon goes to Paris, then, via Switzerland and Italy, to Tunis.

Under the pseudonym of 'Dr Farès', works as psychiatrist at the hospital of La Manouba, then creates the Psychiatric Day Clinic at Charles-Nicolle General Hospital.

June: joins the FLN press office.

5 June: holds an FLN press conference accusing the French of the Melouza massacre (now attributed to the FLN).

September: becomes a member of *El Moudjahid*'s editorial committee.

Travels to Rome, returning to Tunis 21 September.

---

[1]This letter is often dated December, but according to the detailed chronology of Fanon's life from 1954 to 1959 prepared for the French secret services, the letter was written in July, a date presumably derived from the actual letter that Fanon had sent to the Resident Minister ('Fonds Foccart' Archives de la Présidence de la République: Secrétariat général des Affaires africaines et malgaches et de la Communauté (1958–1974). Fonds Élysée, Affaires politiques, Afrique « hors champ » 1958–1974. Afrique occidentale britannique 1959–1971. Carton: AG/5(F)/2213 Ghana 1960–1962). Henceforth 'Fonds Foccart'. For internal evidence that suggests an earlier date for the letter, see also *The Psychiatric Writings from Alienation and Freedom*, p. 285.

1958   June: General de Gaulle takes power in France, visits Algiers and calls for a referendum to be held in September in order to establish the 5th Republic. Martinique votes to continue to be part of the French Community.
September: establishment of the Provisional Government of the Algerian Republic (GPRA). Travels to Rome.
December: Fanon is a member of the FLN delegation to the All-African People's Congress in Accra. 15 December returns to Tunis via Lisbon and Rome.

1959   March: Fanon speaks on 'National Culture and the War of Liberation' at the Second Congress of Black Writers and Artists in Rome. He calls for a 'literature of combat'.
April: Travels to India with Ferhat Abbas, then flies to Cairo and then Casablanca.[2]
May: voyage to Rabat, Morocco, passing through Rome and Madrid; his destination is the ALN (Algerian National Liberation army) military base of Ben M'Hidi located at the border. He is injured in a car accident.
July: he returns to Rome for some hospital treatment; he survives an assassination attempt at the hospital by a commando of La Main rouge (French secret services).
August: returns to Tunis for ALN political meetings.
October: publication of *L'An V de la révolution algérienne* by Éditions François Maspero, without Fanon's introduction. Three months after publication, the book is seized by the police.

1960   February: named itinerant ambassador of the Provisional Government of the Algerian Republic (GPRA) in Africa, based in Accra, Ghana.
April: Fanon gives a talk at the Afro-Asiatic Solidarity Conference, in Conakry; then another at the Positive Action Conference for Peace and Security in Africa, in Accra.
June: he speaks at the Conference of Independent African States, in Addis Ababa.
September: he takes part in the Pan African Congress in Léopoldville (Kinshasa) in the newly independent Congo Republic.

---

[2]Fonds Foccart.

October: takes a flight from Accra to Monrovia; he is informed that the plane for Conakry is full and that he has to take an Air France flight; suspecting a trap, he opts to travel by road to Bamako. He writes a travel diary on the road as he goes to Mopti, Douentza, Gao and then to Tessalit on the Algerian border to identify a possible entry route for the ALN into Algeria via the south.

He returns to Accra and writes 'The Stooges of Imperialism' for the GPRA (published in December in the information bulletin of the Algerian Mission in Ghana).

December: Fanon returns to Tunis for medical tests; he is diagnosed with leukaemia.

1961   January: Assassination of Patrice Lumumba in the Congo. Foundation in Algeria of the Secret Army Organization (OAS). Spring: a stay in Moscow for medical treatment. April: returns to Tunis and writes *Les Damnés de la terre*. He writes to Maspero to ask him to ask Sartre to write a preface. May: his article 'Concerning Violence' is published in *Les Temps modernes*. During the summer: he gives lectures on Sartre's *Critique de la raison dialectique* to the ALN forces stationed at the Tunisian border.

July: Fanon travels to Rome. Simone de Beauvoir and Claude Lanzmann come to meet him at the airport. He meets Sartre with whom he speaks for three days straight. His last meeting with Édouard Glissant, in Rome.

July-September: Sartre writes the preface to *Les Damnés de la terre*.

October: Fanon travels to Rome again, meets Sartre for the last time, and then flies to Washington for medical treatment. He has to wait a week before being admitted to the Clinical Center, National Institute of Health, Bethesda, Maryland (Washington). October: publication of *Les Damnés de la terre* in Paris by François Maspero.

6 December: Fanon dies.

7 December: the police in Paris seize copies of *Les Damnés de la terre*.

1962   3 July: Declaration of Algeria's independence.

1964   Publication by Maspero of *Pour la révolution africaine*.

Index